# Privatization in Malaysia

## Regulation, rent-seeking and policy failure



In recent years, privatization has fallen out of favour in many countries because the underlying political factors have not been well understood. This book examines Malaysia's privatization programme, focusing on how political constraints resulted in the failure of four major privatizations: the national sewerage company (IWK), Kuala Lumpur Light Rail Transit (LRT), national airline (MAS) and national car company (Proton). It considers why developing countries such as Malaysia might want to embark on privatization, the factors that lead to policy failure and what is needed to make it work. It shows clearly that political motives driving privatization often dominate purely economic considerations, and thus it is necessary to analyse privatization within the specific country context. It argues that failure in the Malaysian case was due to political considerations that compromised institutional design and regulatory enforcement, leading to problems associated with corruption. It concludes that privatization does not necessarily improve incentives for efficiency or enhance the finance available for capital investment, and that successful privatization depends on the state's institutional and political capacity to design and manage an appropriate set of subsidies. Overall, this book is a comprehensive examination of privatization in Malaysia, providing important insights for understanding the political economy of this process in other developing countries.

**Jeff Tan** is a political economist at the School of Oriental and African Studies, University of London. His other research interests are in regulation, state capacity, industrial policy, institutions and governance.

**Routledge Malaysian Studies Series**
Published in association with Malaysian Social Science Association (MSSA)

**Series Editors:**
Mohammed Hazim Shah, University of Malaya
Shamsul A.B., University Kebangsaan Malaysia
Terence Gomez, United Nations Research Institute for Social Development, Geneva

The Routledge Malaysian Studies Series publishes high quality scholarship that provides important new contributions to knowledge on Malaysia. It also signals research that spans comparative studies, involving the Malaysian experience with that of other nations.

This series, initiated by the Malaysian Social Science Association (MSSA) to promote study of contemporary and historical issues in Malaysia, and designed to respond to the growing need to publish important research, also serves as a forum for debate on key issues in Malaysian society. As an academic series, it will be used to generate new theoretical debates in the social sciences and on processes of change in this society.

The Routledge Malaysian Studies Series will cover a broad range of subjects including history, politics, economics, sociology, international relations, geography, business, education, religion, literature, culture and ethnicity. The series will encourage work adopting an interdisciplinary approach.

**The State of Malaysia**
Ethnicity, equity and reform
*Edited by Edmund Terence Gomez*

**Feminism and the Women's Movement in Malaysia**
An unsung (r)evolution
*Cecilia Ng, Maznah Mohamad and tan beng hui*

**Governments and Markets in East Asia**
The politics of economic crises
*Jungug Choi*

**Health Care in Malaysia**
The dynamics of provision, financing and access
*Edited by Chee Heng Leng and Simon Barraclough*

**Politics in Malaysia**
The Malay dimension
*Edited by Edmund Terence Gomez*

**Privatization in Malaysia**
Regulation, rent-seeking and policy failure
*Jeff Tan*

# Privatization in Malaysia

## Regulation, rent-seeking and policy failure

**Jeff Tan**

Routledge
Taylor & Francis Group
LONDON AND NEW YORK

First published 2008
by Routledge
2 Park Square, Milton Park, Abingdon, Oxon OX14 4RN

Simultaneously published in the USA and Canada
by Routledge
605 Third Avenue, New York, NY 10017

*Routledge is an imprint of the Taylor & Francis Group, an Informa business*



Typeset in Times New Roman by
RefineCatch Limited, Bungay, Suffolk



*British Library Cataloguing in Publication Data*
A catalogue record for this book is available from the British Library

*Library of Congress Cataloging in Publication Data*
Tan, Jeff, 1965–
Privatization in Malaysia : regulation, rent-seeking, and policy failure / Jeff Tan.
p. cm.—(Routledge Malaysian studies series ; 6)
Includes bibliographical references and index.
1. Privatization—Malaysia. 2. Privatization—Malaysia—Case studies.
3. Malaysia—Politics and government. I. Title.
HD4300.6.T36 2007
338.95951′05—dc22

2007012482

ISBN13: 978–0–415–42821–7 (hbk)
ISBN13: 978–0–415–54537–2 (pbk)
ISBN13: 978–0–203–93480–7 (ebk)

**Dedicated to my parents, Tan Siew Soo and Yeoh Siew Hong**

# Contents

# Tables

# Acknowledgements

I would like to thank the British Council for the British Chevening Scholarship which allowed me to undertake my PhD. I am very grateful to Mushtaq H. Khan for agreeing to supervise my research at the School of Oriental and African Studies (SOAS), and for his insight, stimulating discussions, and faith in me. I am also indebted to Jomo K.S. for his invaluable guidance, constant support, encouragement and feedback. Finally, I want to thank Edward Terence Gomez for his time and support in getting my research published.

# Abbreviations

| | |
|---|---|
| AFTA | Asian Free Trade Agreement |
| AFTK | Available freight tonne kilometres |
| APTK | Available passenger tonne kilometres |
| ARP | Area road pricing |
| ASEAN | Association of Southeast Asian Nations |
| ASK | Available seat kilometres |
| ASN | Amanah Saham Nasional (National Unit Trust Scheme) |
| ATK | Available tonne kilometres |
| BBMB | Bank Bumiputra Malaysia Bhd |
| BEC | Bumiputra Economic Congress |
| Bhd | Berhad (limited company) |
| BNM | Bank Negara Malaysia (Central Bank) |
| BO | Build-operate |
| BOD | Biochemical oxygen demand |
| BOO | Build-operate-own |
| BOT | Build-operate-transfer |
| BPIMB | Bank Pembangunan dan Infrastruktur Malaysia Bhd (Development and Infrastructure Bank) |
| BPPP | Bahagian Pembangunan Perakunan dan Pengurusan (Planning Research Development Unit, National Audit Division) |
| BT | Build-transfer |
| CBU | Completely built up |
| CDRC | Corporate Debt Restructuring Committee |
| CEPT | Common Effective Preferential Tariff |
| CIC | Capital Issues Committee |
| CIMB | Commerce International Merchant Bankers Bhd |
| CKD | Completely knocked down |
| CMGI | Commerce MGI Sdn Bhd |
| CPA | Central planning area |
| CVLB | Commercial Vehicle Licensing Board |
| Danaharta | State asset management company |
| DBKL | Dewan Bandaraya Kuala Lumpur (Kuala Lumpur City Hall) |
| DGSS | Director General of Sewerage Services |

| | |
|---|---|
| DOE | Department of Environment |
| DoR | Department of Railways |
| DRB | Diversified Resources Bhd |
| DSS | Department of Sewerage Services |
| EBIT | Earnings before interest and tax |
| EC | European Community |
| EIB | European Investment Bank |
| EMS | Engine management system |
| EON | Edaran Otomobil Nasional |
| EPF | Employees Provident Fund |
| EPSFD | Economic Planning & Social Facilities Department |
| EPU | Economic Planning Unit |
| FTDKVP | Federal Territory Development & Klang Valley Planning Division |
| GSP | Generalized Scheme of Preferences |
| HICOM | Heavy Industries Corporation |
| HOV | High occupancy vehicle |
| HPU | Highway Planning Unit |
| IATA | International Air Transport Association |
| IBD | International Business Division |
| ICA | Industrial Coordination Act |
| ICAO | International Civil Aviation Organization |
| ICP | Inter-departmental Committee on Privatization |
| ICU | Implementation and Coordination Unit |
| IFC | International Finance Corporation |
| IPC | Infrastructure Project Company |
| IPP | Independent power producer |
| IWK | Indah Water Konsortium |
| JBIC | Japan Bank for International Cooperation |
| JICA | Japan International Co-operation Agency |
| JIT | Just-in-time |
| JKR | Jabatan Kerja Raya (Public Works Department) |
| JPJ | Jabatan Pengangkutan Jalan (Road Transport Department) |
| KCT | Klang Container Terminal |
| KEJORA | Lembaga Kemajuan Johor Tenggara (South East Johor Development Authority) |
| KfW | Kreditanstalt für Wiederaufbau |
| KL PRT | Kuala Lumpur People Rapid Transit |
| KLIA | Kuala Lumpur International Airport |
| KLSE | Kuala Lumpur Stock Exchange |
| KLTG | Kuala Lumpur Transit Group |
| KTMB | Keretapi Tanah Melayu Bhd (Malayan Railways) |
| KWAP | Kumpulan Wang Amanah Pencen (State Pension Fund) |
| LLM | Lembaga Lebuhraya Malaysia (Malaysian Highway Authority) |
| LOA | Lease of asset |

| | |
|---|---|
| LoS | Level of service |
| LPPJ | Road Transport Licensing Board |
| LRT | Light rail transit |
| LTA | Land Transport Authority |
| LTAT | Lembaga Tabung Angkatan Tentera (Armed Forces Savings Board) |
| LTD | Long-term debt |
| LTL | Long-term lease |
| MARA | Majlis Amanah Rakyat (Council of Trust for Indigenous People) |
| MAS | Malaysia Airlines |
| MBO | Management-buy-out |
| MC | Mitsubishi Corporation |
| MCA | Malaysian Chinese Association |
| MHS | Malaysian Helicopter Services |
| MIC | Malaysian Indian Congress |
| MIDA | Malaysian Industrial Development Authority |
| MMC | Mitsubishi Motor Company |
| MoED | Ministry of Entrepreneur Development |
| MoF | Ministry of Finance |
| MoHA | Ministry of Home Affairs |
| MoT | Ministry of Transport |
| MoW | Ministry of Works |
| MRT | Mass Rapid Transit |
| MTI | Ministry of Trade and Industry |
| NCF | Net cash flow |
| NEL | North East Line |
| NEP | New Economic Policy |
| NFPEs | Non-financial public enterprises |
| NIE | New Institutional Economics |
| NPL | Non-performing loan |
| NWW | North West Water |
| OBA | Off-budget agency |
| OEM | Original equipment manufacture |
| OSA | Official Secrets Act |
| PAP | Privatization Action Plan |
| PBT | Profits before tax |
| Pernas | Perbadanan Nasional (National Corporation) |
| PFI | Private finance initiative |
| PMD | Prime Minister's Department |
| PMP | Privatization Master Plan |
| PNB | Permodalan Nasional Berhad (National Equity Corporation) |
| PPP | Public–private partnership |
| PROTON | Perusahaan Otomobil Nasional |
| PSD | Public Service Department |
| PTF | Privatization Task Force |

| | |
|---|---|
| PUTRA | Projek Usahasama Transit Ringan Automatik |
| RAC | Railway Asset Corporation |
| R&D | Research and development |
| RIDA | Rural Industrial Development Authority |
| RM | Ringgit Malaysia (Malaysian ringgit) |
| ROA | Return on assets |
| ROE | Return on equity |
| RPK | Revenue passenger-km |
| RTO | Road Transport Ordinance |
| SCB | Siam Commercial Bank |
| Sdn Bhd | Sendirian Berhad (private limited company) |
| SEDC | State Economic Development Corporation |
| SIA | Singapore International Airlines |
| SMI | Small- and medium-scale industry |
| SMRT | Singapore Mass Rapid Transit |
| SOA | Sale of asset |
| SOE | State-owned enterprise |
| SS | Suspended solids |
| SSA | Sewage Services Act |
| STAR | Sistem Transit Aliran Ringgan |
| STL | Short-term lease |
| STP | Sewerage treatment plant |
| TAC | Track access charge |
| TC | Technical committee |
| TNB | Tenaga Nasional Berhad |
| TOC | Train operating company |
| TRI | Technology Resources Industries Bhd |
| TRTA | Teito Rapid Transit Authority |
| UDA | Urban Development Authority |
| UMNO | United Malays National Organisation |
| USPD | Usahasama Proton-DRB Sdn Bhd |
| UTD | Urban Transportation Department |
| VDP | Vendor Development Programme |

# 1 Introduction

## Why privatize?

The debate over privatization is essentially the debate over the relative efficiency of the state versus markets and private property in the allocation of resources. Privatization is said to improve efficiency by changing the structure of incentives, reducing the possibilities of damaging state interventions, improving monitoring and introducing competition. The mainstream literature has largely focused on the correlation between privatization and performance (by comparing public and private firms) and on establishing the causality between private ownership and performance. However, the results of privatization have been mixed, with the evidence of efficiency gains inconclusive. These approaches are also usually hampered by methodological difficulties and there is a lack of general consensus on the correlation between privatization (private ownership) and economic performance.

Methodological problems arise from attempts to measure performance, in particular key variables (e.g. allocative efficiency), the use of criteria which mostly favours the private sector, interpreting financial profitability and the absence of common agreement on what constitutes successful performance given the often multiple objectives and different goals of public enterprises. In particular, it is often unclear whether improved efficiency is due to a change in ownership or structural changes which accompany privatization, especially increased competition. Evidence of improved performance has also been limited to certain sectors with industry-specific conditions, telecommunications being one of the few such instances, and it is unclear whether these can be replicated in other sectors.

As a result, a growing body of literature has found that the evidence 'does not support any general proposition about the superiority of private over public ownership or vice versa' (Vickers and Wright 1989: 23, cited in Tatahi 2003: 90) and 'there exists neither compelling theoretical reasons nor unambiguous empirical evidence for either developed or developing countries suggesting the pervasive "inefficiency" of public enterprises' (Chang and Singh 1992: 42), with 'no clear-cut evidence that public ownership necessarily results in inferior performance' (Chang and Singh 1993: 34). Several important international surveys on the performances of public versus private enterprises conclude that in a competitive environment, private and public firms do not differ significantly in their economic performance (see Millward and Parker 1983; Borcherding *et al.* 1982, cited in Tatahi 2003). Other studies also point to competition and regulation as more important or at least necessary if privatization is to be more efficient (Vickers and Wright 1989; Caves and Christensen 1980; Faere *et al.* 1985; Atkinson *et al.* 1986; Yarrow 1986; Vickers and Yarrow 1988; Bishop and Kay 1989; Beesley and Littlechild 1989; and Martin and Parker 1997, all cited in Tatahi 2003: 80; Cook and Uchida 2003; also see Hemming and Mansoor 1988; Vickers and Yarrow 1991; Parker and Kirkpatrick 2003).

Despite this, privatization continues to be widely accepted in principle, and the failure of privatization in developing countries has been normally attributed to institutional weaknesses leading to problems of patronage and corruption. The conditions for successful privatization are then said to depend on strengthening institutions, democracy, transparency and accountability. However, these explanations are restricted by a narrow understanding of what privatization and regulation entail, based on an apolitical and ahistorical reading of the constraints facing developing countries, and grounded in theoretically flawed arguments about the incentive benefits of privatization.

We make two main claims. The first challenges the theory that privatization improves incentives by aligning residual control (ownership) with residual returns (profit). It will be argued that the private sector, both in developed and developing countries, is often unable and unwilling to finance projects with high capital costs such as infrastructure provision on its own, making it necessary for the state to share risks even after privatization. In addition, the provision of public goods or services (such as urban transit and sewage treatment) in developing countries is often not profitable, partly because universal service obligations require that these should be affordable. A subsidy may then be required, even by a very efficient operator, if the tariff customers are willing to pay is less than the minimum cost the producer can achieve. But a subsidy may also allow inefficiency to survive, particularly in sectors with insufficient competition. These state interventions dilute incentives because there is no longer a direct relationship between management quality and profits, thereby necessitating regulation. However, asymmetric information will prevent regulators knowing for sure whether an adequate level of efficiency has been achieved. In principle, tough regulators can still achieve efficiency over time in a number of ways, for instance, by setting tariff reduction targets with fixed levels of subsidies. But the success of these strategies depends on the credibility of the regulator's threats that failure to achieve targets may result in the selection of a different operator or the imposition of a financial penalty. The success of privatization will then depend on institutional prerequisites for effective regulation that can maintain incentives for performance in a context where the state is still providing subsidies and sharing risks.

This brings us directly to the second and related claim: privatization necessitates continued and often even greater state intervention in terms of maintaining some subsidies, perhaps creating new ones, devising new methods of regulation and coordinating certain sectors such as rail networks. Regulation will not only involve promoting competition and enforcing rules, but also managing subsidies, setting targets, changing property rights and laws and other interventions that go beyond the simple but standard textbook understanding of regulation. In addition to the issues already discussed, developing countries often also face a shortage of domestic capitalists, and governments will often be engaged in developing entrepreneurial capacity. States in successful developers have played a central role in the emergence of the capitalist class. Privatization in this context can also be seen as a process that aims to facilitate the emergence of domestic capitalists and to that extent, it usually has a political motivation in addition to the standard economic ones. It is our contention that the political motive often dominates, and has to be understood on its own terms.

When the issue of emerging domestic capitalism is introduced, we have an associated problem of catching up, as discussed in the late development literature (e.g. see Amsden 1989; Wade 1990). When new domestic capitalists are encouraged to take over advanced technologies, their initial productivity is expected to be low, till they have had the opportunity of learning-by-doing (see Arrow 1962). This means that we can expect a further set of subsidies to be required, this time temporary subsidies that also need to be monitored and withdrawn over a short period of time to create both the opportunity and incentive for catching up (as discussed in the literature on late industrialization and infant industries). This presents different regulatory challenges, with the state needing to ensure that subsidies are conditional upon performance targets being met. This is because the presence of a regulatory structure or intent does not guarantee success as regulatory failure can be the result of institutional failure (e.g. poor incentive structures) or political failure (e.g. ineffective implementation of subsidy withdrawal). This means that effective regulation will depend on the state's political capacity just as much as, or even more so than, its institutional capacity. This is because the failure to enforce conditionality is usually due to the state's political failure to impose discipline on capitalists.

Thus state failure in the context of privatization can occur before or after privatization and we will refer to these as ex ante and ex post state failures. Ex ante failure can often be unavoidable given the problems of asymmetric information, shortage of entrepreneurs and political considerations, all of which potentially affect the choice of privatization and candidate. It is therefore critical that the state is able to correct any mistakes ex post, through policy changes, tweaking regulatory structures, devising and enforcing conditionality for new or existing subsidy structures, and so on. This ex post failure can provide a more useful explanation for the failure of privatization in developing countries. That is to say, successful privatization will depend on the state's political capacity, in particular its ex post capacity to correct mistakes. Understanding the sources of the state's appropriate political capacities will then allow us to explain better how successful the state has been in managing privatization, and the conditions that need to be met for improving the chances of success in the future.

Theories addressing state failure and the literature on the developmental state provide a useful framework to analyse factors that are important for effective state intervention. The success of the East Asian developmental states has been generally attributed to the state's autonomy to develop and implement policy, combined with networks of information exchange with productive groups (particularly capitalists), which enabled it to both identify areas of necessary intervention, and then implement these interventions effectively (e.g. see Johnson 1982; Wade 1990; Evans 1994; Weiss 1998; Woo-Cummings 1999). State capacity in this context will then depend on the nature of the state–society relationship, and the strength of the state in relation to the group(s) it engages with. In developing countries, a capitalist class is often absent or very weak, and the state–society relationship will usually involve the exercise of influence and the exchange of information with 'unproductive' groups. Regardless of the state's potential for eventual success, its allocation of resources is likely to be through patron–client networks rather than formalized or institutionalized channels since states in late developers rarely have the qualities of Weberian states. The nature of these patron–client networks, and the relative strength of the state in relation to the groups that are accommodated within these networks (which depends on the broader balance of power between groups and classes in society), will affect how and to whom resources are allocated, and most crucially, determine the state's capacity to ensure efficient outcomes by enforcing discipline (e.g. see Khan 1998). The latter approach suggests that the analysis of the prospects and performance of privatization needs to be located in a country context, looking specifically at the nature of social relations and the balance of power in society and within the networks of governance in which decisions about privatization and the regulation of rules and subsidies take place.

This book seeks to explain why privatization may fail by looking at the political motivations behind this, and the constraints on the state's political capacity to manage subsidies associated with privatization. The discussion will take place on two levels. Broadly, we examine the role of (and motivations behind) privatization in the context of state attempts to create domestic entrepreneurial capacity, looking at the problems of institutional and political failure. Specifically, we apply this analytical framework to explain Malaysia's privatization performance and the failure of four of its largest privatizations: Indah Water Konsortium (IWK, the operator of the national sewerage system), Kuala Lumpur's Light Rail Transit (LRT), Malaysia Airlines (MAS, the national airline) and Proton (the national car company).

Malaysia's privatization programme between the mid 1980s and mid 1990s was amongst the most extensive in the developing world, widely publicized, hailed as a success story, and promoted as a model for other developing countries. However, subsequent state bail-outs, and the financial failure and eventual renationalization of these four privatizations by 2000, reveal that this conclusion was premature. Failure here has been generally blamed on the problems of patronage and corruption associated with weak institutions. While this focus on political factors is useful, it does not consider the specific economic and political challenges related to efficiency and redistribution which the state sought to address through privatization. We will examine the failure of privatization in the context of these challenges by asking three central questions: Why privatize in developing countries? Why may privatization fail? What is needed to make privatization work?

A careful reading of Malaysia's economic history and political economy reveals that changes *within* the Malay middle class – as opposed to changes in the balance of power between Malays and other ethnic groups – are critical for understanding Malaysia's economic policy-making and performance vis-à-vis its privatization strategy. This perspective allows us to identify the drivers of Malaysia's privatization programme, the motivations behind this, the subsequent constraints on the state's disciplinary capacity, and how this affected the institutional arrangements and outcomes of privatization. We argue that the drive for a massive privatization strategy was in response to economic inefficiencies but more crucially came from changes in social relations within the Malay middle class that led to increased competition for resources within the ruling Malay party. The emergence of new factions shifted the balance of power, and privatization facilitated the redistribution of resources away from beneficiaries of the state's previous redistributive policy in favour of emerging factions centred on key political leaders. This personalized and gradually undermined the previously centralized patronage network, and led to a growing moral hazard problem as the political leadership became increasingly unwilling or unable to discipline its close supporters. The nature of the changes within these patron–client relationships also affected the choice of privatization sectors and candidates, and most crucially, the state's ability to implement corrective policy or enforce discipline.

This approach allows us to locate our case studies within what we argue is the appropriate political context, while avoiding some of the methodological pitfalls of cross-country and cross-industry comparisons which typify much of the literature. The case studies will offer both a broader discussion of the challenges for privatization in the respective industries as well as a detailed examination of the specific case. Each case study is assessed on its own terms, but within a common analytical framework with performance measured against economic general indicators (efficiency, capital investment and financial performance) as well as indicators specific to each industry and in relation to official objectives. This provides for much richer sources of data, while taking into account non-economic factors which allow us to make useful comparisons and to draw policy lessons. The case studies provide the evidence to support our two main claims that: 1, privatization in developing countries typically necessitates the continuation of state financial support for a variety of reasons; and 2, successful privatization will depend on the state's capacity, in particular its ex post political capacity, to correct ex ante failure and to manage the appropriate subsidy regimes.

The book is structured as follows. Chapter 2 examines the main arguments for privatization. These are shown to be problematic, as they do not identify the political motivations for privatization in developing countries, and fail to account for the political reasons why privatization may fail. The typical recommendations to strengthen institutions do not address the main problems that drive regulatory failure in countries like Malaysia. The chapter then examines sources of state capacity, looking at social relations and the balance of power specific to the country.

Chapter 3 provides the background to understand the political context in which privatization was undertaken in Malaysia, looking at both economic and political imperatives in order to properly locate the subsequent case study chapters. Malaysia's privatization programme will be examined within the theoretical framework presented in Chapter 2, applying the three central questions to the Malaysian case. A discussion of the country's redistributive New Economic Policy (NEP) shows that this was both a consequence and a cause of changes in social relations, in particular the growth of and increasing differentiation within the Malay middle class. This provides the context in which to understand the drivers of the Malaysian government's privatization strategy. The drivers came from both the growing political demands of a new Malay upper middle class, and the challenges faced by the government in managing the public sector. The chapter then provides some background and details of Malaysia's privatization programme, and evaluates its performance from 1983–2000. The results, measured against official objectives, will be shown to be mixed, with privatization in particular failing to develop a dynamic Malay capitalist class. We then trace the failure of Malaysia's privatization programme to the state's ex ante and ex post failure, and suggest why the latter is of far greater consequence for the success of privatization in Malaysia.

Chapters 5–7 present the case studies on IWK, the Kuala Lumpur LRT, MAS and Proton respectively. The first half of each case study will examine the challenges posed for privatization, provide the background to each of these decisions to privatize, and assess performance based on official objectives. The second half of the case studies then examines the problems, looking at the state's ex ante and ex post failure as explanations. Failure in each case was due to both types of state failure, but we argue that the state's ex post failure was the key factor explaining the eventual failure of the four case studies. Chapter 8 summarizes the main findings and presents the conclusions.

# 2 Privatization, rents and rent-seeking

Privatization is argued to provide better incentives and monitoring through the clear designation of property rights, while also reducing damaging state interventions. Improved efficiency as a result is then seen to encourage the private owner or operator to undertake much-needed capital investment. However, privatization does not necessarily lead to the clear designation of property rights, reduce state intervention or enhance the private financing of capital investment. This is because the private sector is often unable or unwilling on its own to meet the high cost of capital investment associated with typical privatizations (e.g. sewerage and water services). This is especially so in developing countries where there is in addition a shortage of entrepreneurial capacity. Furthermore, the ability of the private sector to meet capital investment targets will in part also depend on projected revenues based on cost-covering tariffs. However, cost-covering tariffs are usually politically unfeasible for many critical services. High capital costs and the inability of tariffs to cover high operational costs will then require state subsidies which in turn dilute incentives associated with private ownership unless they are combined with additional and credible incentives and sanctions.

In addition, governments in developing countries will often be attempting to create domestic capitalists due to a shortage of entrepreneurial capacity but also because of political pressure from groups contesting for resources. This will require additional subsidies for learning (also known as 'rents for learning') in order to develop entrepreneurial capacity, and in the long term, promote efficiency and technological 'catching up'. The processes involved here have elements similar to the process of (primitive) capital accumulation in early capitalism (e.g. see Marx 1979) in addition to the regulatory issues raised in the privatization of public sector enterprises in advanced countries. As such, privatization will often be closely tied in with state motivations and the political forces behind this. Here, the mainstream literature on privatization suffers from several shortcomings when attempting to explain the failure of privatization in developing countries because it tends to largely ignore the political context and hence political motivations which often drive privatization. These can affect both the character of privatization (what is privatized, how and to whom) and determine the type and efficacy of related institutions that are important for the success of privatization. Economic theories explaining the success or failure of privatization have generally ignored related literature on why institutions fail and why weak institutions persist (e.g. see Alavi, H. 1982; Khan 1997, 1998, 2000b).

While effective regulation is seen as central for successful privatization, the discussion in the literature is limited in scope, focusing on institutional prerequisites, with regulation viewed as a second-best option in the absence of competitive markets. Proposed institutional solutions focus on strengthening relevant institutions to promote transparency and accountability, and a regulatory framework which safeguards the private sector from political intervention and which promotes competition (e.g. see Vickers and Yarrow 1991; Clague 1997b; Williamson 2000). This does not address the problems related to the management of subsidies, especially in relation to the learning processes necessary for creating a viable private operator. Here the privatization literature fails to identify some important conditions for effective regulation in developing countries because it does not begin by identifying some of the key motivations for privatization, including state attempts to develop domestic entrepreneurs.

A further problem is that these institutional preconditions are often unrealistic for developing countries as they are based on a partial reading of problems in an ahistorical and apolitical framework of analysis. Implicitly, this means that institutions are benchmarked against existing Western standards, but these institutions were themselves the outcome rather than the cause of specific patterns of economic development in developed countries (e.g. see Chang 1999). As such, their prescription is unrealistic, as almost no developing country is able to meet these conditions. The mainstream approach to governance and regulation is also more concerned with how to improve the efficiency of service delivery rather than how to accelerate the process of dynamic change which is a necessary part of the development process (Rowthorn and Chang 1993; Khan 2004). The latter has historically required a different type of interventionist capacity, in particular connected with the efficient provision and regulation of dynamic rents that accelerate growth and ensure successful structural transformations (e.g. see Amsden 1989; Wade 1990; Aoki *et al.* 1997; Khan 2000a, 2000b).

Effective regulation is thus central to privatization but its treatment needs to go beyond measures to overcome market failure and strengthening institutional structures to include discussion of sources of state failure and inadequate state capacities with respect to the specific transformational tasks that the state is trying to achieve. Whether privatization leads to capital accumulation or capital consumption by the new owners will depend on the design of incentive structures (including rents to support learning, the management of long-term subsidies and/or terms of risk-sharing), and the ability of the state to enforce effective and credible sanctions for non-performance. The outcome of privatization, including what is privatized, how, to whom, and more crucially, the performance of privatized entities, will thus be determined by both institutional and political factors.

Failure can then be either due to poorly structured incentives (institutional failure) or well-structured incentives which are not effectively implemented (political failure). Institutional failure usually relates to mistakes made ex ante (e.g. failure to ensure the viability of the privatization project in the first place) while ex post failure refers to the failure to correct mistakes and enforce discipline. As the choice of privatization and candidate will be constrained by political considerations and imperfect information, particularly in developing countries, the state's (ex post) political capacity is usually more critical for successful privatization outcomes. The perception that privatization will reduce the role of the state is therefore misguided because privatization in fact necessitates continued and effective state intervention, and indeed the enhancement of regulatory capacity in key areas. The main concern should then be to ensure that the state has the capacity to intervene effectively, in particular, to correct mistakes.

Unfortunately, the analysis of politics in the privatization literature is limited, and restricted to ex ante political constraints (i.e. opposition by groups with vested interests such as politicians and trade unions) (e.g. Cook and Kirkpatrick 1988; Bienen and Waterbury 1989; Roland 1994; Shirley 1997), focusing on weak political and economic institutions. There is a growing recognition of the need to take into account political power and conflict arising from existing social relations (e.g. Cook and Minogue 1990; Parker 2001; Parker and Kirkpatrick 2002, 2003) and an emphasis on institutional compatibility (e.g. Kessides 2004). However, discussion of political factors tends to centre on the problem of corruption and remains largely uninformed by theory and with little analytical priority. We will build on the existing privatization literature but also draw from developmental state theories to provide a theoretical framework to explain the problem of institutional and political failure.

Theories addressing state failure and the literature on the developmental state provide a more useful framework to analyse factors that are important for effective state intervention, looking in particular at the East Asian developmental states which Malaysia sought to emulate. The lessons that can be gleaned from this suggest that effective state intervention depends on the compatibility of institutions and patterns of intervention with the balance of political power in society. The strength of the state in relation to various competing groups in society is critical for understanding the outcome, because it can help to determine whether the state is able to resist challenges from those who stand to lose out from the proposed changes, and whether critical incentive structures can be effectively enforced. The analytical priority of political factors in our analysis is justified because without an understanding of the political constraints, it is difficult to identify the institutional interventions that may be effective, or to explain why particular institutions do not work in that context. This approach can explain why weak institutions may often persist where the state lacks the political capacity to enforce, as it is unlikely that it can change institutions if it is unable to implement policy in the first place. It is therefore important to locate the analysis of institutional changes such as privatization within an analysis of the political constraints facing the state in a specific country.

This chapter seeks to identify the important conditions for successful privatization by critically examining theory and the evidence of privatization in developing countries. It will ask the following questions: Why privatize in developing countries? Why may privatization fail? What is needed to make privatization work? This will provide the framework to explain Malaysia's privatization experience and the four case studies in the following chapters. The chapter is divided into four sections. The following section briefly looks at the reasons why developing countries would want to privatize, and compare this with the main arguments for privatization. It will be argued that most of the conventional theories of privatization very often do not identify the real motivations of privatization in specific developing countries and are therefore unable to analyse the very problem they seek to address.

The next section examines why privatization may fail, looking at conventional (institutional) arguments. Many of these arguments are problematic because the institutional preconditions identified are based on ahistorical and unrealistic benchmarks and ignore the realities of the development process, in particular the specific political constraints faced by specific countries. This requires an analysis of state capacity, looking in particular at how this is affected by the (changing) balance of power in society. The fourth section seeks to identify some of the conditions for successful privatization, looking at both institutional and political capacity. We argue that while an appropriate institutional design is necessary, political capacity is more important as this is far harder to correct if not in place, and also determines the quality of institutions and the ability of the state to strengthen weak institutions.

## Why privatize in developing countries?

### *Conventional arguments for privatization*

Arguments in favour of privatization are based on the efficiency claimed for private property rights, principal agent theories comparing asymmetric information problems under public and private ownership, and public choice theories looking at the ways in which objectives and outcomes are determined in bureaucracies. These theoretical developments came about in response to poor public sector performance, escalating operational and capital costs, and state fiscal constraints in both advanced and developing countries (Batley 1996). These theories mostly showed that, where feasible, private provision (and market choices) was socially preferable and superior to public provision or production (Windsor 1996). Privatization improved efficiency by: 1, changing the objectives of the firm's ultimate owners; and 2, reducing the possibilities of continuous government intervention (Hakim *et al.* 1996b; Payson and Steckler 1996; Stottmann 2000). This improved the monitoring of managerial performance (Vickers and Yarrow 1991) thereby addressing the problems of poor operational and financial performance of state-owned enterprises (SOEs) and the underinvestment in infrastructure.

### *Clearly designated property rights*

According to property rights and principal agent theories, private ownership is superior to public ownership because clearly defined property rights provide incentives for monitoring and improving efficiency through the alignment of residual control (ownership) and residual return (profit) (Alchian and Demsetz 1972). This is because there are a series of principal–agent problems in public enterprises. All citizens are joint owners of the residual and are therefore the ultimate principal. They have to contract with government, their agent, to manage public enterprises, but government in turn has to contract with managers, who have most of the residual control rights. The government's problem as principal is that it is unable to provide the appropriate incentives to the agent (managers of SOEs) to exert effort in monitoring the performance of workers and employees in a context of asymmetric information. Private ownership is seen as the most efficient way to align incentives because the owner of the residual thereby gains effective residual control rights (Alchian and Demsetz 1972). This alignment is attenuated with shareholding, where the residual owners and control rights again become separated, but specific mechanisms such as the market in managers, takeover threats and regulation ensure that managers in shareholder-owned companies have better incentives and compulsions for monitoring than managers in public enterprises. Different forms of privatization can improve incentives by transferring responsibility and risk to the private sector. Hence, while the public sector bears all the commercial risks in a service contract, this risk is shared in the case of a lease, and fully assumed by the private sector in build-operate-transfer (BOT) and build-operate-own (BOO) contracts, and divestitures.

### *Reduced state intervention*

Private ownership is also shown in these models to enable a more credible promise for the state not to intervene, thus providing beneficial incentive effects for employment and investment (Sappington and Stiglitz 1987a). According to public choice theory, the state is intrinsically inefficient and perpetually overburdened and underdisciplined (Linder 2000), and 'public enterprises are inefficient because they address the objectives of politicians rather than maximize efficiency' (Boycko *et al.* 1996: 309). SOEs are seen to be constrained by the behaviour of politicians and bureaucrats who pursue their own utility rather than the public interest. As such, political motives usually outweigh efficiency considerations (Krueger 1990; Vickers and Yarrow 1991), and any economic intervention by the state is viewed as a potentially counter-productive policy response and an invitation to rent-seeking behaviour. The greater the degree of regulation, the more private resources are absorbed by rent-seeking activities (Krueger 1974, 1990; Buchanan 1980).

Because SOEs, through the allocation of rents, are seen as a vehicle to redistribute wealth or promote politically motivated redistributive arrangements (Jones and Mason 1982), privatization is desirable as it 'effectively drives a wedge between politicians and managers' by depoliticizing firms and making it too costly for politicians to subsidize them (Boycko *et al.* 1996: 318). By placing some distance between the government and producer and substantially increasing the transaction costs of such interventions, privatization is said to make more credible the promise not to use public funds to subsidize losses (Sappington and Stiglitz 1987a; Stiglitz 1996). This also has beneficial effects by subjecting the firm to the discipline of the market. Privatization therefore limits government intervention by changing 'the residual rights of intervention' and altering the incentives to intervene (Sappington and Stiglitz 1987a: 80).

### *Financing capital investment*

The increasing cost of infrastructure development has required new financing solutions, and privatization has been promoted as a way of mobilizing resources and investing them cost-effectively to meet the growing needs of developing countries while also overcoming existing inefficiencies. Privatization is seen as suitable for high-cost, capital-intensive infrastructure projects where cost is the main concern and where there are limited externalities (Heilman and Johnson 1992; Rosenau 2000b) because private ownership is said to provide more incentives or make it easier to implement cost-covering tariffs, thus making the project more viable. The private sector is said to offer potential efficiency gains (needed to turn around or restructure failing public enterprises), new sources of funding (leveraged development) and project revenue enhancement (World Bank 1994; Hakim *et al.* 1996b; Payson and Steckler 1996). While governments may have access to cheaper credit, this is argued to be insufficient to outweigh inefficiencies arising from lax financial discipline, leading to cost overruns and delays in infrastructure construction (World Bank 1994). In this case, an efficient private operator who can reduce cost and raise efficiency can theoretically raise money more cheaply as lenders face lower default rates.

## ***Privatization problems***

These well-known arguments for privatization are, however, problematic because the private sector is often unable or unwilling to finance capital investment on its own, thereby necessitating state subsidies. Subsidies will also be needed for welfare reasons and to promote learning. These subsidies potentially dilute incentives, thereby requiring continued state intervention in the form of regulation and subsidy management. As such, privatization does not lead to the clear designation of property rights or finance capital investment, especially in developing countries, and it does not reduce state intervention.

*Subsidies for capital costs, welfare and learning*

The benefits of privatization are premised on the clear designation of property rights where the private owner, as the residual claimant, has full incentives to improve efficiency as this impacts directly on his or her residual returns. This, however, requires that the private owner must either be able to control revenue and/or bear risks. In reality, these incentives are diluted and full divestitures have been limited because of: 1, the high capital costs and significant externalities associated with large-scale projects such as in infrastructure; 2, welfare concerns (which constrain the implementation of cost-covering tariffs); and 3, the lack of entrepreneurial capacity (which necessitates learning and 'catching up').

Contrary to privatization providing new funding sources for capital-intensive projects, large capital investments usually require some public financing. This is because infrastructure development is characterized by long-term contracts involving durable assets with high sunk costs, asset lumpiness, long gestation periods and uncertainty. Being capital-intensive means that turnover compared to investment is low, while long lead times mean that the financing requirements during the initial stages of the work are high (Fayard 1999) yet revenue is low in the early years of the operation. Consequently, many infrastructure projects which offer positive economic and social benefits cannot break even (Poole 1996; Fayard 1999). Additionally, a higher price elasticity for demand leads to uncertain revenues, with investors expecting a higher rate of return given the higher risk (Payson and Steckler 1996). Private sector financing also costs more due to the possibility of default, project-specific risks and limited liability (Sappington and Stiglitz 1987a; Daniels and Trebilcock 2000). As a result, the private sector faces great difficulties in financing such high-cost, long-gestation projects without government guarantees (to secure long-term loans) and tax breaks (to reduce the tax burden at the beginning of the loan period) (Windsor 1996; Fayard 1999; Dunn 2000). The state must therefore either reduce the private sector's share of the cost, or its risk, to ensure the project is viable for private sector participation (Heilman and Johnson 1992).

In contrast, the state can keep costs down by providing long-term loans, given that long maturity is more important than low interest rates (see Fayard 1999) (provided that moral hazard problems can be mitigated because the state as a financier is likely to be perceived as a weaker enforcer of changes in management than a private financier). This is complicated by the perceived need for government financial assistance to encourage private participation to ensure that projects that have negative net private present value are undertaken (Daniels and Trebilcock 2000). This may also involve monopoly pricing or profit guarantees to attract investors or ensure project viability (e.g. see Kessides 2004).

Given the difficulties the private sector faces in financing capital intensive projects, privatization has increasingly involved some form of public–private partnership (PPP) (see Supiot 1996; Sparer 1996 and 1998; Saltman and Figueras 1998, all cited in Pongsiri 2001: 14), with the actual number of complete divestitures being small, especially in sectors such as rail where concessions have been the dominant form of private participation (Kessides 2004). A striking feature of PPPs is the high degree of government financial assistance because of the very high capital costs and the need to subsidize public goods or compensate for positive externalities. Despite the promise of private sector investment in infrastructure with privatization, 'utility operators around the world are having an extraordinarily hard time securing the financing needed to maintain and expand services' (Kessides 2004: 11), and subsidies and grants play an increasingly significant part of infrastructure investment in developed countries.

The sharing of risks leads to risk-incentive trade-offs as private incentives are reduced where the risk is transferred back to the state (Heilman and Johnson 1992; Daniels and Trebilcock 2000). As risks have largely been borne by the public sector, there can be no clear designation of property rights as the owner 'cannot capture the whole social and economic benefits generated' nor would such a designation ensure efficiency and high levels of investment (Fayard 1999: 12–13). This means that the owner's 'residual' depends just as much on government decisions as on performance in monitoring the work process, and this can significantly dilute the incentives to monitor in the absence of adequate institutional arrangements and regulation. Where government subsidies finance the project, the government may constrain design and construction options, but more importantly may be unwilling to let the project fail or terminate concessions given the 'essential' nature of public services and political repercussions of interruptions in their provision.

Operational subsidies will be needed where the private operator cannot charge cost-covering tariffs or fares. Cost-covering tariffs are usually politically sensitive but remain a central element of investment-oriented regulation as this is seen to encourage efficient actions by consumers, suppliers and investors, promote financial viability and increase access to affordable services (Kessides 2004). Past pricing policies by SOEs and subsidy mechanisms are seen as seriously flawed as they undermined the financial viability of utilities, leading to chronic underinvestment and a deterioration in service quality as subsidies are poorly targeted while distorted prices impose significant costs (Kessides 2004). As underpricing leads to underinvestment, privatization is said to require aligning prices with underlying costs to attract investors, particularly if the private sector is expected to invest in rehabilitating the system or expanding coverage (Kessides 2004).

The case for cost-covering tariffs is thus twofold. On the one hand, this is needed to expand affordable services and access, especially for poor people. However, this will involve raising service charges which impact upon poor people. To counter this, it is argued that subsidized services (e.g. water, electricity and telecommunications) largely benefit the middle and upper classes, and hence increased prices mainly affect these groups rather than the poor. The privatization of utilities in Latin America, for example, is argued to have hurt mainly the middle class (Morley 2000, cited in Cornia 2003). On the other hand, it is argued that 'many poor people would be willing to pay for efficient services if they were offered', and regulatory impediments to financial viability are said to be eliminated when utilities are allowed to charge appropriate prices in a competitive environment (Kessides 2004: 50–51).

In reality, cost-covering tariffs are often not possible because much of the population in developing countries have a limited ability to pay for basic services, and tariff increases usually encounter strong resistance (e.g. see Parker and Kirkpatrick 2002: 16; Estache 2003; Kessides 2004), not least from the middle class. Not surprisingly, privatization has become increasingly more unpopular, for example in Latin America and Sri Lanka (Zeufack 2004). As such, the government is obliged to guarantee universal service provision of basic services even after privatization. The general unwillingness of populations in developing countries to pay for higher service charges is the reason why governments have been unable (as opposed to unwilling) to implement cost-covering tariffs. Subsidies will therefore be necessary for operational viability if universal service obligations and public unwillingness to pay higher charges prevent the implementation of cost-covering tariffs or fares.[1] This is not to argue that cost-covering tariffs are unimportant in order to attract private participation, as demonstrated by the withdrawal of UK firm Biwater from a planned water project in Zimbabwe in 1999 because consumers were too poor to pay the necessary tariffs to meet the company's profit projections (Parker and Kirkpatrick 2002). Rather, the choice is between cost-reflective tariffs which are politically difficult to implement, or lower prices but with subsidies to guarantee returns for private investors. Welfare and political considerations mean that the state will need to subsidize capital and operational costs to help make privatization commercially feasible for the private sector to invest in infrastructure.

Subsidies will also be required because many developing countries lack the entrepreneurial capacity in terms of depth (capabilities and technologies) and breadth (a large enough pool of potential entrepreneurs) (e.g. see Jones and Mason 1982: 25). Capital formation is not limited by political risk (i.e. the threat of state predation) (e.g. see Bates 2001) but rather the lack of domestic capitalists. As such, privatization is likely to be undertaken where the state is engaged in developing entrepreneurial capacity, and this will require subsidies for learning and 'catching up'. Rather than merely implementing measures to encourage private investment, governments will then need to help the private sector in developing countries to acquire technological and entrepreneurial skills, which requires learning-by-doing. The operation of enterprises during this critical period usually requires direct or indirect state subsidies (i.e. rents for learning or conditional subsidies) (e.g. see Amsden 1989; Wade 1990; Aoki *et al.* 1997; Khan 2000a, 2000b).

### *Regulation and management of subsidies*

The necessity for subsidies discussed above will require continued, and in some areas, enhanced state intervention, both ex ante and ex post. The state must be able to ensure that correct decisions are made ex ante in relation to what is privatized, to whom and how, the types of subsidies required, and the appropriate regulatory framework. This will depend largely on its institutional capacity and available information to make the right technical decisions. However, the state must also be able to make and implement decisions post privatization in response to ex ante mistakes and changing entrepreneurial capacity (in the case of the management of learning rents). This will entail some element of ex post state discretion involving qualitative judgements which are often arbitrary (i.e. how high to set targets, how much subsidy to provide, how much pressure to apply, when to withdraw subsidies, and when to replace private sector operators with new ones).

The management of learning rents in developing countries will therefore entail a very different type of regulation involving political judgement and not just technical requirements. This will require more dynamic regulatory structures to respond to changing entrepreneurial capacity, and to push entrepreneurs to levels previously not achieved and which cannot be achieved in the public sector. Regulation here is thus not just about providing a stable and predictable environment to encourage private investment, or to protect consumer welfare in monopoly environments, but also to manage rents, especially those related to promoting learning and developing entrepreneurial capacity. The ability of the state to intervene ex post to correct ex ante mistakes and respond to changing circumstances will depend on the political context (in particular the balance of power in society that may allow or prevent some types of disciplining of entrepreneurs).

## ***Political motivations for privatization***

We have argued that privatization entails continued state intervention in terms of providing implicit and explicit subsidies. Successful privatization will then depend on how well the state can design and manage these subsidies. As discussed above, the ability of the state to intervene effectively, particularly to correct ex ante mistakes, will be politically circumscribed, depending on the state's strength in relation to the groups receiving subsidies. This will in turn depend on the political context in which privatization is undertaken. Here, conventional arguments for privatization are based on the assumption that developing countries privatize mainly for economic reasons (e.g. see Hemming and Mansoor 1988; Kikeri *et al.* 1994; Plane 1997). The failure here to account for the political motivations behind privatization restricts our understanding of the character of privatization in many developing countries in terms of what is privatized, how and to whom, and the effectiveness of related institutions and state intervention, which are central to our assessment of privatization. As such, this approach cannot explain why privatization may fail, and why weak institutions persist.

Privatization is an inherently political process as 'what is privatized and how represents the state's continuing intervention within the economy, favouring certain capitals at the expense of others' (Fine 1997: 376; also see Vickers and Yarrow 1991). Different constellations of political interest will thus produce different levels of political response to pressure for privatization (Cook and Minogue 1990: 29; also see Cook 1997). Privatization may be undertaken as part of state attempts to develop domestic entrepreneurial capacity to meet developmental objectives, or be politically motivated (e.g. by powerful groups contesting resources and political leaders wishing to secure support through the distribution of economic resources to these groups). Decisions to 'establish, retain or divest a public enterprise are thus not made in a political vacuum' and 'ownership and control of economic units are instruments for advancing certain interests and frustrating others' in the struggle for power among various interest groups (Jones and Mason 1982: 16; also see Cook and Kirkpatrick 1988). As politics will drive decisions to privatize (Parker and Kirkpatrick 2003), who benefits depends on which groups are more powerful and influential. The nature and outcome of privatization will therefore be affected by the balance of power in society. So, while there may often be economic (fiscal and efficiency) reasons, privatization will usually be pushed through by groups which stand to gain the most and will only be introduced if it is politically feasible to do so, namely where the balance of power in society favours its introduction.

This balance of power, and the character of the groups contesting and potentially benefiting, will in turn shape the nature of a country's privatization programme. In developed countries, privatization is usually awarded to existing capitalists most capable of financing and running former state enterprises. This is not the case in developing countries where there is a lack of entrepreneurial capacity and where groups contesting for privatization projects may not be capitalists but often members of an 'unproductive' intermediate class who are politically powerful or well-connected. This will invariably affect how privatization is undertaken in terms of the chosen industries, mode of privatization, choice of candidates as future owners, the choice of regulatory structure, and performance (outcome), particularly where privatization is used to develop domestic capitalists. This allows us to address one of the paradoxes in public choice theory: why should politicians and bureaucrats support privatization if this is not in their interest? Here, privatization will be politically motivated where it offers opportunities for certain groups (including politicians and bureaucrats) to capture resources. Understanding the political context and motivations for privatization thus helps explain the character of privatization which allows us to then determine why privatization may fail and what conditions are necessary for it to work.

## Why may privatization fail?

Conventional arguments for privatization blame failure on weak political and economic institutions, the problems of patronage and corruption associated with these, and arbitrary state intervention in many developing countries. As a result, privatization is characterized by poor choices, poor implementation and weak regulation, with a lack of credible commitment to contracts or policies. There are two problems with this explanation. First, it does not locate institutional failure within a country's political context nor account for political motivations. This is important given that institutions are the outcome of historical and political factors. This will then allow us to explain why weak institutions may persist, and to come up with more appropriate solutions to improve the state's regulatory capacity. Looking at a country's political context will also help us correctly identify the motivations for privatization. As discussed in the previous section, privatization will often be politically motivated, especially in developing countries. This will affect what is privatized, how and to whom. Second, and as a result of this, privatization will entail regulation which goes beyond conventional views of regulation in the context of market failure. Hence, rather than simply promoting competition and safeguarding property rights (to encourage private investment), regulation will be needed to deal with diluted incentives arising from subsidies for capital costs, welfare considerations and learning (to develop domestic entrepreneurial capacity).

The success of privatization then depends on the effectiveness of state regulation in the context of managing these subsidies. This will depend on the state's institutional and political capacity. The failure of privatization can thus be due to institutional or political failure. As mentioned earlier, institutional failure refers to the absence of, or weaknesses in, political and economic institutions which affect the choice, implementation and regulation of privatizations. Political failure refers to the inability of the government to enforce regulation. As we shall see, both explanations of failure are based on different conceptions of what privatization involves, and thus provide different recommendations for successful privatization. Both institutional and political failures represent state failures which can occur before (ex ante) or after (ex post) privatization. It will be argued that political failure, in particular the state's ex post failure, is more serious and provides a more useful explanation for the failure of privatization because mistakes are bound to occur ex ante due to informational constraints and political considerations which affect the choice of privatization.

## *Conventional explanations of failure*

### *Weak political institutions*

The view that failure is due to weak institutions is grounded in the New Institutional Economics (NIE) which seeks to explain (market) failure in terms of transaction costs, imperfect information, the structure of property rights and collective action problems (Clague 1997a; Williamson 2000; also see Bardhan 1989b). For the NIE, underlying the failure of privatization in developing countries is the problem of political interference which is seen to undermine regulatory independence, thereby affecting private investment and incentives. Governments in developing countries are viewed as corrupt and incompetent, lacking credible commitments not to intervene, failing to safeguard property rights and being incapable of implementing proper, consistent regulatory procedures. As a result, privatization in developing countries is poorly implemented and regulated, lacking regulatory independence and credibility, and subject to widespread corruption, regulatory and political capture, and arbitrary political intervention (Tullock 1967; Stiglitz 1971; Krueger 1974; Bhagwati 1982; Laffont 1996, cited in Kessides 2004: 80; Daniels and Trebilcock 2000).

Corruption, patrimonialism, cronyism and clientelism are seen to create serious problems for public administration in developing countries (Theobold 1990, cited in Parker and Kirkpatrick 2002: 13; also see Boeker 1993, cited in Plane 1997: 364; Cook and Kirkpatrick 1995; Parker and Kirkpatrick 2003). Corruption has been blamed for the failure of privatization in Zambia and many parts of Africa, India and a number of transitional economies (Tangri 1999; Tangri and Mwenda 2001; Craig 2000, 2001, all cited in Parker and Kirkpatrick 2002: 14; University of Greenwich 2001; Meseguer 2002, both cited in Parker and Kirkpatrick 2003). The absence of regulatory independence is also argued to be a major reason for the failure of privatization in developing countries, made difficult by deliberate government actions and a lack of understanding of the importance of separation of powers (Kessides 2004). Regulatory capture is associated with a weighting which favours producer over consumer surplus, while political capture occurs when regulation becomes a tool of self-interest within government or the ruling elite. The latter is considered a much greater risk given the problems of credible commitment, history of arbitrary administrative intervention, and discretionary use of executive power said to characterize developing countries (Stiglitz 1998, cited in Parker and Kirkpatrick 2002: 8; Pongsiri 2001; Kessides 2004).

The state's lack of credibility to commit to contracts or policies is attributed to weak political and economic institutions which safeguard contracts and property rights (e.g. see Clague 1997b; Williamson 2000). The absence of democracy and transparency means that 'policies are changed by absolute decree with no prior notice' and 'bureaucrats may have a great deal of discretion in the application of business regulations', with their decisions being unpredictable (Clague 1997b: 25–26). The underlying assumption here is that state intervention is potentially damaging and the state is prone to predation, which makes it necessary to limit the scope of state intervention to the enforcement of contracts and property rights, while making credible the threat not to confiscate or intervene arbitrarily.[2]

Here, democracy is the best way to safeguard property and contractual rights by preventing arbitrary state intervention (e.g. see Clague *et al.* 1997; Haggard 1997; Bates 2001). Democracy is said to reduce the incentive of political leaders to redistribute because the majority or ruling group has a more 'encompassing interest' in society's productivity (e.g. see Olson 1997; Olson and Kahkonen 2000). An autocrat, in comparison, may also have an encompassing interest in the society, but is seen to have the power and incentive to unilaterally confiscate assets whenever he has a short-term horizon. The literature does not explain why democratically elected leaders should have longer-term horizons given their usually limited terms in office compared to many autocrats, or how democratic institutions could provide such a credible commitment not to confiscate (e.g. see Przeworski and Limongi 1993). Instead, it is argued that a democracy provides for more secure property and contract enforcement rights because it constrains political leaders from repressing the political rights of opponents or eliminating the vital interests of losers given that political tenure is limited (Clague *et al.* 1997; Olson 1997; Olson and Kahkonen 2000; Leftwich 2002).

### *Weak economic institutions*

The benefits of privatization come from changed incentives for privatized firms which depend on the competition and regulation facing such firms (Vickers and Yarrow 1991). The fundamental privatization theorem states that 'when certain conditions are satisfied, government involvement cannot improve upon the performance of the private market' (Sappington and Stiglitz 1987a: 568). Here, privatization failures are analogous to market failures, and have been blamed on weak economic institutions in developing countries (compared to developed countries), exacerbated by political interference and corruption as discussed above. It is for these reasons that the relationship between privatization, incentives and efficiency are believed to be less clear-cut, and the differences between public and private ownership in developing countries is less distinct than in countries with stronger institutions and private sectors.

A number of regulatory failures have been identified, based on a comparison of institutional structures between developed and developing countries (see Noll 1999; Stern and Holder 1999; Cook 1999; Brownbridge and Kirkpatrick 2000, all cited in Parker and Kirkpatrick 2002: 2). Developed countries are seen to have competitive product, capital and labour markets; protected and well-defined property rights; well-understood standards of business conduct; and relatively high standards of probity in public administration. In contrast, developing countries are said to be characterized by imperfectly competitive and incomplete markets; underdeveloped capital markets; weak management and patronage in appointments; poorly protected private property rights; weak business ethics; and low standards of public administration, including cronyism and corruption (Parker and Kirkpatrick 2003: 23).

Furthermore, regulatory frameworks in developing countries are seen as fragmented and lacking in coherence (Kessides 2004), constrained by the lack of technical expertise, insufficient institutional preconditions (including a lack of checks and balances, and weak auditing, accounting and tax systems), a resistant political and administrative culture, and opposition from organized labour (Parker and Kirkpatrick 2002; Kessides 2004). A study of infrastructure regulation in six Asian developing countries (Bangladesh, India, Indonesia, Malaysia, Pakistan and the Philippines) found significant weaknesses in coherence, independence, accountability, transparency and predictability (Stern and Holder 1999, cited in Kessides 2004: 91).

### *Problems with conventional explanations*

Conventional explanations focussing on institutional failure essentially look at ex ante failure, namely mistakes made before privatization. This includes the state's failure to determine the viability of a privatization project and is usually, though not wholly, related to information and institutional failure. Decisions may be based on insufficient or incorrect information, and/or the government may choose to privatize without the necessary institutions or procedures in place. The emphasis here is on strengthening institutions to encourage private investment (by reducing corruption and arbitrary political intervention) and promoting efficiency (by maintaining competitive pressures). This usually involves good governance measures at the broader level (i.e. democracy, transparency and accountability), and substantive procedures in the case of privatization (i.e. transparent selection, clearly specified contracts and predictable regulation). This approach is problematic because ex ante mistakes will invariably occur as a result of information constraints, thereby compromising the choice of candidates, contract specification and regulation. Furthermore, while these measures are desirable in themselves, they are based on an ahistorical reading of institutional development and a restricted view of privatization in developing countries which do not take into account political factors and why privatization may be undertaken.

*Information constraints*

Arguments to improve institutional arrangements are based on conventional explanations of privatization failure as a result of weak institutions. As such, proposed solutions generally emphasize the need to strengthen the selection process, contract specification and regulation. However, the state's ability to make the correct decisions in these three areas will be constrained by imperfect information.

Conventional explanations stress the importance of transparency and competition in the selection process (e.g. see Kikeri *et al.* 1994). Competitive bidding is central as it ensures transparency and the most efficient outcome by stimulating interest across a broad range of potential partners. Awarding a concession to the bidder proposing the lowest future tariff levels, for example, indicates the highest efficiency. However, competitive bidding is dependent on the quality of available information and incurs significant transaction costs which the government must shoulder (Weber 2002). Information is needed so that bids are realistic and viable (in terms of risks to the private sector) as poor-quality information results in underbidding and renegotiations (Stottmann 2000). More crucially, a transparent selection process (even if this was politically possible) does not guarantee that the chosen candidate will be the most efficient as the government is unable to properly screen applicants due to asymmetric information. Here, the winning bidder may not be the most efficient, conform closest to government objectives or be the one who values the asset the most, but simply the most optimistic about the future price of the asset, the best at price discrimination or the most likely to default on promises (Sappington and Stiglitz 1987a; Stiglitz 1996); or may have the greatest ex post bargaining ability, especially if there is the possibility of renegotiation (without competition) (Kessides 2004).

The requirements for domestic ownership or control in developing countries also mean that expertise is usually secured through a technical partnership with a foreign party. This means that the local owner or concessionaire need not have the requisite expertise or experience so long as this can be obtained from overseas. Hence, selection here will not necessarily be on the basis of the most competitive bidder but rather the best politically connected bidder. Indeed, this is an important criterion for foreign companies seeking a local partner to secure privatization contracts in developing countries.

More importantly, inappropriate candidate choice may not lead to failure if this can be remedied through learning rents and clearly specified incentives and penalties. The key difference between developed and developing countries in the context of asymmetric information is that inappropriate candidates can be more easily disciplined through the threat of replacement in the former where there are less constraints on entrepreneurial capacity. The institutional design of the process of divestment can also matter. For example, if the enterprise is first leased out before being privatized, non-performing candidates may be more easily replaced (e.g. the concession can later be given to someone else), but reallocation may not be as easily carried out if outright privatization is the first step. As ex ante mistakes will invariably occur in the selection process, transparency is less important than the state's capacity to correct mistakes arising from political and information constraints.

Successful privatization is also argued to depend on contract specification to clearly allocate risks and establish accountability. The contract needs to address the problems arising from the divergent interests of the government and private sector, and an incentive-accountability structure is needed especially when partners have separate interests (Rosenau 2000b). How risk is shared is directly related to the incentive structure of the contract (Heilman and Johnson 1992).

However, contract design is also constrained by imperfect information, namely the inability to specify all future contingencies, leading to incomplete contracts (where it is not possible to fully specify incentives and risks) and inevitable contract renegotiation. Ex post contract renegotiations are therefore likely where the quality of information is poor at the start, and the possibility of early renegotiation may in turn lead to unrealistically low bids (Dnes 1995, cited in Kessides 2004: 106). The high incidence of contract renegotiation has been blamed on political interference, opportunistic behaviour and flawed contract design (Guasch *et al.* 2003, cited in Kessides 2004: 107). However, as it is neither possible (due to asymmetric information and the inability to predict the future) nor desirable (in terms of the flexibility to deal with the circumstances arising from future uncertainties) to design complete contracts, governments and firms agree to performance standards that can be modified to fit contingencies, with contracts often providing loopholes or relying on loose parameters of fulfilment (MacNeil 1978, cited in Weber 2002: 49). As such, contract renegotiation (and post-contract opportunism) almost always remains a reality (e.g. see Parker and Kirkpatrick 2002).

Furthermore, contract renegotiation appears to result in regulatory, as opposed to political, capture in developing countries (Kessides 2004). Evidence shows that contract renegotiation has been high in Latin America, especially in transport (where 50 per cent of contracts were renegotiated) and water (75 per cent renegotiations), with two out of every three of these requested by the operator and leading to increased tariffs or reduced investment (Estache 2003). The ability of the state to enforce contracts then becomes more important than actual contract design as '(e)ven the best contracts – those that clearly specify terms of fulfilment and breach – must be enforceable in order to be effective in practice' (Weber 2002: 48).

This is especially important as contracts are not only limited by incomplete information but also by the limits of liability and enforcement. As there are bounds on the losses the contractor can be forced to bear (e.g. due to bankruptcy laws or political considerations), the contractor may renege on the contract rather than deliver. Hence 'with feasible penalties for failure that are dwarfed by the social losses that would result from failure, the private producers cannot be induced through monetary means to invest the appropriate level of effort to prevent failure' (Sappington and Stiglitz 1987a: 573). Contract enforcement is further limited by the prohibitively high costs of enforcement and the perception of being anti-business and deterring potential investors (Weber 2002). The key condition here is thus one of contract enforcement and credible sanctions by the state to ensure that the private sector fulfils its obligations, especially where subsidies are involved. The failure to do so, rather than poor contract specification, provides a better explanation why privatization may fail.

Finally, successful privatization will depend on the regulatory framework. Regulation is needed as it is not possible to fully specify incentives and risks in a contract, and because the natural monopoly features of public infrastructure projects limit competition and hence incentives for efficiency. Regulation is thus conventionally seen as necessary to address three broad classes of market failure: imperfect competition, imperfect information and externalities (Sappington and Stiglitz 1987b). Following from this, the discussion of regulation is largely restricted to preserving incentives for efficiency in the absence of competition. Competition is seen as preferable to regulation because competitive markets are believed to generate superior knowledge of consumer demands and producer supply costs. In other words, the social welfare results of regulation remain 'second best' as the regulator does not have sufficient information to regulate optimally to maximize social welfare (Sidak and Spulber 1998, cited in Parker and Kirkpatrick 2002: 8). As such, measures to promote competition such as through unbundling and isolating monopoly segments is preferred as these also reduce the need for regulation (World Bank 1994; Kessides 2004).

Here, the emphasis is on 'good governance' measures (independence, transparency, predictability, accountability and credibility) in order to safeguard the private sector from arbitrary interventions, thereby providing a stable and predictable environment which encourages private investment (e.g. see Levy and Spiller 1993). A set of substantive procedures follow from these guiding principles aimed at promoting regulatory independence, accountability, commitment and credibility (e.g. freedom from political interference; adequate funding; judicial appeals; transparent decision-making processes) (Parker 2001; Smith 1997, cited in Kessides 2004: 85). Discussion of the state's regulatory capacity has therefore generally focused on narrow technical and institutional requirements, namely financial and human resources (i.e. qualified personnel with regulatory expertise) and coherence (i.e. clearly defined responsibilities between different agencies and government departments), with the choice of regulation dependent on the regulatory authority's technical capacity and available information. For example, both price cap regulation and rate of return regulation[3] require extensive and reliable information on all aspects of the utility business to determine the appropriate benchmark (or price cap) and rate of return, while sophisticated regulatory training and technical ability are needed to calculate realistic benchmarks.

However, regulation will be compromised by imperfect information. By sharing some of the capital costs or subsidizing the operator in return for lower tariffs, the private owner's residual return no longer has a one-to-one relationship to effort in management. The presence of asymmetric information means that managers are much better informed about industry conditions and their behaviour can be monitored only imperfectly (Vickers and Yarrow 1995). This makes it even more difficult to determine the operator's actual costs and profits, and hence, the appropriate amount of subsidies or level of price cap. This creates disincentives by encouraging the operator to artificially inflate costs. Privatization therefore does not solve the problems of incentives and monitoring, and entails greater regulation to monitor these subsidies, particularly to ensure that performance targets are met. And if the state has to monitor and sanction subsidies, this raises precisely the types of questions about incentives and constraints in the state sector that were used to explain the underperformance of public enterprises in the first place.

More critically, this is a narrow view of what regulation entails in privatization. Regulation will also involve managing subsidies and enforcing discipline to ensure performance targets are met, and not just safeguarding private investment and promoting competition. The issue of rent management becomes central to the regulatory framework if these rents are to lead to efficient outcomes (Khan 2004). Effective regulation depends not just on institutional capacity but more so on the state's political capacity, as regulatory effectiveness is constrained by the capacity of governments to enforce regulatory rules (e.g. see Cook 1999). This includes the power to efficiently allocate – and reallocate – property rights and subsidies (i.e. to replace owners and concessionaires, or withdraw subsidies) and implement difficult decisions depending on the type of privatization and sector.

In developing countries, this may involve coordinating capital and operational decisions to integrate sectors such as transport networks, and overriding public opposition to tariff or fare increases if this is needed to ensure commercial viability. It may also require the political capacity to provide subsidies with the appropriate credible threats to prevent moral hazard problems and sustained inefficiency of the private sector replacing the inefficiency of the public sector. The state's ability to subject firms to market discipline therefore depends not just on its regulatory capacity (e.g. see Kessides 2004) but more explicitly its effective political capacity (see Khan 2004), especially as high-density narrow-interest groups may develop, leading to pressure for protection and other types of subsidies (Olson 2000; also see Krueger 1990). From this perspective, the failure of privatization is due to the state's ex post failure to correct mistakes and manage rents. A broader view of privatization and regulation must therefore take into account the political context and motivations behind the decision to privatize.

*A historical view of institutions*

Conventional institutional recommendations are unrealistic as they are benchmarked against Western norms that do not account for the political realities in developing countries nor explain the performance of countries in East Asia which industrialized without these institutions in place. For that matter, they do not even reflect the experiences of advanced countries at similar stages of their economic development (e.g. see Chang 2002; Huber *et al.* 1993).

There is no clear correlation between governance indicators (such as democracy and transparency/low corruption) and performance (e.g. see Przeworski and Limongi 1993; Khan 2004). This claim is a fairly recent one given that democracy (i.e. universal suffrage and the freedom to form unions) was historically seen to threaten property rights (Przeworski and Limongi 1993). Rather, democracy in Europe was the outcome of shifts in the balance of class power as a result of capitalist development which transformed the class structure, enlarging the working and middle classes (e.g. see Huber *et al.* 1993). That is to say, institutions are a product of both social, economic and political history, and current conditions (e.g. see Parker 2001), and institutional change depends on the nature of social relations and the balance of power in society, with the emergence of efficiency-improving arrangements affected by redistributive considerations (Bardhan 1989b; Parker and Kirkpatrick 2002). This perspective gives us a different set of insights when we try to make sense of the constraints facing privatization strategies.

The experiences of advanced countries and late industrializers during their transition to capitalism demonstrate that the allocation of new property rights, through political processes that implicitly grants some individuals massive rents, is an important part of the process of capital accumulation (Khan 2004). This process has not been transparent and indeed, corruption has played a historical role in the emergence of the entrepreneurial class in Europe (Bardhan 1997). In the case of South Korea in the 1980s and 1990s, more recent evidence reveals substantial corruption was involved in the allocation of new property rights or rents. As competition for resources will be intense and thus more heavily contested in developing countries, the creation of new property rights (e.g. through privatization) is unlikely to be allocated through transparent processes but instead in personalized and partisan ways, and through patron–client networks (Khan 1998, forthcoming).

As such, anti-corruption measures will be difficult to implement as it may not be in the interest of the state or powerful groups. Moreover, where non-capitalist or unproductive groups are politically dominant, efforts to promote good governance institutions such as democracy may simply lead to political capture by these groups becoming easier. Political and nationalistic considerations also prevent privatization to specific ethnic groups or foreign interests (Cook and Kirkpatrick 1988; Parker and Kirkpatrick 2003), further limiting the pool of acceptable candidates. As such, focusing on corruption ignores the intrinsically political nature of privatization which often cannot be undertaken using transparent processes. Here, weak institutions are often the outcome of political factors as well as a cause of failure.

### *Political failure*

As privatization entails continued state intervention, its success depends on the effectiveness of this intervention. This includes the institutional capacity to make the correct ex ante decisions relating to the choice of candidates, contract specification and regulation. However, as discussed in the previous section, ex ante decisions will invariably be compromised by imperfect information and the political context in which privatization is undertaken. This can affect state decisions and institutional arrangements, leading to poor or incorrect choices. Thus, while it is important for the state to have the institutional capacity to make the right decisions, it must more importantly be able to implement these, correct any ex ante mistakes which result from information constraints, and respond to changing entrepreneurial capacity in relation to the management of learning rents. That is to say, privatization can fail because: 1, the state has failed to clearly specify terms and conditions of subsidies, thereby failing to preserve incentives for the private owner or operator; 2, the state may make the correct decisions but be unable to implement these, in which case failure will be in enforcing conditions which must accompany any subsidy programme; and/or 3, the state is aware of decisions which turn out to be incorrect ex post, but is unable to rectify these. The failure to implement policy and to correct ex ante mistakes represent ex post political failures, and this can provide a more useful explanation for the failure of privatization in the context of developing countries.

The political motivations that usually drive privatization in developing countries can explain why ex ante failure often occurs (e.g. where privatization proceeds despite the lack of sufficient information and viability, or without proper institutions in place) as powerful interests 'may be pushing some forms of privatization that are economically not sensible but politically difficult to avoid' (Roland 1994: 1161). This will affect the choice, implementation and regulation of privatizations, as well as the accompanying institutions. The persistence of weak institutions (i.e. weak procedures, regulatory frameworks and regulatory capacity) may, in this perspective, be a reflection of a wider political failure on the part of the state to strengthen institutions given the existing balance of power in society. The choice of privatization will be in part shaped by the strength of groups which stand to gain. Hence, where there are powerful but 'unproductive' groups, privatization could involve non-competitive sectors, usually infrastructure construction or former state monopolies. This has often been the case in developing countries.

This means that the efficiency gains from private operations or ownership is not guaranteed, and successful privatization will depend on state support to help finance the privatization, subsidize any operational losses where cost-covering tariffs may not be possible, and promote learning in order to develop the necessary entrepreneurial capacity to run the enterprise efficiently. This is more important than the choice of candidate because the lack of skills and capital can theoretically be addressed through learning rents and state subsidies. Whether privatization leads to learning and efficiency gains will therefore depend on the ability of the state to manage these subsidies. This entails a different sort of regulation, one which requires the institutional capacity to make the right decisions, but more importantly, the political capacity to credibly enforce sanctions where performance targets are not met (Khan 2004), especially where implicit subsidies are involved in the determination of the sale price, and where there are learning rents to develop entrepreneurial capacity. Rather than committing not to intervene, the state may also have to intervene arbitrarily and possibly even reallocate property rights where necessary. The failure to do so represents the state's ex post failure and is more important as this is more difficult to correct than institutional or ex ante failure.

In the case of developing countries, it may be difficult to reallocate an enterprise to an alternative entrepreneur because appropriate alternative entrepreneurial capacity may not be available and political constraints may prevent reallocation of assets away from powerful or well-connected individuals. As there may be no efficient entrepreneurs ex ante, and in some cases no entrepreneurs at all in that particular sector, the allocation of resources through privatization is bound to involve some degree of arbitrariness in developing countries. The purpose of privatization is indeed often to create entrepreneurs. Thus the choice in most developing countries is not between unproductive and productive entrepreneurs, but rather to ensure how 'one can transform into the other depending on the relationship with the state and the state's ability to effectively enforce growth-enhancing institutions' (Khan 2004: 34).

In other words, there is no reason why inappropriate candidates cannot be made productive provided there are sufficient incentives, learning rents and credible state sanctions. (Conversely, it is crucial that the state is able to ensure that productive groups do not become unproductive.) In addition, the state's ex post capacity may be further constrained by public service obligations and also national considerations. This can lead to moral hazard problems where privatization involves important enterprises (e.g. a national airline) or projects (e.g. public infrastructure) as it cannot easily substitute non-performing private owners, yet it is also politically unfeasible to let the enterprise or project fail, even more so if this involves the provision of a public good (e.g. water or sewage treatment). The choice then is between subsidizing the private firm in order to ensure continued service provision or, as a last resort, renationalizing the project. Here, renationalization represents the ultimate failure of privatization. The state's political failure to manage subsidies in this context can therefore provide a more important explanation for the failure of privatization.

Without accounting for this type of political context, the discussion of corruption and 'good institutions' is also meaningless as the persistence of weak institutions cannot be explained. As privatization policies are embedded in social relations, 'cultural and political assumptions and factors related to privatization need to be analysed . . . in a dynamic perspective in their own right, allowing for a fuller understanding of how they relate to the privatization process' rather than being treated 'simply as barriers to economic development' (Torp and Rekve 1998: 91, cited in Parker and Kirkpatrick 2003: 16). This can account for regulatory or political capture in small, poor countries where the regulator is more likely to be too weak to avoid capture by powerful interest groups (Noll 2000c, cited in Kessides 2004: 102), and in societies with a culture of cronyism and clientelism, particularly in developing countries with strong family loyalties, clan systems and cultural norms favouring relationship contracting (Guasch and Hahn 1999: 137, cited in Parker and Kirkpatrick 2002: 13). The failure to correctly identify these sources of state failure has partly accounted for the mixed performance of privatization in developing countries.

Many aspects of state failure particularly in the context of privatization can usually be traced to political constraints posed by the balance of power in society. Even when regulatory institutions appear to be appropriate, they may fail because of an incompatibility of the institutions with the existing balance of power that prevents effective implementation (also see Levy and Spiller 1993: 249). As the state's political capacity, in particular its ex post capacity to enforce sanctions and discipline, is central to the success of privatization in developing countries, it is important to examine the sources of, and constraints on, state capacity in order to identify the factors that may lead to state failure. These will then enable us to prioritize the important conditions for successful privatization.

The discussion of state capacity has been central to developmental state theories.[4] These theories provide useful lessons by examining the sources of state capacity and the state's ability to manage (learning) rents. The discussion here is closely related to the conditions in which privatization may be undertaken in developing countries. Here, state capacity has been defined in terms of the strength or capacity to implement economic policies effectively, and ability to exercise a large measure of control over the behaviours of domestic and foreign capital (Koo and Kim 1992). The state must be able to manage conflict (e.g. between different segments of capital), allocate resources to the most productive sectors and enforce discipline. It must be able to construct economic rules that advance the long-term interests of capital and technological character of the nation as a whole, and as such, promote growth (Pempel 1999: 142). The success of the East Asian late industrializers (initially Japan, and later Taiwan and South Korea) has been attributed to the state's 'embedded autonomy' – the combination of an autonomous bureaucracy (i.e. 'Weberian bureaucratic insulation') and thick external ties to the economy's organized agents (Evans 1994: 96). That is to say, the state needs to be insulated enough to be able to independently formulate and implement policy, but also connected to productive groups in society.

Bureaucratic capacity, coherence and autonomy from societal forces are said to provide the ability to devise long-term economic policies without interference from private interests. This 'coherent meritocratic bureaucracy' is said to have strong internal networks based on a strict selection process requiring formal competence rather than clientelistic ties or traditional loyalties (Johnson 1982; Evans 1994). It is the implementation of strategies by a comparatively autonomous technocratic elite and the institutionalizing of close relationships between business leaders and state officials in the formation of a dynamic export-oriented regime of capital accumulation that is seen to characterize the developmental state (Johnson 1982). As capital accumulation demands close connections to private capital, such connections have to be with industrial capital, enabling state elites to incorporate these powerful groups in the state's economic project (Evans 1995).

The nature of this state–capital relationship is seen as one of 'strategic interdependence' between both parties, where there is a mutually dependent relationship between government and big business (Barzelay 1986, cited in Choi 1993: 23–24) and in which both must feel that their own success depends on the fortunes of the other partner (Vartiainen 1999). The concept of the developmental state means that 'each side uses the other in a mutually beneficial relationship to achieve developmental goals and enterprise viability' (Johnson 1999: 60). The state's embedded autonomy is seen to provide it with the 'infrastructural power' or 'transformative capacity' to coordinate industrial change by 'penetrating' and 'extracting' resources from society and allocating them to desired ends, shaping incentives through coordinated decision-making to 'elicit desired behaviours' (Mann 1991, cited in Felker 1998: 87; Weiss and Hobson 1995; Weiss 1998; also see Rodrik 1995 and Bardhan 2000). Here, state capacity is not about strong or authoritarian states or coercive power to forestall political challenges, but rather 'negotiative power' to negotiate rudimentary reciprocity between political and economic actors (Weiss and Hobson 1995). The diversity in state structures, state-economic linkages and interstate relations inform the autonomy, strategies and capacities of modern states to facilitate industrial change (Weiss and Hobson 1995).

However, the relationship between the state's autonomy and its capacity is ambiguous (e.g. see Crone 1995; Fine 2003), where state capacity is often equated with autonomy or insulation (e.g. see Mackie 1995; Gomez 2002b), and state autonomy linked with efficiency (e.g. see Rowthorn and Chang 1993). It is also unclear whether a developmental state is autonomous or responsive to capitalist interests. On the one hand, this positive state–capital relationship is seen to allow the state to implement policies in favour of business (Koo and Kim 1992). South Korea's developmental policies in the 1960s and 1970s are said to derive largely from the consistency of its policy implementation in favour of large capital which in turn ensured business confidence and a favourable investment climate, with both business cartels and state economic bodies 'committed to high growth, realising that they would have to swim or sink together' (Pempel 1999: 164). On the other hand, the South Korean state was also largely autonomous of business since it could choose to damage business interests (e.g. as in the case of the Kukje chaebol) when state demands for bribes or political subservience were not met (Khan 2004: 178).

What is important here is the nature of the state's relations with social groups and the composition of these social groups. In some cases, there may not even be a capitalist class to undertake economic investment. Where capitalists are absent from these groups, the task of the state is to transform selected candidates into capitalists. This will involve the creation of new property rights (e.g. through privatization) and supported with learning rents and other subsidies. The state's ex ante ability to select winners in this context will very likely be determined by its political strength relative to those contesting (e.g. see Cook and Minogue 1990; Haggard and Maxfield 1999). The main lesson from the South Korean case is that effective state intervention was possible because the state could enforce decisions by penalizing poor performers and rewarding good performers (Pempel 1999). Here, the state could allocate and reallocate property rights and subsidies because South Korean history was such that organizationally powerful intermediate class social factions who could be purchased to protect inefficient industries were simply absent, and at the same time, there was a sufficient pool of potential candidates for the capitalist class which allowed the state to replace non-performing capitalists relatively easily. As such, resources could be allocated without significant political constraints to efficient entrepreneurs, and these were also the entrepreneurs who could offer the highest payoffs to the state (Khan 1998). In principle, the state could enforce both predatory and developmental actions, but chose the latter as this offered bigger payoffs in the long run.

In contrast, most developing countries typically have powerful factions, often led by unproductive social groups who can, for a price, protect inefficient enterprises. These countries also have a far more limited pool of qualified candidates to select from and impose discipline on through the threat of replacement. These conditions can effectively constrain the state's ex post ability to transform those initially selected into efficient capitalists through the efficient management of rents. State capacity thus does not only depend on the state's reach (its connections with capitalist groups or other productive relationships) but also its ability to overcome political constraints (i.e. resistance to disciplining). Hence, while the South Korean state could maximize rents extracted from capitalists and at the same time ensure compliance with productivity maximization, many developing country states are faced with the problem of incompetent (non-capitalist) candidates who are also harder to discipline.

As the state's connection with society in developing countries may not be production-oriented alliances but rather with unproductive 'non-capitalist' classes created and brought together by the colonial legacy and struggle for independence, these groups have had to be accommodated. These groups have been variously described as 'a well-educated but economically unproductive professional class' (Pempel 1999: 169–170), the 'educated salaried middle classes' (Alavi, H. 1982: 299), and the intermediate class left behind in the development process (Khan 1998: 19), whose political role is of considerable importance, organizing resistance and developing ways to 'modify certain market outcomes "politically"' (Alavi, H. 1982: 299; Khan 1998: 19). State capacity therefore not only depends on the state's relationship with segments of capital but also on political constraints posed by other groups in society outside the 'developmental alliance'.

Furthermore, the state–society relationship in developing countries is not formalized or 'institutionalized' (as has been argued by some in the South Korean case [e.g. see Evans 1994]) but personalized, usually between patrons and clients. Patron–client relationships are repeated relationships of exchange between specific patrons and their clients. The nature of this relationship (in terms of how it is likely to influence economic decisions) depends on the objectives and ideologies of the patrons and clients; the number of potential clients and their degree of organization; the homogeneity of clients; and the institutions through which patrons and clients interact, including the degree of fragmentation of institutions (Khan 1998: 23–26). More critically, the relative power of patrons and clients can determine how resources are allocated. In South Korea, it was possible for the state to extract the maximum economic payoff while ensuring that resource allocation was efficient because clients of the state both in the business sector and in politics were weak. Inefficient clients could not defend themselves and the state had no interest in defending them.

However, where the patron is politically weak, inefficient clients may easily survive because clients in this context may be offering political support (or the absence of political opposition) rather than an economic payoff. This political corruption may be necessary to ensure stability but can also be growth-reducing. This depends in part on the degree of centralization, with centralized corruption being potentially less harmful (Bardhan 1997; also see Shleifer and Vishny 1993) as reflected in the different impact of corruption on economic growth in South Korea and South Asia (e.g. see Khan 1998). Patron–client networks in India and Pakistan reveal the substantial political power of clients from intermediate 'non-capitalist' classes whose necessary accommodation made it more difficult for the state to reallocate rents more efficiently. This partly explains the persistence of inefficient rents in the Indian subcontinent (Khan 1998, undated).

## What is needed to make privatization work?

Privatization will entail state intervention to finance capital costs, subsidize any operational losses where cost-covering tariffs may not be possible, and to promote learning in order to develop the necessary entrepreneurial capacity to run an enterprise efficiently and for technological catching up. Whether privatization leads to learning and efficiency gains will therefore depend on the ability of the state to manage these subsidies. Here, the state's ex post capacity to correct ex ante mistakes is more important than its capacity to make the correct ex ante decisions in the first place. This is because ex ante decisions relating to selection, contract specification and regulation will be constrained by political factors and incomplete information. From this perspective, rather than its institutional capacity, the state's political capacity will be more important to correct ex ante mistakes and implement policy and enforce conditionality essential for the success of any subsidy programme

### *Political capacity*

The management of rents necessary for successful privatization in developing countries will require that the state is able to deliver the appropriate credible threats, including reallocating property rights by replacing owners where performance targets are not met. It may also need to enforce contracts (where the private operator or owner reneges) and coordinate capital and operational decisions to integrate sectors such as transport networks. And it will need to override public opposition to tariff or fare increases if this is needed to ensure commercial viability, or provide and enforce conditional (operational) subsidies. As discussed in the previous section, all these will depend on the strength of the state in relation to the private owner or concessionaire, which in turn will be determined by the balance of power in society, and specifically, the compatibility of related institutions with this.

The assessment of state capacity must therefore take into account the country's political context, looking specifically at how patron–client relationships affect the allocation of economic resources and the capacity of the state to enforce discipline. The persistence of weak policies and institutions, and the failure of efficient institutional change, lies in the balance of power in society between social factions and classes (Brenner 1976, 1985; Bardhan 2000), and in particular, 'powerful interest groups opposed to change who can impose unacceptable costs on others or the state' (Khan 2004: 33). This is because the effectiveness of institutional capacities 'depends on their compatibility with the underlying distribution of power' and enforcement requirements need to be compatible with existing power structures for institutions to perform efficiently (Khan 2004: 35). In other words, to be effectively enforced by the state, institutions must be 'compatible with or cannot be opposed by powerful interests within society' (Khan 2000a; also see Shirley 1997). Privatization should therefore not be pursued if the state lacks the political capacity to override the interests of powerful but unproductive groups who could resist necessary efforts to sustain or improve performance in the new private sector. The incompatibility of the enforcement requirements of particular institutions with pre-existing social power structures can explain why similar state policies and institutions can lead to very different outcomes.

The overriding condition for successful privatization then is the state's political capacity to implement the necessary institutions required for enforcing compliance with productivity-enhancing regulations. As this will largely depend on the existing political conditions in a country, and the technologies of the enterprises being privatized, the assessment of state capacity will entail a careful political, economic and historical analysis of that country. Where privatization is being driven by powerful interests, it is important to identify the dynamic elements or groups who may form productive alliances with the state and contribute to the process of capital accumulation. This could mean that it may not be possible or even desirable to blindly pursue transparent processes and other 'good governance' measures, even more so if unproductive groups stand to gain by using this to mobilize factional support for their own ends.

This does not mean that moves towards greater transparency and accountability should not be pursued as ends in themselves, only that we should not expect these moves to result in an environment necessarily more conducive for successful privatization, or indeed for economic development in general. Instead, a more complex analysis is needed to understand the very specific political and economic challenges facing developing countries. This also requires a broader view of regulation which recognizes the importance of promoting learning and capital accumulation. A long-term solution would have to 'help productive forces within developing countries organize' (Khan 2004: 34) and some privatizations can assist in accelerating these social changes.

### *Institutional capacity*

Having determined the state's political capacity to implement policy, we can then look at the institutional requirements. The three most important institutional requirements that follow for successful privatization are: 1, project viability and privatization design; 2, regulatory and contract design; and 3, selection. The ranking of these institutional conditions are based on an assessment of which institutions, if poorly structured, would prevent the others from functioning; and which conditions, if not met, could be most, or least, easily corrected. Following this line of reasoning, we could argue that a transparent selection process, regulatory independence and clearly stipulated contracts will not overcome the problems arising from a lack of project viability, especially if there are no measures in place to make an unviable project more viable. On the other hand, as argued earlier, inappropriate candidate choice may not lead to failure if this can be remedied through learning rents and clearly specified incentives and penalties.

*Project viability and privatization design*

The most important institutional condition is the capacity to determine whether an enterprise or project is financially feasible and commercially viable. This requires:

- identifying the problems to be solved in order to determine the aims and most appropriate mode of privatization;
- determining operating and capital costs and projected revenue;
- ensuring that the deal can be properly financed, without creating an unrealistic debt burden which may affect operations and capital investment;
- determining tariff conditions (level and structure, subsidy arrangements, collection performance, disconnection policy) and consumer preferences, affordability and willingness to pay (Stottmann 2000).

The issue of project viability is separate from that of candidate selection because the provision of certain public goods is often not commercially viable and has traditionally been subsidized as a result, usually for welfare reasons. This is the case for sewerage services and urban rail networks which usually require capital and operational subsidies, especially in developing countries, in order to keep tariffs affordable or politically acceptable. Similarly, airlines and auto manufacture are extremely difficult sectors, characterized by regular failures in the face of inherent industry problems. In these circumstances, we argue that even the most suitable candidate is unlikely to make a fundamental difference to the commercial viability of the privatization as ongoing state subsidies will be needed, and success needs to be measured against second or even third best outcomes. These examples are discussed in further detail in the case study chapters. In addition, the state will usually have to make these enterprises attractive enough for the private sector to participate, usually by providing sufficient subsidies together with incentives and compulsions for improving management and efficiency. However, if the state could have operated the enterprise more efficiently in the first place, there would be no reason to privatize.

The mode of privatization will depend on the level of information, regulation and monitoring, with regulatory capacity determining which privatization option is most appropriate. For example, it is possible to proceed with limited information in the case of service and management contracts with fixed fees, while management contracts with performance incentives require sufficient information to define incentives. Leases, BOT contracts and concessions require good system information, and in the case of divestiture, very good system information is essential. A strong regulatory framework is essential for divestiture, concessions, BOT contracts and leases, and is needed to monitor service and management contracts. A concession or BOT contract would therefore be difficult to implement where regulatory capacity is weak, the regulatory environment uncertain, and information poor. Finally, cost-covering tariffs are regarded as necessary in the case of a lease, concession or divestiture. In reality, this will depend on the willingness of consumers to pay higher charges and the capacity of governments to impose these or, failing that, provide operational subsidies which will require careful monitoring and enforcement of conditions.

In the case of a utility, key parameters in assessing performance include:[5]

- its present and projected service area;
- current operating and maintenance cost;
- current characteristics of the service;
- current tariff levels and structure and collection efficiency;
- current and projected consumption;
- a basic inventory of the assets and their condition and serviceability;
- human resources;
- the capital cost of improvements and annual expenditure necessary to achieve intended service levels;
- availability of funding for service improvements through grants, equity and loans; and
- the additional operating costs due to system expansions, considering the efficiency gains that private operations might achieve.

The most important condition here is determining consumer preferences, affordability and willingness to pay, and where cost-covering tariffs are needed, implementing measures to change public attitudes towards (higher) user charges. It is also crucial to ensure that measures are in place to make the project commercially viable through subsidies where cost-covering tariffs cannot be implemented. This last point is important because, as mentioned above, some projects such as urban rail networks may be economically desirable but may not necessarily be financially or commercially viable. This will entail careful privatization design and clearly specifying conditions for subsidies, performance parameters and investment levels.

### *Contract and regulatory design*

The second most important institutional condition is a contract which clearly stipulates obligations and penalties, and in tandem with this, an effective regulatory framework which effectively monitors performance and enforces appropriate penalties for non-compliance. A contract should clearly specify obligations (completion date, security, penalties for defaults in performance, a payment schedule based on satisfactory completion of sequential stages), and incorporate pricing and subsidies in contractual commitments to make these more predictable (Daniels and Trebilcock 2000). To safeguard against contract renegotiation, careful provision must be made to deal with unexpected events over the life of the contract. This includes conditions under which adjustment can be made; guidelines determining when and under what conditions contract renegotiation must occur (rather than price or service adjustment by agreement or by regulatory discretion); the process by which renegotiation must be initiated and conducted; and a definition of clear arbitration provisions (Stottmann 2000). The regulator's technical capacity will depend entirely on the quality of personnel and regulatory expertise. Regulatory staff should have the technical ability to specify the conditions of supply (access and possible exclusion), tariffs, prices and service/product quality, investment and profits (returns on capital), technical standardization and operational rules. This will in turn require adequate financial resources to attract and retain skilled professionals.

### *Selection*

Least important in the context of privatization in developing countries is a transparent selection process as this is limited by inadequate and asymmetric information and often constrained by quite substantial costs associated with open bidding. Auctions can reduce information problems when valuing highly idiosyncratic assets (where there are no obvious benchmarks to determine the minimum return required) but work best where the allocated good is stable and well defined. Furthermore, bundled goods which typify many infrastructure projects pose competitive bidding design problems (Daniels and Trebilcock 2000).

Transparency will also be sacrificed in competitive negotiations where the government invites proposals from selected bidders to meet specific service objectives. This may be favoured where projects have many possible technical variations which the contracting entity may want to explore without being bound by standard solutions required by competitive bidding (Stottmann 2000), and to reduce the costs of organizing competitive bidding (and where the government may favour a few candidates). Similarly, in direct negotiations, the project proposal originates from the private sector. This may be needed to attract innovative projects and secure private sector involvement in smaller cities and towns where the cost of entering competitive bidding may be high relative to the expected returns (Stottmann 2000), but can also be an easy way to secure privatization funds.

Obviously there needs to be a minimum standard of competence. The prequalification of bidders arguably serves to ensure that potential bidders have the technical and financial capacity, and a track record performing similar tasks, thereby weeding out inappropriate firms before they prepare costly proposals. However, the shortage of entrepreneurial capacity in developing countries means that bidders often do not have the experience or technical or even financial capacity which in turn requires some form of foreign technical partnership and/or state support in the form of financing and learning rents. The ability of the selected candidate to deliver will then depend on the nature of any technical agreements and the structure of incentives and penalties, and most of all, on the state's capacity to enforce these. The relative importance of these will clearly depend on the country context, industry and period.

Having established these conditions for successful privatization in developing countries, we can now proceed to explain Malaysia's privatization experience in the next chapter. The following four chapters will then look in detail at the failure of four case studies to determine what factors were responsible and what conditions needed to be in place for their successful privatization. As we shall see, Malaysia's privatization programme generally failed to meet many of the institutional criteria above due to the political constraints and the nature of patron–client relationships. However, failure was ultimately due to the state's inability to correct ex ante mistakes and strengthen weak institutions because its (ex post) political capacity was constrained by the balance of power in society.

# 3 Institutional and political failure

## Privatization in Malaysia

Between the mid 1980s and mid 1990s, Malaysia's privatization programme was one of the most extensive in the developing world, both in terms of scale and scope. By 2001, the state was restructuring, bailing out and taking over major companies involved in privatized enterprises or projects. This culminated in the renationalization of four of the largest privatizations (subject of the subsequent case study chapters). What happened? Failure occurred on two levels (institutional and political) before (ex ante) and after (ex post) privatization. These failures can best be explained by asking why Malaysia privatized in the first place because political motivations will affect privatization decisions, institutional arrangements and outcomes. This is turn requires an examination of the country's political context, namely changes in social relations and the balance of power, and how these constrained the state's capacity to make the correct ex ante and ex post decisions.

From the literature, we can identify a number of key changes in social relations that affected the development of policy in general and towards privatization. The emergence of a Malay middle class was directly responsible for the introduction of redistributive policies under the New Economic Policy (NEP) in 1971 to foster and accelerate the development of an ethnic Malay capitalist class. These policies were driven by an 'ethnic imperative' to create Malay entrepreneurs, and involved an 'efficiency trade-off'. This led to public and private sector inefficiency, but also longer-term problems due to the lower efficiency of the Malay capitalists that the government sought to patronize. The NEP also substantially increased the size of the middle class and transformed the nature of patron–client networks. This increased competition for resources in the ruling Malay party, UMNO (the United Malays National Organisation), which in turn centralized and personalized patron–client networks around a few key leaders. The emergence of a group of influential entrepreneurs in this context was a key factor in the decision to privatize because their support in intra-party leadership contests was crucial. Privatization was an extension of the NEP and closely related to state attempts to foster and accelerate the development of an ethnic Malay capitalist class. These political factors were eventually to also compromise privatization policies and the accompanying institutions.

However, while the literature touches on political motivations, this tends to be divorced from the political and economic context. Specifically, it does not adequately address the key challenges facing the state, and the nature of constraints on its (ex post) political capacity to correct mistakes. It will be argued that while policies were largely driven by an ethnic imperative (which was politically necessary to accommodate the demands of an emerging Malay middle class), the government also pursued broadly developmental policies (e.g. see Lall 1995; Jomo and Gomez 2000) and, through privatization, sought to address both economic (efficiency) and political (redistribution) concerns that had arisen under the NEP. Here the government faced two related challenges. The first was to promote learning in order to develop a dynamic capitalist class capable of successfully running privatized companies or projects, and furthering the process of capital accumulation. Learning was also necessary for technological acquisition for catching up, especially in the case of infant industries or technology-intensive sectors. Secondly, the government also needed to ensure the commercial viability of privatized enterprises and projects, especially where these involved high capital costs, large externalities and social considerations discussed in the previous chapter. As conditional subsidies were needed to facilitate learning and/or ensure commercial viability, the success of privatization depended on the government's political capacity to impose credible subsidization strategies and enforce compliance, including withdrawing subsidies and even reallocating property rights where conditions were not met.

The question then is whether privatization improved the government's political capacity to better address economic inefficiency by promoting learning (e.g. through conditional subsidies). This was not in general what we observe in Malaysia, where the government has historically failed to implement or even stipulate conditionality. The constraints on the government's ability to do so then become a crucial explanation for the failure of privatization strategies. As discussed in Chapter 2, privatization can be said to improve firm performance by reducing the possibility of state interventions (e.g. subsidies, bail-outs) thereby subjecting the firm to the discipline of the market. However, this crucially does not improve the government's disciplinary capacity which will be needed to effectively manage subsidies. In the case of Malaysia, privatization did not substantially change the relationship between the government and enterprise. Rather than a more 'arm's length' relationship, the national and economic significance of many of the larger projects or enterprises meant that the government was unlikely to allow these to fail. In the case of three of the case studies (Kuala Lumpur LRT, MAS and Proton), privatization was also inappropriate as it could not address inherent industry-related problems.

Furthermore, the emergence of the new Malay middle class (under the NEP) increased conflict over resource allocation and altered the balance of power. Growing political contestation in UMNO increased the importance of patron–client networks in intra-party contests, resulting in more centralized and personalized patron–client relationships as the Prime Minister sought to consolidate power. This in turn compromised the state's political capacity to correct mistakes or discipline the private sector by creating moral hazard as privatization beneficiaries were closely associated with key members of the leadership, even acting as proxies in some cases. As a result, inefficiencies were tolerated and failure even rewarded. These inefficiencies, inherited from the NEP, subsequently affected learning and technology absorption.

This chapter will examine how changing social relations (reflected in changing patron–client relationships) shaped privatization and its accompanying institutions, and constrained the government's ex post political capacity to correct mistakes and enforce discipline. The following section locates Malaysia's privatization programme in the context of the NEP, which was itself the outcome of the country's changing social relations. This provides the necessary context for examining why Malaysia privatized, looking specifically at the problems of public and (Malay) private sector inefficiency, and changing social relations arising from the NEP. This is followed by an assessment of the performance of Malaysia's privatization programme, looking at *how* it failed. The next section then examines why privatization failed by identifying constraints to the government's institutional and political capacity posed by ethnic redistribution, crony capitalism and the balance of power. The final section summarizes the main arguments and locates the four case studies in the context of state capacities to promote learning and commercial viability, briefly outlining the privatization and industry challenges in each case, and identifying reasons for failure and necessary conditions for successful privatization.

## Why did Malaysia privatize?

### *The political context*

Malaysia's privatization needs to be understood in terms of government attempts to meet economic and political challenges related to growth and redistribution. This was first officially sanctioned under the NEP which sought to promote Malay capital accumulation by increasing Malay opportunities for ownership participation, jobs and business. The NEP and its legacy have shaped Malaysia's political economy since. It is therefore important to examine the specific historical and political circumstances leading to the introduction of the NEP in order to explain why privatization was undertaken within the context of redistributive policies. The NEP is generally regarded as a policy shift in response to inter-ethnic inequality which led to the 1969 'race riots'. However, a closer examination of the decade after independence reveals NEP-type policies already in place, and the emergence of an increasingly impatient and vocal Malay middle class which was already benefiting from these policies.

The origins of the NEP can be traced back to British colonial rule which emasculated Malay political and economic power, enabling British companies to dominate commerce, banking and services, and to own almost all the major tin mines and plantations. The Chinese were prominent only in small and medium-sized businesses (retail trade, small construction, restaurants) (Puthucheary, J. 1960; Lim 1985; Bowie 1991), with Malays confined to agriculture, and remaining economically weak. However, despite overwhelming economic control by British capital (see Puthucheary, J. 1960; Tan, T.W. 1982), emerging inequalities were perceived along ethnic lines (e.g. see Jesudason 1989; Bowie 1991), partly because Chinese businesses were conspicuous in the countryside where they took over rural transportation and rice milling (Lim 1981), and acted as intermediaries between British capital and the Malay peasantry.

In the lead-up to Independence, British colonial authorities repressed left-wing nationalist groups and instead encouraged the formation of ethnic-based political parties led by conservative, pro-British middle class elements. These groups were represented mainly by Malay aristocrats (in UMNO) and the Chinese and Indian bourgeoisie (in the Malaysian Chinese Association, MCA and Malaysian Indian Congress, MIC, respectively). Power was handed to these three parties as part of the Alliance Party, with Independence conditional on British economic interests being guaranteed, and an inter-communal consensus, where the majority Malay population retained political power and special privileges in return for citizenship rights and economic freedom for non-Malays.

As a result, Independence did not alter the pattern of economic control by British companies, with the government's First Five Year Plan (1956–60) committed to free enterprise and attracting foreign investment (Lim 1985; Rasiah and Ishak 2001), the latter motivated by UMNO's desire to curb Chinese expansion (Gomez 1999). Between 1957 and 1960, public expenditure was mainly on infrastructural development (50 per cent) and agricultural and rural development (23 per cent), with only 1.4 per cent allocated to commerce and industry development (Lim 1985). Early state intervention was geared towards improving the poor socio-economic position of Malays by promoting new economic activities (through public enterprises with redistributional objectives), expanded education and public employment opportunities, and rural development and infrastructure (Salleh and Meyanathan 1993, cited in Lall 1995: 530) in order to secure political support (Lim 1985; Jomo 1990).

Nonetheless, there were already attempts to redress ethnic economic imbalances with the Federal Constitution's guarantee of Malay 'special rights', the first legal action to create a Malay bourgeoisie (Lim 1985). However, the lack of success here led to pressure from aspiring Malay businessmen, and resulted in greater support for Malay businesses through protection (quotas for business licences, employment and education), assistance (credit, training and business premises), and acquisition (corporate ownership) (see

Lim 1985). This included 30 per cent Malay quotas on company boards, preferential access for transport and timber licences, and 25 per cent quotas for government contracts (Lim 1985; Shamsul 1986). Almost all Malay businessmen, regardless of type,[1] were either created by the state or at the least with crucial state support (Jomo 1993a) and were heavily dependent on the state which remained in control (Ho 1988).

The emergence of an increasingly vocal Malay business class was itself the outcome of a growing Malay middle class since independence. This included the increase in Malay teachers (with 80 per cent of the Federation of Malay Teachers Association belonging to UMNO), Malay businessmen,[2] and a fourfold increase in junior civil servants (Clarke 1964, cited in Neuman 1971: 229). Changes over a ten-year period before 1970 show that the Malay middle class grew at a faster rate than the non-Malay middle class, being 'able to benefit as much in sharing in the significant increase in the middle- and upper-income groups' (Tan T.W. 1982: 124–125, 325; also see Shamsul 1986) and enjoying the highest rate of household income increase between 1957 and 1970 (Snodgrass 1972, cited in Ho 1988: 106; also see Aris bin Othman 1977).[3] Even the slow progress of Malay equity from 2 to 6 per cent in seven years was 'phenomenal' given the small base (Tan T.W. 1982).

Tangible and significant benefits, including extremely fast and unusually high rates of post-Independence benefits, served to heighten expectations and aspirations, and contributed to the Malay middle class's impatience. For this group, the stakes were high and their reactions sharpest following 'modest' changes in ownership and control of the economy since 1957[4] (Tan T.W. 1982; Gomez and Jomo 1997), and as a result of their frustration at the inability of the civil service to continue absorbing the emerging university graduates who then turned to commerce (Jomo 1990). Increasing inter-ethnic inequality (partly a reflection of the Malay rural demography) and constraints faced by Malay businesses led to calls for direct state intervention and the creation of Malay capitalists.

Demands for greater government intervention in favour of economic redistribution for Malays came not from lower-income groups, but middle- and upper-middle-income Malays (Tan T.W. 1982; Toh and Jomo 1981, cited in Puthucheary, M. 1984: 218). This group began to exert pressure through the Associated Malay Chambers of Commerce,[5] Kuala Lumpur Petty Traders Association, and UMNO[6] (Lim 1985; Ho 1988; Jesudason 1989), and secured the support of then Deputy Prime Minister Tun Abdul Razak who introduced the Bumiputra Economic Congress (BEC) (Puthucheary, M. 1984). Demands made at the first BEC in 1965 led to the establishment of Bank Bumiputra (to provide Malays with credit facilities), and the reorganization of the Rural Industrial Development Authority (RIDA) in the form of MARA (the Council of Trust for Indigenous People). Delegates at the second BEC in 1968 even threatened to cause political instability if Malays were not given their share of the economy, and demands made here were subsequently incorporated in the NEP (Lim 1985; Searle 1999).

The Alliance Party's failure to secure a two-third parliamentary majority in the 1969 elections was seen as a direct threat to Malay 'special rights' and provided the emerging Malay middle class with the opportunity to push for redistributive policies in favour of Malays (Hua 1983; Jomo 1990). It also provided UMNO with the tactical mobility and strength to replace the original communal settlement and pursue policies which could not have been implemented earlier in a bureaucracy part-controlled by British-trained civil servants and expatriates (Ho 1988), and was supported by a shift in the balance of power within UMNO MPs and legislators towards Malay vernacular teachers,[7] former government clerks, local party cadre and small businessmen (Goh 1971; Ahmad 1985; Neuman 1971).

The thrust of the NEP was largely shaped by demands from the emerging Malay middle class. Hence, while it officially aimed to eradicate poverty irrespective of race, the NEP's main focus was to benefit this group by restructuring society to eliminate the identification of race with economic function. This involved the redistribution of wealth to the Malay middle class through substantial increases in education, (public) employment and business opportunities, and the ownership of share capital in the corporate sector, with the aim of creating Malay capitalists (Rasiah and Ishak 2001). Greater access to education through a quota system facilitated Malay employment in the public sector, which expanded rapidly as a result.[8]

Increasing government control and ownership of the banking sector influenced lending patterns and ensured compliance with lending targets for Malays[9] (Chin and Jomo 2000). Low interest rates, easy credit[10] and preferential lending aimed to assist Malay businesses, while the state made even larger funds available despite the poor track record of Malay businesses (Jesudason 1989). Risky forms of collateral were accepted, and it was also not uncommon for the Malay partner to acquire shares without the cash payment of capital but with the future earnings of allotted shares (Tan T.W. 1982). Malay ownership was also facilitated through the state acquisition of shares which provided the quick control of well-managed, profitable companies[11] as well as training for a new generation of Malay managers. The initial process of increasing Malay corporate ownership centred on the 1968 Capital Issues Committee (CIC) which set share prices, usually below market price, for Malay individuals and SOEs, and the 1975 Industrial Coordination Act (ICA) which required companies to set aside 30 per cent of shares issued for Malay equity (Jesudason 1989).

### *Reasons for privatization*

The political imperative to develop (Malay) entrepreneurial capacity through the quick transfer of assets to state agencies (and the desire to bypass the Chinese business sector) entailed an efficiency trade-off which led to public and private sector inefficiency. As NEP programmes to support Malay capitalists were essentially the extension of (unsuccessful) pre-NEP policies

(Shamsul 1986), it created a dependency on continued state support, increasing patronage and rent-seeking. While these inefficiencies were tolerated during a period of high economic growth in the 1970s, they were not sustainable in the 1982 economic recession. The government sought to address these problems through privatization.

However, while public sector reform is usually associated with episodes of economic downturn, the rapid pace of privatization post-1986 can be described as 'reform without downturn' (Campos and Esfahani 1996: 208). In short, there were other (non-economic) reasons for privatization. These related to changes in the composition of Malay society, namely the emergence of a new Malay middle and business class which increased competition for resources within UMNO, and ultimately pressure for changes in the redistributive process in favour of emerging Malay capitalists aligned with particular factions of the political leadership. Public sector inefficiency and economic crisis facilitated the policy shift but privatization was ultimately politically motivated, reflecting a shift in the balance of power which allowed a new group of businessmen-cum-politicians and professionals contesting for political power in UMNO to reward supporters. (UMNO's leadership itself increasingly came from business and professional backgrounds, reflecting the changes in the composition of the party's membership.) Privatization thus represented a change in the way resources were controlled and allocated, and was in part driven by the factional struggles in UMNO and supported by an emerging group of big businessmen which stood to benefit from the sale of state assets at the expense of those who continued to rely on NEP-style assistance and hand-outs.

### *Public sector inefficiency*

Privatization was in part a response to public sector problems and state fiscal constraints, in particular the unsustainability of public sector expansion under the NEP (Jomo 1993a). To meet NEP redistribution and employment targets, the public sector expanded into one of the largest in developing countries by the late 1970s (Wilson 1999). Between 1970 and 1983, the bureaucracy grew fourfold to 521,818 employees, public sector expenditure increased over tenfold to RM35.4 billion in 1982, and the number of SOEs increased from 109 to 656 by 1980 (Khoo B.T. 1995). The expansion of the public sector was such that even federal government officials were uncertain how many public enterprises had been established in the early 1980s, not just by the federal and state governments, but also by various statutory bodies, regional development agencies and similar public sector bodies.

By 1983, two-thirds of government expenditure was spent running twenty-seven of the largest public enterprises (Khoo K.J. 1992). In 1984, the Ministry of Public Enterprise could only report the annual returns of 269 out of 900 public enterprises, whose accumulated losses came up to RM137.3 million (Supian 1988; Kamal and Zainal 1989). Public sector borrowing, including loans from domestic agencies, increased from RM26.5 billion (1980) to RM100.6 billion (1986). The economic burden of this large, financially draining public sector became unsustainable with the global recession in the 1980s, with falling oil prices (1982–86), the collapse of the tin market (1985), and declining prices of other major exports (after 1984) substantially increasing the budget deficit from RM120 million (1981) to RM3.5 billion (1987) (Gomez and Jomo 1997). Under pressure to implement fiscal austerity measures as well as economic reform, the government offered financially weak public enterprises the option of closure, rehabilitation or privatization (Gomez 1994).

Public enterprise performance was hampered by ambiguous criteria and unclear, often contradictory and multiple objectives (e.g. redistribution and employment generation versus efficiency); a lack of coordination on the different levels (state and federal, municipal and regional, and between ministries); a serious shortage of competent and experienced Malay managerial expertise; and the absence of proper guidelines on selection and monitoring of management performance (Puthucheary, M. 1984). Little attention was given to viability and managerial competence (Jesudason 1989). Directorships were not based on management ability and experience but political and bureaucratic considerations (Ismail and Osman 1991) and led to the emergence of self-aggrandizing rentier managers, rather than disciplined, competent and entrepreneurial administrators (Gomez 1994; Jomo 1995; Gomez and Jomo 1997). Easy access to credit encouraged SOEs to operate on high gearing ratios without adequate pre-investment planning or first developing expertise (Puthucheary, M. 1984), while government bail-outs[12] and protection from market forces bred complacency and resulted in a bloated bureaucracy, inferior services, major inefficiencies, low productivity, limited innovation and high costs (Ismail and Osman 1991; Felker 1993; Gomez and Jomo 1997). Ethnic considerations entailed an efficiency trade-off, where incentives to attract foreign investment lacked technological and performance conditions (Rasiah and Ishak 2001). State agencies were not interested in building up an indigenous technological capacity, preferring easy access to foreign partners and technology (Jesudason 1989). The eagerness to promote redistribution created distortions for the efficient functioning of SOEs, subsequently adversely affecting both efficiency and distributive equity (Gouri *et al.* 1991). As a result, most SOEs became commercially unviable, and there remained real problems of state entrepreneurship without the basic technical and managerial attributes (Jesudason 1989).

### *Private sector inefficiency*

Privatization was also a response to other constraints posed by state-driven capital accumulation under the NEP, in particular related inefficiencies in the private sector. Government efforts to promote entrepreneurship through affirmative action under the NEP actually discouraged learning.

Positive discrimination in education led to low internal social rates of return and low social productivity of schooling, while the lowering of university entrance requirements for rural (Malay) students led to the concentration of Malays in the liberal arts and social sciences (Bruton 1992). This created a major obstacle for effective Malay entry into modern industry and necessitated civil service expansion to absorb Malay graduates (partly also to compensate for the slack demand in the private [manufacturing] sector) (Meerman 1979, cited in Bruton 1992: 251; Bruton 1992).

The government believed that entrepreneurship could be learned through ownership and management, supported by preferential treatment. It sought to create Malay entrepreneurs by taking over established firms in order to provide new owners with ready-made companies (Bruton 1992). This quick control of profitable companies by state agencies increased de facto Malay equity ownership and provided training for Malay SOE managers. However, the government also minimized risk and provided windfall gains (through share purchase) for Malay entrepreneurs, and there was little interest or understanding of specific training, accumulated experience, or trial and error (Bruton 1992, 1998). This insulation from market competition and easy access to finance undermined the possible disciplining experience of business management, while the speed of asset acquisition by new Malay businessmen undermined their learning-by-doing (Jesudason 1989; Gomez and Jomo 1997).

The lack of skills and previous learning base meant that the government was unable to address the issue of absorbing complex organizational and production processes necessary for technological upgrading and industry linkages (Bruton 1992; Lall 1995). Unlike South Korea, Malaysia did not have large industrial conglomerates or many (non-resource-based) major manufacturers with strong records of international competitiveness to undertake industrial upgrading (Jomo and Tan 1999). More crucially, unlike South Korea, subsidies were allocated without performance conditions. As a result, greater economic opportunities and state protection under the NEP did not increase business acumen or produce a class of dynamic Malay capitalists (Gale 1981; Jesudason 1989; Bowie 1991; Khoo B.T. 1995; Crouch 1996; Gomez and Jomo 1997). Rather, it perpetuated Malay dependence on the state, creating a 'subsidy mentality' among businesses, with a 'permanent middle class' dependent on the government (Jesudason 1989; Kamal 1989; Khoo B.T. 1995). Government attempts to create large (Malay-controlled) conglomerates thus mainly resulted in their move into non-tradable sectors.

Learning failure, subsidy dependence and rentier behaviour led to inefficiency and a lack of productive base, often characterized by divestment for quick profits (Jesudason 1989; Gomez 1999) or 'Ali-Baba' (Malay–Chinese) relationships where Malays handed over control and management of companies to non-Malays in exchange for salaried directorships (Bruton 1992). Many Malay businessmen were highly geared on loans and were too dependent on preferential share allotments acquired under the NEP, lacking managerial and financial skills, particularly in project implementation and management, and undertaking questionable projects (Bruton 1992; Khoo B.T. 1995). Malay businessmen also faced capital, skilled labour and market limitations, and competition from SOEs and Chinese businesses. By the end of the 1970s, many businesses had failed despite significant support, and demands grew for more protection and assistance in the form of easier credit, lengthier grace periods for loan repayment, more training, better business premises, etc. (Bruton 1992).

There were also wider economic problems. While the economy continued to register high growth rates, this was largely due to external factors (e.g. higher commodity and oil prices), with Chinese and foreign investment declining following the Industrial Coordination Act (ICA) (Bowie 1988). Structural problems emerged by 1980 with low private investment (which increased the public sector share), slow growth in agricultural productivity, land constraints, highly concentrated manufacturing and shallow foreign-led export sectors with weak linkages, labour shortages in agriculture along with urban unemployment, slow technological progress (beyond original equipment manufacture [OEM]) and technology transfer problems (Bruton 1992; Lall 1995; Rasiah 1998). According to the government's Industrial Master Plan (Malaysia 1983a), restructuring under the NEP adversely affected industrialization and was cited by US investors as the most serious disincentive to invest in the country (Schlossstein 1991).

### *Changing social relations*

While privatization was partly in response to NEP inefficiencies, it did not seek to fundamentally change the NEP's redistributive policies, or the nature of state–capital relations. Instead, privatization was to be implemented within the context of the NEP. As such, economic motivations are insufficient to explain why privatization was introduced. Rather, privatization was ultimately motivated by political considerations related to changes in social relations and the increasing competition in UMNO. The recession intensified the conflict over resources in UMNO, particularly between predominantly small businessmen who continued to rely on state subsidies and an emerging group of big businessmen and former SOE managers who stood to benefit from privatization and who were closely connected to the new political leadership, itself increasingly represented by former businessmen such as Finance Minister Daim Zainuddin. Mahathir Mohamad also represented a break from previous prime ministers, coming from a professional (as opposed to aristocratic) background and was staunchly pro-business and anti-state.

The motivations for privatization here can be partly traced back to the personal motivations of individual leaders (e.g. see Gomez 2002b). Privatization decisions were widely believed to have personally benefited Daim, while Mahathir and Deputy Prime Minister Anwar Ibrahim were more likely to have been politically motivated, with privatization presenting opportunities to reward their supporters, thereby securing political support (e.g. see Yusoff 1990; Gomez 1991, 2002c). Where economic redistribution was previously centralized through the party (e.g. see Khan 2000b), privatization allocated resources increasingly through personalized patron–client networks centred on certain political leaders.

Increasing competition for resources can be traced to the substantial growth in the Malay middle class which changed the composition of UMNO's membership and altered the balance of power within the party, shifting power away from the bureaucracy (Leigh 1992; Felker 1998). This was facilitated in part by the 1982 recession (e.g. see Jomo 1993a, 1994) which enabled Prime Minister Mahathir to centralize authority, bypass the bureaucracy to initiate state–business relationships and eventually introduce privatization. Central to this was the support of an influential segment of NEP-nurtured Malay state managers, businessmen and the new Malay middle class. The expansion of the Malay middle class was a direct result of the NEP. 'Between 1970 and 1990 the proportion of the Malay workforce working in middle-class occupations more than doubled from 12.9 to 27.0 per cent' (Crouch 1993: 142) and, by one estimate, increased by more than tenfold between 1970 and 1998 (see Jomo 1999b). Malay representation increased in eight prized professions[13] (from 5 per cent in 1970 to 25 per cent in 1988) (Jomo 1990), managerial posts[14] (especially in the commercial and industrial sector) (Ismail and Osman 1991), and among university graduates (who moved into business following the exhaustion of employment opportunities in the public sector) (Jomo 1990).

The emergence of the Malay middle class pushed UMNO to assert itself, eventually establishing the party's political and economic hegemony. This was made possible by UMNO's direct involvement in business, with the formation of Fleet Holdings in 1972, the party's own holding company, in order to establish its financial independence from the Malaysian Chinese Association (e.g. see Yusoff 1990; Bowie 1991). Under the NEP, the government was initially able to centralize redistribution without state capture due to a unified party elite under a strong leadership which had the support of a large middle class and rural populace (as a result of bureaucratic expansion and rural development) (Leong 1991, cited in Felker 1998: 90). This centralized patronage allowed UMNO to control resources, providing benefits to its supporters and strengthening party loyalty (Jesudason 1989; Crouch 1992; Khoo K.J. 1992; Felker 1998). The government was also able to strengthen and insulate the state's planning and economic agencies,[15] with bureaucrats controlling resources through the management of state assets, and initially with minimal private business influence on economic policies (Felker 1998; Leong 1991, cited in Felker 1998: 90).

Despite its continued dependence on the state, the Malay business class grew in organization and influence (Jesudason 1989), with the growing number of Malay businessmen fostered by the NEP becoming an increasingly important element in the Malay political elite by the 1980s. This was reflected in the changing composition of UMNO leaders from politicians and 'administocrats' to a combination of politicians and businessmen (Leigh 1992), with significantly more Malay politicians active as businessmen (on their own and on UMNO's behalf) and Malay businessmen active in politics after the NEP (Ho 1988). Corporate restructuring increased Malay share ownership from 1.5 per cent in 1969 to 19.4 per cent in 1988, and individual share ownership among Malays increased to 67 per cent.[16] State efforts to control the 'commanding heights of the economy' (e.g. plantations and tin mines), driven by concerns with finding the quickest way to accumulate assets and control well-managed, profitable companies, also created a powerful group of former state managers increasingly active in business (Jesudason 1989).

The late 1970s saw the emergence and transformation of the Malay bourgeoisie from primarily directors – not owners – of large corporations (before the mid 1970s) to Malay millionaires (Lim 1985), with professional and trustee Malay executive directors becoming prominent by the late 1980s (Searle 1999). This shift in power was accompanied by changes in the occupational background and outlook of UMNO leaders and grassroots members, with schoolteachers and other local leaders replaced by businessmen and university-educated professionals produced by the NEP (Crouch 1992; Searle 1999). 'Middle-class elements' were able to completely take over UMNO by the early 1980s (Jomo 1999b), and by the time privatization was introduced, there was already a large Malay middle class, including a younger, more professionally trained managerial cadre whose support was important, and who had to be accommodated (e.g. see Milne and Mauzy 1999). However, as mentioned in the previous section, this group did not necessarily represent a dynamic, independent capitalist class, being the product of state policies which sought the quickest and easiest way to create capitalists. As such, they continued to be dependent on state support but were also increasingly impatient and ambitious.

The changing composition of the Malay middle class altered patron–client relationships and reshaped the internal politics within UMNO local branches. UMNO's expansion into business established the party's economic dominance and financed intra-party/leadership contests by securing votes through the allocation of contracts to supporters. Increasing economic patronage changed the nature of the patron–client relationship, transforming local UMNO representatives into political patrons. Elected members of parliament who were previously political patrons (providing political support in return for economic benefits) greatly increased their control of the district development machinery, allowing them to become economic patrons, distributing development benefits and purchasing continued support (Shamsul 1986). While Malay businessmen were heavily dependent on their access to government patronage, they became an important force in the internal politics of UMNO through the party's extensive patronage network (Khoo K.J. 1992; Crouch 1992; Aziz 1997), increasing bitter factional struggles for nomination and outbreaks of violence at UMNO branch and division meetings after 1984 (Shamsul 1986). Although factions were already present in all levels of UMNO (Ahmad 1985), the rise of 'money politics' was closely related to (if not a direct result of) the NEP (Shamsul 1986). This resulted in a series of bitter contests between 1981 and 1987, culminating in the leadership challenge and open party split in 1987 (Khoo K.J. 1992; Crouch 1992).

Conflict arose between state agencies[17] and small Malay contractors, and timber merchants and businesses (Lim 1985; Bowie 1988), with SOEs frequently encroaching into areas where Malays were already operating or could easily move into (Bruton 1992). (This eventually compelled the state to trim back the role of SOEs, focus on heavy industries, and finally divest ownership to Malays [Lim 1985].) The main conflict though appeared to be between two factions (e.g. see Malek 1986). The pro-'distribution' faction, comprising small and medium Malay businessmen, and the 'bureaucratic class', were concentrated primarily at the branch level of UMNO and within various Malay chambers of commerce, heavily dependent on access to patronage, and favoured continued state intervention. This group was most affected by the government's response to the 1980s recession which included the tightening of credit,[18] austerity measures, the suspension, restructuring or shelving of State Economic Development Corporations (SEDCs) (Searle 1999) and centralization of assets.

The so-called pro-'growth' faction, on the other hand, involved a coalition of political and business elites. This included a cadre of NEP-trained Malay businessmen whose support for privatization facilitated the shift to narrow and personalistic policy networks in order to bypass formal bureaucratic channels, enabling politicians to take over control of state-held assets from technocrats and bureaucrats (Shamsul 1986; Felker 1999; also see Gomez 2002b, 2002c). This group is said to have grown independent of state sponsorship and patronage, viewing the NEP as imposing market distortions and obstructions to growth and new business opportunities (e.g. see Khoo K.J. 1992; Crouch 1992; Khoo B.T. 1995; Searle 1999). Certainly there were government concerns about the sustainability of redistributive policies in the context of a recession and existing inefficiencies, and privatization shifted the focus away from the NEP's 'redistribution with growth' to an emphasis on 'growth with redistribution'. However, the economic rhetoric was also largely to justify redistributive policies in favour of an emerging faction within UMNO that was closely aligned to a segment of the political leadership and increasingly benefiting from patronage as a result. This led to the gradual erosion of the Ministry of Trade and Industry's powers through the transfer of profitable enterprises to trust agencies directly under the Prime Minister's control[19] and transfer of UMNO shares and assets to the new UMNO treasurer and Minister of Finance Daim Zainuddin (Yusoff 1990; Khoo K.J. 1992).

Privatization therefore needs to be understood in terms of the contest for and conflict over the control and allocation of resources, including rents. This was in turn influenced by the changing social relations. Here, Mahathir's victory in intra-party struggles – especially in 1987 following the introduction of privatization – owed much to the successful creation under the NEP of a 'Malay rentier-business cadre' who stood to benefit (disproportionately) from greater business opportunities following privatization, and whose support was crucial (Jomo 1993a; Felker 1993). This group of prominent and rich businessmen can be traced back to two key NEP institutions, Peremba and Fima, where they served under Daim and Mahathir respectively. Peremba was co-founded by Daim before Mahathir appointed him as Finance Minister. It was the property development arm of the Urban Development Authority (UDA) and was set up to train Malay managers and entrepreneurs (*Malaysian Industry*, January 1996). Fima was set up in 1972 as a quasi-government food production company, with Mahathir as its chairman and later director until his appointment as Prime Minister.

Privatization provided this new group of businessmen with opportunities for rent capture at the expense of the pro-'distribution' faction because they were closely connected with the political leadership. These rents included significant implicit subsidies in privatization contracts which were difficult to capture under the NEP where state ownership and (bureaucratic) control restricted rents mainly to broad-based subsidies and cheap credit. Privatization also presented a segment of the political leadership with the opportunities to reward its supporters, thereby securing future support at party elections (e.g. see Gomez 1990, 1991). All this is not to say that economic reasons were not important. Rather, it was these political factors and motivations which affected the character of Malaysia's privatization programme, including its performance and the types of institutions, and the government's ability to promote learning and ensure commercial viability.

## Malaysia's privatization programme (1983–2000)

The discussion above allows us to make sense of Malaysia's privatization programme. Announced in 1983, privatization represented a change in how resources were allocated within UMNO as a result of a shift in the balance of power and was as such to be implemented within the context of the NEP's redistributive policies. Privatized public sector assets were to provide the basis for further corporate growth of the Malay private sector, and ownership conditions were to reduce ownership imbalances between Malay and other interests (Malaysia 1985; Galal *et al.* 1994b), mainly through fostering Malay entrepreneurs and through the transfer of state-owned assets to individuals.

Officially, privatization aimed to:

1 relieve the government's financial and administrative burden;
2 improve efficiency and productivity through competition and employee incentives;

3 facilitate economic growth by increasing the role of the private sector in development;
4 reduce the size and presence of the public sector; and
5 help meet NEP targets by providing opportunities for restructuring the ownership pattern.

However, it is the final objective which accounts for some of the main features of the privatization programme. Privatization was characterized by a non-transparent selection process, weak regulation and the lack of complete divestiture (Malaysia 1991b). Decisions and regulation remained highly centralized and personalized, reflecting the increasingly personalized patron–client networks, while the mode and sectoral distribution of privatization allowed the government to continue directing economic activity and promote capital accumulation methods consistent with the preferences (and abilities) of the new Malay middle class. Despite its scale and scope, privatization involved relatively few (complete) divestitures and a predominance of contracting out, focusing mainly on the non-tradable sector (e.g. construction and property development), as well as completely new projects initiated by the private sector.

All these facilitated easy capital accumulation by supporting economic activity in rentier sectors, but affected the performance of privatization because the government failed to address inherited inefficiencies and promote learning and commercial viability due to constraints posed by patron–client networks. As a result, by 2001, the government begun scaling back the programme following the failure and renationalization of several large privatizations and public companies involved in these, signalling the end of its 'owner-manager' model by replacing the private owners with professional (state) managers (e.g. see *The Star*, 10 August 2002; Kennedy 2002).

### *Background and main features*

The government defines privatization as the transfer to the private sector of activities and functions which have traditionally rested with the public sector. This applies to enterprises already owned by the government and to new projects normally implemented by the public sector (Malaysia 1991b), and requires the transfer of management responsibility, assets (or the rights to use assets) or personnel. The four main modes of privatization are sale of assets or equity; lease of assets; management contracts; and build-operate-transfer (BOT) and build-operate (BO) (Malaysia 1991b). However, privatization is also broadly defined to include partial divestitures (with the government retaining majority ownership); joint public-private sector ventures; schemes to draw private financing into construction projects (e.g. highways and low-cost housing schemes); licences to operate in sectors previously exclusive to the public sector (e.g. TV broadcast, telecommunications); contracting out of public services (e.g. garbage collection); contracted leasing of public properties; corporatization; and management-buy-out (MBO) (Jomo 1990). In addition, the chosen mode was to reflect the requirements of national objectives.

On paper at least, there were clear privatization procedures. The Privatization Task Force (PTF) monitored progress of feasibility studies, established technical committees, coordinated the privatization of SOEs and advised the Inter-departmental Committee on Privatization (ICP) (Ismail and Lee 1990; Malaysia 1991b). The ICP (technically the highest decision-making body) made recommendations to the Cabinet, and was responsible for planning, monitoring, coordinating and evaluating the implementation of the privatization programme. Decisions were based on 'feasibility' and 'desirability'. Feasibility was determined by the ease of privatization (in terms of SOE-restructuring and legal or regulatory changes) and attractiveness to the private sector (in terms of its competitive market position, growth potential and financial profile). Desirability was based on government priorities for economic development and improvements in the provision of goods and services. Privatization could be initiated by the government or private sector. Government-initiated privatization normally required a detailed study to determine viability and mode of privatization before a tender or negotiations with a single party where circumstances warranted. In the case of private sector-initiated privatization, the first promoter to submit a detailed feasibility study to the PTF had the exclusive rights to negotiate with the government. This was designed to reward private sector initiatives and innovations (Malaysia 1996). Nonetheless, private sector-initiated privatization was to be only considered under circumstances where the proposer offered a unique cost-effective solution or potential savings, or possessed technical know-how, patent rights or some other component essential to the proposal (e.g. see Jomo 1994: 75).

To support this, new modes of privatization were introduced (e.g. build-transfer [BT] and asset swap) to facilitate the privatization of land development and 'accommodate the requirements of more innovative proposals submitted by the private sector' (Malaysia 1996: 203). As such, rather than merely representing a transfer of activities and functions to the private sector, privatization often resulted in completely new projects developed by the private sector which may not have otherwise been undertaken by the state.[20] This does not reduce the government's financial burden or the size of the public sector, or improve efficiency, but does increase the role of the private sector and is consistent with NEP targets. The private sector-initiated approach helped expedite implementation and encourage private sector proposals. The Privatization Master Plan (PMP) identified 234 privatization proposals initiated by the private sector, of which 109 were implemented (Malaysia 1996; also see Jomo 1994).

Gauging the exact scale of Malaysia's privatization programme is difficult because the data does not include every public sector activity or function transferred to the private sector. For example, privatization implemented prior to 1983 'for reasons of efficacy of execution of activities rather than to consciously achieve some national objectives', and which do not involve the transfer of assets or personnel, is excluded (Malaysia 1991b: point 21), even if these transferred activities to the private sector. This includes contracts on a turnkey basis and contracting out of services by municipalities and other government organizations (e.g. security, cleaning, laundry and maintenance of hospital facilities) undertaken between 1986 and 1990 (Malaysia 1991a; Jomo 1994). Smaller privatizations (of less than 500 employees) and divestments since 1981 are also often excluded from official statistics, including the first state divestments where equity in 45 companies was transferred to Permodalan Nasional Berhad (PNB, the National Equity Corporation) and Amanah Saham Nasional (ASN, the National Unit Trust Scheme), and equity in another 120 companies to private parties in 1981. Similarly, corporatization is sometimes excluded, while non-financial public enterprises (NFPEs) were only categorized under the public sector in the Fifth Malaysia Plan (1986–90) (Malaysia 1986).

Furthermore, there is no comprehensive list of privatizations on a state or federal or municipal level, with information largely scattered and restricted following amendments to the Official Secrets Act (OSA) to cover government tender documents (Jomo 1994). This limits access to details of privatization tenders, contracts, estimates of project value and names of beneficiaries, especially given the practice of using nominees.[21] The exclusion of these privatizations from official records, and the data problems, tend to under represent the actual scale of privatization (itself a reflection of the degree of state intervention under the NEP, with SOEs involved in almost every economic sector) (see Adam and Cavendish 1995; Plane 1997: 352).

Nonetheless, the available evidence allows us to outline some broad features of Malaysia's privatization programme. Privatization was characterized by the overwhelming number of Malay beneficiaries, in line with the objective of 'restructuring the ownership pattern in the economy'. Here, the mode and sectoral distribution of privatization was also consistent with the preferences of the Malay middle class in general, focusing largely on sectors where Malay enterprises were most concentrated, namely in 'construction' (the largest privatized sector), 'government services', and 'wholesale and retail trade, hotels and restaurants' (Table 3.01; also see Ho 1988).

Furthermore, although divestiture (through the sale of equity) was the method with the highest privatizations (109 out of 328 in 1983–2000) (Table 3.02), this was a relatively small number and restricted to partial divestiture, where the government disposed only a small fraction of the public sector during the first decade, with only a fraction of the shares going into private hands (Galal *et al.* 1994b). In the case of majority divestiture, the government often retained effective control through a 'golden share' (a special rights redeemable preference share), with management largely unchanged (Ho 1988; Jomo 1994). Instead, privatization largely involved contracting out. Officially there were 79 privatizations through contracting

*Table 3.01* Malaysia: Number of privatized projects by sector, 1991–2000

| *Sector* | *Privatizations* | *Share of total (%)* |
|---|---|---|
| *1991–1996* | | |
| Agriculture and forestry | 16 | 7.8 |
| Mining and quarrying | 10 | 4.9 |
| Manufacturing | 31 | 15.2 |
| Construction | 46 | 22.5 |
| Electricity, gas and water | 14 | 6.9 |
| Transport, storage and communications | 22 | 10.8 |
| Wholesale and retail trade, hotels and restaurants | 23 | 11.3 |
| Finance, real estate and business services | 13 | 6.4 |
| Government services | 11 | 5.4 |
| Other services | 18 | 8.8 |
| Total | 204 | 100 |
| *1996–2000* | | |
| Agriculture and forestry | 8 | 8.2 |
| Manufacturing | 2 | 2 |
| Construction | 27 | 27.6 |
| Electricity and gas | 12 | 12.2 |
| Transport | 16 | 16.3 |
| Water and sewerage | 4 | 4.1 |
| Wholesale and retail trade, hotels and restaurants | 6 | 6.1 |
| Finance, real estate and business services | 3 | 3.1 |
| Government services | 20 | 20.4 |
| Total | 98 | 100 |

*Source:* Adapted from Malaysia (1996: 204, Tb 7–1); Malaysia (2001a: 185).

out (BOT/BOO/BT) in 1983–2000 (Table 3.02), the highest method of privatization after sale of equity and sale/lease of assets. For reasons discussed earlier, this figure may be much higher when other BOT/BOO/BT projects related to infrastructure, construction and property development are included. (For example, there were around 47 major privatized road projects, and based on UMNO's list of privatizations alone, 60 property or construction-related privatizations.)[22] This emphasis on contracting out (in non-tradable sectors, mainly in construction and property development) offered secure rents and was again consistent with the sectors in which many Malay companies were active.

Despite the procedures on paper, privatization remained highly centralized and personalized in practice. Where some allocations were made by the Ministry of Trade and Industry in the 1980s, this prerogative was increasingly exercised by the Ministry of Finance (MoF) in the 1990s. This followed Mahathir's consolidation of power and his appointment of close friend Daim Zainuddin as Finance Minister. While the expanded scope of privatization allowed for numerous methods of privatization which spread transfers as

*Table 3.02* Malaysia: Number of privatized projects by mode, 1983–2000

| *Method* | *1983–90* | *1991–95* | *1996–2000* | *1983–2000* |
|---|---|---|---|---|
| Sale of equity (SOE) | 4 | 94 | 11 | 109 |
| Sale/lease of asset (SOA/LOA) | 5 | 39 | 35 | 79 |
| Build-operate-transfer (BOT) | 9 | 21 | 15 | 45 |
| Build-operate-own (BOO) | 1 | 18 | 10 | 29 |
| Build-transfer (BT) | 0 | 5 | 0 | 5 |
| Corporatization (COR) | 0 | 13 | 9 | 22 |
| Management contract (MC) | 5 | 9 | 11 | 25 |
| Management buyout (MBO) | 2 | 5 | 7 | 14 |
| Total | 26 | 204 | 98 | 328 |

*Source:* Adapted from Gomez and Jomo (1997: 84) for 1983–90; Malaysia (1996: 202–204) for 1991–95; and Malaysia (2001a: 185) for 1996–2000.

widely as possible among Malays, these privatizations were usually restricted to services and small divestitures and contracts. Instead, a large proportion of privatization, including some of the largest, was allocated through non-transparent procedures to a relatively small group of capitalists, both Malay and non-Malay (many who received training in NEP institutions and were connected to the political leadership, in particular the Prime Minister and Finance Minister) (see Ho 1988; Jomo 1990; Gomez 1990, 2002c; Barraclough 2000) and to politically favoured state institutional investors and nominee companies (see Goh and Jomo 1995: Table 7.9). Furthermore, the MoF retained majority ownership of key privatized companies including the two largest companies on the Kuala Lumpur Stock Exchange (KLSE), Telekom Malaysia and Tenaga Nasional Berhad (TNB, the national power company).

Regulation was similarly personalized (rather than formalized), with some private owners reporting directly to Mahathir.[23] This can account for the generally weak, often absent, regulatory framework and *ad hoc* nature of government intervention, often by different ministries/ministers, but with the Prime Minister having overriding authority. The low emphasis on regulation meant that regulatory authorities were hampered by insufficient autonomy and technical expertise, and limited to safety regulations with relatively little economic regulation. Regulatory design was further complicated by multiple (often social) objectives and weaknesses in competition policy (see Lee, C. 2004), as well as institutional fragmentation and competing agendas (e.g. in the public transport sector). These problems were partly due to technical weaknesses and inherited bureaucratic structures, but also the nature of political considerations related to centralized and personalized patronage systems.

In particular, these institutional characteristics were a reflection of the increasing conflict in UMNO and subsequent authoritarianism discussed earlier. Following Mahathir's narrow re-election as party president in 1987, he consolidated his authority both within UMNO, where he amended the constitution to increase his power (Milne and Mauzy 1999), and in government, with the concentration of power in a few key regulatory agencies directly under the Prime Minister's Department (Searle 1999). UMNO's control of key economic and technocratic agencies of government, specifically the MoF, Ministry of Trade and Industry, and Economic Planning Unit (EPU, located in the Prime Minister's Department) meant that decision-making became increasingly centralized, allowing Mahathir to bypass key bureaucratic interests (Felker 1999) and impose his own views on economic policies, with even the EPU having to defer to the Prime Minister on his choice of key projects (e.g. see Jesudason 1989; Milne and Mauzy 1999). Here, increasing competition did not lead to decentralized patron–client networks but instead prompted Mahathir to strengthen his authority, in part by securing political support through the greater personal control of resource allocation.

### *Privatization performance (1983–2000)*

Assessment of Malaysia's privatization performance is affected by methodological difficulties (discussed in Chapter 2) as well as data problems discussed in the previous section. As a result, evidence is patchy at best and inconclusive. One solution is to measure performance in terms of the official aims of privatization.

#### *Relieving the government's administrative and financial burden*

Privatization saved the government RM122.0–RM132.2 billion in capital expenditure (Malaysia 1996, 2001b; *The Edge*, 18 December 2000) and around RM7 billion in operating expenditure (*The Edge*, 18 December 2000; *Far Eastern Economic Review*, 25 January 2001).[24] While savings on operating expenditure represented less than 1 per cent of operating (current) expenditure, savings on capital expenditure was around 25 per cent of total development expenditure of the public sector from 1981 to 2000 (Malaysia 1986, 1996, 2001b). However, these were only savings in accounting and not economic terms since the money was still spent on capital expenditure through government-guaranteed or soft loans to the private sector (i.e. it was effectively still a loan to the government but through the private sector). Most non-financial public enterprises (NFPEs) and even government development expenditure have been primarily financed by the private capital market, albeit with government-guaranteed loans in the former and government borrowings in the latter.

Furthermore, the state provided RM5.1 billion in soft loans for privatization projects (1983–96) (*The Edge*, 6 November 2000) and RM4.8 billion 'for projects with a high social component' (1991–95) (Malaysia 1996). Most of these soft loans were later transferred back to the state, while 'contingent liabilities' incurred through the guarantee of minimal revenue flows to private operators are believed to have been around RM20–RM30 billion (Jomo 2002). The government's desire to ensure the success of its privatization policy (e.g. by discounting asset prices) also crowded out private demand for capital for non-privatization purposes, as well as the creation of assets (through productive investment) in favour of the transfer of assets (through private acquisition of government stock) (Jomo 2002).

Privatization saw revenue from corporate taxes grow steadily in absolute terms and as a percentage of total government revenue from 1980 to 2000. However, revenue from corporate taxes already exhibited high growth rates before privatization (19 per cent in 1971–75 and 14.3 per cent in 1976–80, where GDP was at 7.2 and 7.8 per cent respectively) and as a percentage of government revenue (20.4 per cent in 1970 and 22.8 per cent in 1975) (Malaysia 1981). Furthermore, corporate tax revenue declined in growth rate and absolute terms in the first seven years of privatization (Table 3.03). There is also no clear evidence that additional recurrent revenues from leases or taxation compensated for the loss of recurrent revenue from the government's more profitable investments (Jomo 1994), especially given the revenue foregone through tax exemptions such as the RM4.5 billion for highway company PLUS (*Asian Wall Street Journal*, 21 December 1998).

The government earned RM21.2–RM23.1 billion from the sale of equity and RM12.7 billion from the sale of assets (Malaysia 1996, 2001b; *The Edge*, 18 December 2000) although the volume of privatization revenue 'remained miniscule during the 1980s' (Cavendish and Mistry 1992: 39, cited in Cook and Kirkpatrick 1995: 297). Furthermore, this does not take into account the very substantial cost of government bail-outs, takeovers and renationalizations, nor the loss of revenue through the undervaluation of public-listed shares[25] (e.g. see Ismail and Lee 1990; Jomo 1994; Goh and Jomo 1995).

Similarly, the transfer of an estimated RM7.45 billion in federal debt to the private sector by 1990 through privatization (Ismail and Lee 1990) needs to take into account the transfer back of outstanding private sector debt through renationalizations and the state purchase of non-performing

*Table 3.03* Malaysia: Revenue from corporate taxes, 1970–2000

| *Year* | *Total (RM billion)* | *% of govt revenue* | *Years* | *Total (RM billion)* | *Growth rate (%)* | *GDP (%)* |
|---|---|---|---|---|---|---|
| 1970 | 0.49 | 20.4 | | | | |
| 1975 | 1.2 | 22.8 | 1971–75 | 0.49 | 19 | 7.2 |
| 1980 | 2.5 | 18.1 | 1976–80 | 1.2 | 14.3 | 7.8 |
| 1985 | 3.9 | 18.6 | 1981–85 | 16.1 | 8.7 | 4.9 |
| 1990 | 4.5 | 15.2 | 1986–90 | 16.9 | 1 | 6.7 |
| 1995 | 11.7 | 23 | 1991–95 | 43.7 | 21.1 | 8.7 |
| 2000 | 13.9 | 22.5 | 1996–2000 | 77.8 | 3.5 | 4.7 |

*Source:* Adapted from Malaysia (1981, 1986, 1991a, 1996, 2001a).

loans (NPLs), many from privatized enterprises or companies involved in privatized projects.[26] By early 2000, the state asset management company Danaharta had acquired RM47 billion worth of NPLs from financial institutions (Chin and Jomo 2001), including RM3.09 billion (the single largest NPL) from Renong (UMNO's holding company and the largest privatization beneficiary) (*Far Eastern Economic Review*, 22 February 2001).

Finally, privatization reduced the size of the public sector by transferring 114,198 employees to the private sector between 1983 and 2000[27] (excluding transfers from privatized SOEs such as hospital and port services) (Malaysia 1996, 2001b). However, as the private sector was not allowed to retrench employees in the first five years, privatization did not address inefficiencies arising from excess staff that were merely transferred to the private sector (Ismail and Lee 1990).

### *Improving efficiency and productivity*

Efficiency gains are typically measured by profit margins, profit–asset ratios, labour and total factor productivity, production and export data, sales performance, capital investment, leverage and dividend policy. Early studies found efficiency gains in the privatizations of Malaysia Airlines (MAS), ports and Sports Toto (the state lottery) (Jones and Fadil 1992, 1994; Galal *et al.* 1994); solid waste infrastructure and services (Lee Y.F. 1997); and improvements in TV broadcasting (Ismail and Lee 1990; Tan C.H. 1991; Mohamad Sheriff 1991, both cited in Ghosh 1999) and Telekom Malaysia (Mohamad Sheriff 1991, cited in Ghosh 1999).

The privatization of three ports (Klang Container Terminal, Penang Port and Johor Port) has been credited for increasing cargo-handling and improving productivity and profits (Ismail and Lee 1990; Malaysia 1991b, 1996, 2001b; Jones and Fadil 1992; Jones 1994; Galal *et al.* 1994b; Singaravelloo 1996). However, much of this improvement was due to output growth, which was the result of exogenous demand shifts, e.g. the increase in the number of ship calls at Malaysian ports as a result of new shipping lines commencing direct calls, and additional services by existing lines (Malaysia 2001b). It is also unclear if privatization of an unprofitable port would have been successful (Hochstein 1996).

Telekom Malaysia reported improvements following corporatization in 1987 and (49 per cent) divestment in 1990, registering steady profit growth for seven consecutive years, increasing returns on assets, and increasing revenue per subscriber, production per employee, direct exchange lines per employee and response to faults/complaints, while also improving existing services and providing new services (Malaysia 1991b, 1996, 2001b). The corporatization of TNB, the national power company, saw a reduction in system losses, and improvements in average fuel conversion efficiency, revenue generated and access to the public (Malaysia 1996, 2001b), and significantly improved infrastructure and strategic investment which reduced power outages (Leary 1998). However, TNB's profitability decreased while cost per unit and cost to public per unit per output increased as a result of unequal power purchase agreements with (private) independent power producers (IPPs) (*Malaysian Business*, 1 September 1993; *The Sun*, 2 January 1996; *New Straits Times*, 8 January 1996, 4 July 1996; *The Star*, 28 December 1996, 5 October 1999, 23 January 1999; *Business Times*, 11 November 1998; Malaysia 2001b). Furthermore, despite divestment, both Telekom Malaysia and TNB remained majority state-owned.

The contracting out of solid waste infrastructure and services improved garbage collection in Kuala Lumpur from 5.7 tons of waste per vehicle per day before privatization to 8.7 tons in 11 municipalities, and resulted in cost savings in nine others (Lee Y.F. 1997). Sports Toto, the privatized lottery fund, expanded and introduced new products as well as registered gains amounting to 11 per cent of predivestiture sales (to 1990) from improved marketing to expand market share (Galal *et al.* 1994b; Jones 1994). Revenues from levies on the privatized lottery were three times greater (in real terms) than revenue from the former SOE (Kikeri *et al.* 1994). However, it is not entirely clear that Sports Toto's performance was the result of privatization and not other factors, particularly given that 'minimal efforts were taken by the government to expand operations in view of the [unIslamic] nature of the company's activity' (Ismail 1991: 624).

Overall, the evidence here is small (given the scale of privatization), selective (often restricted to a few same case studies or sectors) and employs different measurements. The diverse modes of privatization and different entities privatized also make pre- and post-privatization comparisons or comparisons with similar SOEs difficult if not impossible. It is also sometimes not clear whether efficiency gains, where these took place, were the result of privatization or favourable macroeconomic conditions.

### *Facilitating economic growth*

Privatization is argued to have facilitated economic growth through corporate expansion and greater utilization of growth opportunities through private sector motivation (Malaysia 1991b). This was reflected in overall levels of private investment, corporate and industry growth, and market capitalization. Private investment increased absolutely and in terms of its share of total investment and GNP (1983–97). Private investment growth rates also exceeded GDP growth rates after 1986. However, although the increase in private investment is most likely the result of privatization (particularly in the case of large BO/BOT infrastructure projects in the late 1980s and early 1990s) (Malaysia 1991b), private investment was already growing rapidly and constituted over 60 per cent of total investment from 1970 to 1980 (Table 3.04).

*Table 3.04* Malaysia: Private investment, 1970–2000

| *Year* | *Private investment (RM billion)* | *Share of total investment (%)* | *Share of GNP (%)* |
|---|---|---|---|
| 1970 | 1.5 | 67.9 | 12.1 |
| 1975 | 2.5 | 62.3 | 14.1 |
| 1980 | 10.4 | 62.6 | 20.1 |
| 1981 | 11.5 | 55.2 | 20.5 |
| 1982 | 11.4 | 50 | 19 |
| 1983 | 12 | 49 | 18.3 |
| 1984 | 13.3 | 52.6 | 18 |
| 1985 | 12.3 | 53 | 17.1 |
| 1990 | 24.2 | 64.7 | 21.9 |
| 1995 | 57.7 | 71.6 | 28.5 |
| 1997 | 87.9 | 73.8 | 39.2 |
| 1998 | n/a | 57.9 | 18.5 |
| 2000 | 42.9 | 49.2 | 13.8 |

*Source:* Adapted from Malaysia (1981; 1986; 1991a; 1996; 2001a).

Privatization has been credited with enhancing economic growth (Tan C.H. 1991) by releasing resources for corporate expansion through efficiency gains, although no evidence of this has been produced. Growth is also said to have been generated by allowing private entrepreneurship in sectors previously monopolized by the state, and through the multiplier effect, especially in (BOT) road construction, electricity supply, telecommunications and TV broadcasting (Malaysia 1991a, 1991b, 1996, 2001b; Leary 1998). However, the examples of BOT projects and licensed activities merely involve the private sector substituting for what the public sector would otherwise have undertaken at lower cost to users (see Jomo 1989).

Privatization significantly deepened the capital market. The public listing of the thirteen entities privatized by June 1992 raised market capitalization by RM201.1 billion, accounting for 28 per cent of total capitalization and making the Kuala Lumpur Stock Exchange (KLSE) the largest stock market in Southeast Asia and the fourth largest in Asia (*Malaysian Business*, 16 August 1992; *Investors Digest*, November 1992). TNB and Telekom Malaysia alone – the two largest companies on the KLSE – accounted for RM62.08 billion (11 per cent) of market capitalization in 1995 (Tan, C. 1996; Malaysia 1996). Between 1996 and 2000, five newly listed Infrastructure Project Companies[28] (IPCs) raised RM3.5 billion through the issue of new shares (Malaysia 2001b).

However, there is considerable evidence that companies in Malaysia seek stock market listing for signalling purposes, to secure more bank credit on better terms rather than to raise money directly on the stock market. Three quarters of the US$35 billion estimated to have been borrowed from abroad were accounted for by three privatized SOEs (MAS, TNB and

Telekom Malaysia) (Jomo 2002). In any case, there is no clear evidence that privatization in particular contributed to economic growth in the late 1980s (Jomo 1994), and the direction of causality is unclear, with domestic growth coinciding with a period of strong regional economic growth, initially driven by East Asian export-oriented manufacturing investments between 1988 and 1997 (Jomo and Gomez 2000).

### *Reducing the size and presence of the public sector*

The reduction in the size and presence of the public sector is reflected in public sector development expenditure. Privatization reduced the government's economic allocation from 64.9 per cent of total expenditure (1986–90) to 50.6 per cent (1991 95) and public expenditure in commerce and industry, transport, communications, energy and public utilities from 23.4 to 17.5 per cent. However, after an initial reduction in government expenditure between 1981 and 1985, the level of government spending (as a percentage of GNP) remained constant throughout 1986–95 where the bulk of privatizations took place (Table 3.05). Furthermore, public expenditure increased across the board with total public sector expenditure (as a percentage of GNP) increasing to above 1986–90 levels following the Asian financial crisis. Privatization also did not reduce the state's involvement in the economy in terms of the number of public enterprises which increased from 736 to over 1,000 between 1986 and 1989, while the value of government investment undertaken by public sector agencies increased from RM2.5 to RM5.7 billion (1981–87) (Malaysia 1989; Gomez and Jomo 1997).

### *Meeting NEP redistributive targets*

NEP targets can be measured in terms of capital ownership and control, the economic performance of Malay capitalists, and levels of government support. In absolute terms, privatization was successful in creating a class of Malay capitalists, particularly in contributing to wealth acquisition (Jomo 1993a, 1994). Privatization is said to have increased Malay ownership and

*Table 3.05* Malaysia: Public sector development expenditure (RM billion, current prices), 1976–2000

| *Year* | *Total* | *Share of GNP (%)* | *Economic allocation* | *Main privatization sectors* | *Share of total (%)* |
|---|---|---|---|---|---|
| 1976–80 | 42.8 | | 18.5 | 11.9 | 27.8 |
| 1981–85 | 78.6 | 24.1 | 55.8 | 46.9 | 59.6 |
| 1986–90 | 61.9 | 14.2 | 31.2 | 14.5 | 23.4 |
| 1991–95 | 117.7 | 14.8 | 27.7 | 20.7 | 17.5 |
| 1996–2000 | 215.2 | 16.3 | 47.2 | 47.6 | 22.1 |

*Source:* Adapted from Malaysia (1981; 1986; 1991a; 1996; 2001a).

control of share capital;[29] Malay control of companies on the KLSE;[30] and Malay equity in privatized companies.[31] This centred on transportation (32.2 per cent), construction (27.1 per cent) and agriculture (24.3 per cent) (1996–2000) (Malaysia 2001b), consistent with the sectoral distribution of privatization. However, the total Malay share of capital had risen steadily since 1971, with the biggest growth from 4.3 to 9.2 per cent between 1971 and 1975 (Table 3.06). On the other hand, the increase of the individual Malay share of capital from 5.8 per cent (1980) to 18.6 per cent (1995, before the Asian financial crisis), and increasing concentration of individual share in the Malay stake from 39 per cent (1975) to 67 per cent (1988)[32] (Jomo 1990), coincided with privatization where the government transferred assets from trust agencies to individuals. This was mirrored in the decline in the corresponding share of trust agencies from 6.7 per cent (1980) to 2 per cent (1995) (Table 3.06).

However, despite the steady increase in the Malay share of capital, there have been significant dilutions of Malay interests in privatized enterprises (see Arab-Malaysian Merchant Bank *et al.* 1995: Table 2.16, cited in Jomo 2002). Malay interests divested RM1.79 billion worth of shares in publicly listed companies up to 1993, of which 53 per cent were shares of companies listed during 1990–92, indicating a 'lack of sustaining power of [Malays] to hold the equity in the long-term' and 'the pursuit of short-term capital gains' (Malaysia 1996: 210; 2001b). This suggests that privatization failed to produce a dynamic class of efficient Malay entrepreneurs (Rasiah and Ishak 2001), with Malay participation restricted to property, construction, finance and other non-tradable sectors, and dependent on continued government support and intervention. Failure was reflected in state restructuring, bail-outs and takeovers of companies owned by the small group of Malay capitalists who received the bulk of privatization.

## Why did privatization fail?

From the evidence in the previous section, the performance of Malaysia's privatization programme is mixed at best and clearly failed to meet long-term

*Table 3.06* Malaysia: Malay ownership of share capital (%) (selected years)

| *Year* | *Total* | *Individual* | *Trust agencies* |
|---|---|---|---|
| 1971 | 4.3 | 2.6 | 1.7 |
| 1975 | 9.2 | 3.6 | 5.6 |
| 1980 | 12.5 | 5.8 | 6.7 |
| 1985 | 17.8 | 10.1 | 7.7 |
| 1990 | 19.3 | 14.2 | 5.1 |
| 1995 | 20.6 | 18.6 | 2.0 |
| 1999 | 19.1 | 12.8 | 17.4 |

*Source:* Adapted from Malaysia (1981, 1986, 1996, 2001a).

NEP objectives of creating an independent Malay capitalist class. This is of immediate relevance to our discussion (and the case studies that follow) as it relates to the government's ability to promote learning and commercial viability through privatization in order to address problems arising from the NEP. The literature has attributed failure to the government's ex ante mistakes as a result of ethnic considerations and political patronage which affected rational economic policy, undermining efficiency and promoting unproductive rent-seeking. However, this focus on ex ante mistakes downplays the political (and information) constraints which invariably result in poor privatization decisions in the first place, and which then necessitate ex post corrective measures in the form of regulation and the management of subsidies if privatization is to be successful.

Evidence shows that the Malaysian government has historically lacked disciplinary capacity, failing to withdraw subsidies or protection, for example. Privatization did not improve the government's disciplinary capacity, which continued to be constrained by existing patron–client relationships, the scarcity of capital and social costs of bankruptcy. Failure in the end was due to the state's inability to correct mistakes that were made based on ethnically or politically motivated decisions, or information that turns out ex post to have been flawed. This ex post failure to correct mistakes is more important than the ability to make the correct ex ante decisions and provides a more useful explanation for the performance of Malaysia's privatization programme which was characterized by the government's inability to enforce discipline. Constraints on the government's disciplinary capacity can be traced back to changes in social relations under the NEP and privatization.

## *Ex ante failure*

### *Ethnic redistribution*

The increase in state intervention under the NEP in favour of ethnic redistribution has been associated with a dramatic increase in the scope of patronage and rent-seeking at the expense of rational economic policy (Tan, T.W. 1982; Jomo 1986, 1993a; Jesudason 1989; Jomo and Gomez 2000), with the state unconstrained by social forces, including a weak private sector, and financed by its considerable resources, in particular oil revenues (Jesudason 1989). The Malay-dominated state elite aligned itself with foreign capital (in order to bypass Chinese businesses) in exchange for directorships, joint-ventures, and other passive, essentially rentier, rewards (Lubeck 1992; Henderson and Applebaum 1992b). Consultation between state and business was neglected in favour of inter-ethnic political bargains that benefited an unproductive rentier bourgeoisie beholden to a political patronage system legitimated by ethnic chauvinism and thus hostile to the discipline of market competition (Gomez 1990, 1991; Lubeck 1992).

Rents were largely redistributive and not designed to promote learning, while the process of capital accumulation was channelled to serve political and ethnic imperatives. The result was an inefficient and fragile Malay bourgeoisie as 'political elites were rewarded precisely for breaking the rules of market rationality' and economic inefficiency was compensated by political rewards for UMNO (Jesudason 1989: 99–100). NEP licences, contracts, concessions and political access to enormous funds from the banking system contributed to the rapid growth in the number of Malay businessmen and allowed UMNO to provide benefits to its supporters and strengthen party loyalty (Crouch 1992; Khoo K.J. 1992). This became a more important criterion than technical competence, with party discipline enforced through the threat of recalling loans (Gale 1981; Mehmet 1988; Jesudason 1989; Gomez 1990; Crouch 1992; Gomez and Jomo 1997; Searle 1999). Policy changes (and failure) are attributed to changes in the balance of power between ethnic groups. Increasing state intervention is seen as a result of a breakdown of the 'consociational' framework (Jesudason 1989) or changes in the 'communal settlement' (Bowie 1991) where one ethnic group gains the upper hand, leaving the state unconstrained to act. Here, the state is viewed through 'public choice theory' lenses, comprising self-serving bureaucrats and politicians who abuse their power, especially when unchecked by the private sector.

This analysis of the state independent of social forces (and its assumptions of the motivations of the private sector) is problematic, and fails to identify the political forces behind state actions and the groups or factions which stand to gain or lose. As such, the question of state autonomy is not addressed, and it remains unclear in whose interest the state acts, given that policies have favoured certain groups over others and that the state has also implemented industrial strategies which also benefited non-Malay businesses, sometimes at the expense of Malays. As a result, increasing conflict in UMNO remains outside this framework. This is a crucial point because increasing intra-ethnic, rather than inter-ethnic, conflict has been the main cause of political instability since the 1969 'race riots', and central to how resources have been allocated.

By ignoring this, ethnic accounts break down when attempting to explain privatization. This was less a response to Chinese capital's 'obstructionism' during the NEP (Bowie 1991) and more to changes in social relations within the Malay community, specifically the emergence of the new Malay middle and business class pushing for a shift in resource allocation in its favour. It is in this context that ethnic considerations can partly account for ex ante mistakes related to the choice of candidates, though this needs to be viewed more broadly in terms of learning failure under the NEP (as discussed previously). The NEP was itself the result of political (more so than ethnic) imperatives to accommodate an increasingly impatient Malay middle class. Government policies were the outcome of changes in the balance of power within UMNO rather than between Malays and non-Malays, and state actions were a reflection of this. Privatization was a continuation of redistributive policies, this time benefiting a newly emerged group of businessmen closely associated with a segment of the UMNO leadership, and whose support was crucial in the party's leadership contests. This allowed Mahathir to consolidate his position as party president and push through policies which rewarded his supporters but which also aimed to address efficiency and technological constraints under the NEP. However, for reasons discussed earlier, these political motivations affected ex ante decisions, namely the types of privatization pursued, how (and to whom) this was allocated, and the types of institutions that were created.

### *Political patronage*

Ethnic explanations tend to converge with arguments about political patronage and crony capitalism, but these have tended to be largely descriptive. The 'political business' model, on the other hand, seeks to explain how politicians, and not the state, distribute rents (through the state) by looking at how the changing balance of power between capital and the state affects 'the dynamics of policy-making and policy implementation' (Gomez 2002b: 3, 7). This is an instructive approach which allows us to establish 'the institutions or actors in whom power is centred, and the nature of the relationship between capital and the state', thereby determining how rents are allocated (Gomez 2002b: 7). Political funding by business is central in influencing the distribution of rents through factions (loosely based around a leader) (Gomez 2002b). As a result, privatization increased rent-seeking and money politics, and led to a highly geared and unsustainable conglomerate-style expansion, where the politically powerful dominated financially profitable but rentier activities (Gomez 1991, 2002c; Rasiah 1998, 2001). This was compounded by the absence of an open tender system as a result of a 'first come, first served' policy which allowed the government to allocate resources on the basis of political and personal connections (Jomo 1994). Privatization beneficiaries were not competent enough because their selections were not based on strict economic criteria as political considerations outweighed economic optimality (e.g. see Wedeman 2002).

One of the difficulties in the political business model though is that state capacity is equated with autonomy, with the degree of state independence from capital said to determine the level of corruption and form of rent distribution (Gomez 2002b, 2002c). This assumes that the state can be independent of social forces, and can act and implement policies without political constraints. While the nature of the state's relationship with capital is central to its analysis, the model does not explicitly explain how this relationship affects government policy and capacity. Furthermore, it presumes that the correct choice of candidate would have made a difference. This is similar to Mahathir's arguments in favour of handpicking candidates (to prevent lobbying or outright corruption from influencing policy decisions) (Felker 1998; Mahathir 1998a, 1998b), the main difference being that the political business model emphasizes transparent, as opposed to personalized, selection processes. Here, the leadership was aware of the importance of selection,[33] and believed its choice of rich, successful businessmen 'had already proven their ability to run big operations' and thus their ability to improve the performance of companies to be privatized (Mahathir, quoted in *New Straits Times*, 27 November 1995; also see Mahathir 1998a, 1998b). Failure can then be attributed to ex ante mistakes in the wrong choice of candidates.

However, the arguments are flawed in both cases given the constraints of asymmetric information and available entrepreneurial capacity. It is also debatable whether competitive bidding would even be possible in the context of resistance to change and other political considerations (Ismail and Osman 1991) as increasing political competition and conflict would place political loyalty above economic criteria. Furthermore, a more transparent selection process may not improve the quality of candidates given the lack of entrepreneurial capacity, types of enterprises and serious industry challenges. In terms of our four case studies, it is unlikely that there were more suitable candidates with experience in building and operating a national sewerage or urban rail system, running a major airline or manufacturing cars. The task is therefore not so much to select winners but rather to create successful capitalists in these areas through a combination of incentives and effective sanctions to enforce conditionalities. Here, the government sought to develop a handful of very large industrialists with 'the acumen to accumulate wealth' to contribute to industry and commerce, providing employment and government revenue (Mahathir 1986: 11). This was closely modelled on the successful experiences of South Korea which Mahathir sought to emulate. However, South Korea's success was not due to 'picking winners' but rather 'creating' winners by setting export performance and productivity targets, and withdrawing support whenever performance lagged (Alavi, R. 1996; Wade 2003). This means that the effectiveness and efficiency of government action depends on ex post measures, in particular its disciplinary capacity.

### *Ex post failure*

While ethnic and political factors affected ex ante decisions, the main problem the government faced was in its ex post failure to correct mistakes. This failure to enforce discipline and promote learning appears to be a historical problem, with the state constrained at various periods by different factors, in part related to ethnic and political considerations. However, the literature on ethnic considerations and political patronage is generally divorced from the discussion of the key industrial and technological challenges facing the state which privatization partly sought to address.

There is evidence that the government was aware of ex ante mistakes related to privatization and attempted to address these, suggesting that ethnic and political considerations were tempered by an economic imperative as there were limits to efficiency losses the government was prepared to accept.

As successful privatization requires the state to make the correct decisions and then to correct decisions that turn out ex post to have been incorrect, we need to examine what constrained the government's political capacity to do so in order to explain why privatization failed. Furthermore, as ethnic motivations and patronage networks were largely a result of underlying political forces, it is necessary to examine these political factors, rather than their manifestation, if we are to identify the constraints to the government's ex post political capacity.

Ethnic-based explanations also invariably simplify changing social relations, downplaying the conflict within UMNO which affected the state's disciplinary capacity. Here, aspects of the political business model (Gomez 2002b, 2002c) can offer greater insight by examining the relationship (through patron–client networks) between different segments of capital with factions within the political leadership. We will build upon both these arguments to show how the government's disciplinary capacity was constrained, why the government historically failed to enforce discipline, why privatization did not improve the government's disciplinary capacity, and how this affected the performance of privatization, specifically the four case studies.

### *Disciplinary constraints under the NEP*

Although the NEP allowed the government to centralize redistribution, it also resulted in the overexpansion of the public sector, with the emergence of a small but powerful 'bureaucratic-capitalist elite' capturing rents and exercising considerable influence over policy (Jomo 1986; Mehmet 1988; Bowie 1991; Bruton 1992; Jomo and Tan 1999). This introduced managerial and control problems as state bureaucrats entrenched themselves and resisted government attempts to discipline them, with policy adjustments becoming increasingly more difficult (Bruton 1992). The government sought to address these problems by closing down loss-making SOEs[34] (Tan C.K. 1984) and reducing public expenditure after 1983. However, the public deficit remained high as SOEs were less subject to budgetary discipline (Ismail and Osman 1991; Jomo 2002).

The government's disciplinary capacity has been constrained since the 1970s, with concerns raised in two Malaysia Plans regarding the efficiency losses due to protection (Alavi, R. 1998), and again in 1983 by the Malaysian Industrial Policy Study (Malaysia 1983b) which recommended the halving of average levels of protection (Jomo and Edwards 1993). Despite this, inefficient import-substituting industries continued to receive high (and even increasing) levels of protection without proper evaluation, monitoring or performance conditions, and irrespective of productive capabilities, allowing unsuccessful firms to waste rents (Bruton 1992; Alavi, R. 1996, 1998; Jomo and Tan 1999; Rasiah and Ishak 2001; Rasiah 2001).

Selective state intervention was of a much poorer quality and considerably less effective than in Taiwan and South Korea in the 1960s and 1970s, with little evidence of rent deployment favouring industrialization or productive use, and a reliance on foreign rather than domestic-led manufacturing growth (due to the lack of Malay entrepreneurial ability and the desire to constrain Chinese capital) (Jomo and Tan 1999). The state's failure to direct domestic capital into strategic manufacturing industries adversely affected industrialization (Jesudason 1989; Bowie 1991; Felker 1998; Jomo and Tan 1999), preventing the emergence of an efficient, 'deepening' industrial policy (Jomo and Tan 1999: 303). Instead, rents provided wrong incentives, encouraging efficient companies into protected sectors. Furthermore, foreign-dominated manufactured exports had few production or technological linkages (see Felker 1998: 83). The result was a weak technological base and inadequate human resource development and skills formation (Malaysia 1985). The private sector was unable to provide comprehensive and detailed industry-level information (to guide policymaking) or mobilize large networks of producers to respond to government initiatives and incentives due to the top-down nature of networks (where private sector appointments are based on personal friendship or reputation) and the legacy of ethnically fragmented business networks and representation (Felker 1998).

Central to the discussion of industrialization is thus the process of technological innovation and, related to this, the role of the state. The state needs to underwrite the high cost of information about technology, especially when gains are large, with economies of scale (Jomo and Edwards 1993), and provide incentives for innovation (i.e. Schumpeterian rents) (e.g. see Khan 2000b). However, protection does not guarantee success unless it induces learning (Bruton 1998). The capacity to learn is said to depend on industry's 'collective learning' ability (facilitated by human capital and competitive pressures from exporting) and 'knowledge accumulation' (learning-by-doing), as well as the ability of the government to learn from its mistakes (Bell *et al.* 1984; Jacobsson 1993; Bruton 1998; Kim 2004). More importantly, learning will depend on the government's capacity to enforce conditional subsidies and correct mistakes once identified.

The Heavy Industries Corporation (HICOM) was the government's attempt to address the issue of absorbing complex organizational and production processes necessary for technological upgrading and industry linkages.[35] However, as heavy industries were set up to serve domestic, rather than export, markets, there was no systematic attempt to guide or monitor the technological development process, with the sector characterized by soft budgets (Lall 1995) and the lack of performance targets and conditionalities. Learning was also compromised by the complex nature of the technology, lack of (Malay) skills and desire to bypass Chinese capital. The government later sought to address HICOM's poor performance by replacing the (Malay) management with foreigners and non-Malays in the 1980s, and later privatizing the company (which included its subsidiary Proton). Privatization can therefore be partly seen as an attempt to improve the technological acquisition and industrial upgrading process. The success of privatization then depended on whether the government was better able to enforce discipline in order to address these technological and learning challenges.

*Disciplinary constraints under privatization*

The government tried to address technological and learning challenges through a policy shift in the early 1980s, culminating in the introduction of privatization. The 'Look East' policy in 1981 sought to raise productivity and competitiveness by changing attitudes and work habits (Bruton 1992). This was followed by 'Malaysia Incorporated' in 1983 which aimed to build networks with the organized business sector to improve government-business coordination and engage the private sector in pursuing goals in industrial upgrading. This institutionalizing of direct, high-level, public-private networks also aimed to free policymaking from inefficiencies and inadequate oversight of bureaucratically minded industrial policy of the 1970s and 1980s by centralizing decision-making and rent allocation (Felker 1998).

Privatization facilitated the shift of power away from the bureaucracy by centralizing authority in economic policymaking (in the Prime Minister's Department) and elevating links between political and select business leaders, drawing 'business into greater consultation within clientelist channels at the apex of the political party and government system' (Felker 1999: 104; Leigh 1992). This allowed 'political elites to de-bureaucratise policy-making', rein in SOEs and streamline regulation, and, through the dialogue process with business, discipline the bureaucracy for greater efficiency, particularly in economic regulation (Felker 1999: 104). The government was increasingly unwilling to subsidize broadly, focusing on public-allocated growth opportunities more narrowly among a small group of entrepreneurs through the management of key government-linked projects in order to overcome distributional constraints and inefficiencies (Felker 1993).

This shift occurred in the broader context of greater authoritarianism as Mahathir sought to consolidate power in his party and government in response to increasing intra-party political contestation and his narrow victory in UMNO elections. Growing conflict increased the importance of patron–client networks in winning intra-party contests. The leadership response was to develop more centralized and personalized patron–client relationships (mainly around the Prime Minister and Finance Minister and, to a lesser extent, Deputy Prime Minister Anwar Ibrahim) which also affected privatization decisions and institutional arrangements. Decisions were made by Mahathir and in particular, Daim, widely regarded as the architect behind Malaysia's privatization programme and believed to have named the ('first come, first served') beneficiaries. His continued influence even after stepping down as Finance Minister was reflected in the continued allocation of privatizations to his close associates, some of whom were believed to have been acting as his proxies. Evidence shows that the bulk of major privatizations were awarded to close associates (and even family members) of Daim and Mahathir, strongly suggesting that privatization was used to secure and reward political support (e.g. see Gomez 1990, 1991, 1994, 1997). Daim also allegedly profited personally from some of the biggest privatizations (e.g. MAS, LRT System 2, North-South Highway) which went to his close associates and protégés, some of whom admitted that they were acting as proxies for UMNO (whose finances were controlled by Daim as party treasurer) (Yusoff 1990; Gomez 1991).

Personalized patron–client networks involving vested party and individual interests led to moral hazard, making it difficult to then discipline clients, particularly given the increasing competition and conflict in the party. The more intense the competition, the more dependent the patron was on the client for support, and the more personalized the patron–client relationship became. Mahathir's resort to increasing authoritarianism to reassert central control suggests the lack 'of negotiative power' (i.e. the political capacity to impose discipline on clients through negotiated processes) (see Weiss and Hobson 1995). There were also further moral hazard problems arising from the national or economic importance of many privatizations (e.g. infrastructure, public services) (see Chang and Singh 1997). As such, privatization did not promote a more 'arm's length' relationship between government and enterprise, or improve the credibility of the government not intervening in the likelihood of failure, particularly in the four case studies that follow.

## Conditions for successful privatization

We started out by asking three questions: Why did Malaysia privatize? Why did privatization fail? What are the important conditions for success? These questions are closely related. Motivations for privatization affect privatization decisions, institutional arrangements and performance outcomes. This makes it necessary to locate privatization in a country context in order to identify its motivations, causes of failure and conditions for success. We have argued that Malaysia's privatization programme was motivated by both economic (efficiency) and political (redistributive) considerations, but that the latter was more important. Key decisions (about what was privatized, how and to whom, and about the regulatory framework) were mainly shaped by political factors. As such, Malaysia's privatization programme was driven by redistributive priorities, with the bulk of privatizations going to Malay beneficiaries and focused on non-tradable/non-competitive sectors consistent with the preferences and abilities of this group, namely in construction and services, and mainly through (BOT) concessions. Moreover, many key privatizations, including the four case studies that follow, were awarded to a small group of (mainly Malay) businessmen closely associated with a faction of UMNO's leadership.

Privatization was characterized by non-transparent, personalized selection; undisclosed contracts; weak personalized regulation (also see Leeds

1989, cited in Cook and Kirkpatrick 1995: 306–307; Lee, C. 2004); and a wide scope of modes, including private sector-initiated projects. Conventional arguments attribute these to the problems of patronage and corruption associated with weak economic and political institutions. However, this fails to identify the reasons for weak institutions because it assumes that privatization is largely undertaken for economic reasons and ignores political factors which drive such decisions. The literature on Malaysia examines some of these political motivations but generally attributes failure to ethnic concerns and crony capitalism, failing to explain why weak institutions persist. In fact, privatization decisions ignored (admittedly weak) official guidelines for feasibility and desirability, suggesting that the problem was not just due to institutional failure but also the government's political failure to implement policy.

In contrast to these explanations, we have argued that privatization was politically driven by changes in social relations within the Malay community and UMNO specifically. This can be traced back to the emergence of a new Malay middle and business class under the NEP which led to increasing conflict and leadership contests in the party. The ascendancy of a pro-business faction in UMNO shifted the balance of power and enabled the transfer of the control of state assets from bureaucrats (under the NEP) to politicians. Ongoing conflict over resources in UMNO led to Prime Minister Mahathir consolidating authority by centralizing decision-making and allocating privatization assets to his supporters through increasingly personalized patron–client networks, with regulation similarly centralized and personalized. This allows us to explain the non-transparent processes and inherent regulatory weaknesses which led to ex ante mistakes in privatization decisions and design. The performance of privatization here was affected by the government's ex ante failure to ensure project viability, proper privatization design, contract and regulatory design, and selection as discussed in Chapter 2. However, as these decisions were politically unavoidable (and arguably necessary for political stability), it was more important for the government to be able to correct ex ante mistakes. Here too, the government failed to implement conditionality and enforce discipline, and it is this ex post failure that led to failure in all of our four case studies.

The four failed privatizations to be investigated were thus characterized by the state's ex ante and ex post failures. Ex ante (institutional) failure related to the choice of industry and candidate, weak contract and regulatory design, and non-transparent and personalized selection, with beneficiaries closely associated with individual political leaders (Table 3.07). The privatizations of the Kuala Lumpur LRT, MAS and national car manufacturer Proton, though 'desirable' (in terms of promoting economic development and improving the provision of goods and services) were arguably not 'feasible' (in terms of potential profitability and attractiveness to the private sector) without ongoing state support. The general inability of urban rail networks to meet operational, let alone capital, costs should have made the LRT

*Table 3.07* Malaysia: Privatization beneficiaries and political affiliation

| *Privatization* | *Owner/concessionaire* | *Political affiliation* |
|---|---|---|
| IWK (1991) | Vincent Tan | Daim and Mahathir |
| IWK (1995) | Ahmad Sebi | Daim protégé |
| IWK (1996) | Wan Adli | Unknown, but associate of Vincent Tan |
| IWK (1997) | Ishak Ismail | Former secretary of Anwar's UMNO division |
| LRT 1 (STAR) | Various state agencies | State-owned |
| LRT 2 (PUTRA) | Halim Saad | Daim |
| LRT 3 (KL Monorail) | Vincent Tan | Daim and Mahathir |
| MAS | Tajudin Ramli | Daim protégé (worked for Daim in Peremba) |
| Proton | Yahaya Ahmad | Mahathir protégé |

*Source:* Adapted from Gomez (2002c).

*Note:* IWK had several ownership changes following its privatization.

privatization unattractive to the private sector. MAS faced serious industry challenges (including substantial capital costs, low margins and a cyclical industry) and a loss-making domestic sector which would have made it unfeasible for a private owner. Proton had serious technological and industry challenges, and was uncompetitive, relying on continued protection for its profits.

However, ex ante feasibility problems did not automatically mean that the privatizations would have failed. Rather, it was precisely because of feasibility problems that ex post measures were needed to share some of the risks but also crucially to ensure that efficiency gains and learning (particularly in the case of Proton) took place in order for the privatizations to work. This required the design and enforcement of credible subsidization strategies to preserve incentives for efficiency and learning, particularly given the potentially large and unpayable debt burdens arising from the high capital requirements in all these sectors. The success of such ex post intervention will in part depend on the seriousness of ex ante failure. In the case of poor project or privatization viability, the effectiveness of ex post state intervention will necessarily be limited, and results need to be benchmarked against second-best outcomes.

The fact that privatization proceeded despite the lack of information and feasibility suggests that it was driven by powerful private domestic interests (closely linked with segments of the political leadership) and, in the case of IWK and LRT Systems 1 and 2, by foreign firms (in alliance with influential local businessmen). The willingness of the private concessionaires and owners to take on the privatizations despite these potential problems suggest that they expected the privatizations to be profitable, or for the state to continue subsidizing losses. Evidence from each of the four privatizations indicates that the private concessionaire or owner may have been motivated by potential short-term rents instead of longer-term profits arising from improved operational efficiency. This is most evident in the case of the LRT (where construction costs were higher than comparable regional networks) and Proton (where the company continued to rely on profits from a protected domestic market). Even in the case of IWK, privatization was very likely driven by the prospect of monopoly rents from compulsory sewerage charges. Irregularities at MAS suggest that rents may have been earned from the purchase of aircraft and the creation of subsidiaries. This preference for short-term profits through rent capture was also arguably consistent with the abilities of the private operators, most of whom had no previous experience in these or related sectors.

Here, the government failed to address potential moral hazard problems which made these short-term rents more attractive than potential profits arising from greater efficiency in operations and production. However, this is not to say that failure was due to the poor choice of candidates. As mentioned, the selection of these candidates was politically and economically circumscribed, and also needs to be considered in terms of state efforts to create domestic capitalists. In this context, it was crucial the government had the capacity to manage the subsidies necessary for ensuring that the privatization was viable. It therefore needed credible sanctions to ensure that the privatizations addressed industry challenges (see Table 3.08). Instead, failure was ultimately due to the government being unable to implement the necessary ex post measures to address industry challenges and promote learning. There is evidence that the government attempted but failed to enforce the collection of tariffs (IWK), coordinate investment and public transport policy (LRT), and enforce discipline (Proton, MAS).

Each of these failures highlights the different political constraints to the state's political capacity. With the possible exception of IWK, these political failures can be partly explained by changes in social relations which increased competition for resources in UMNO and changed the nature of patron–client networks, compromising privatization decisions, related institutions and regulation, and ultimately the government's capacity to correct mistakes. The government's disciplinary capacity had historically been weak, and attempts, through privatization, to improve (Malay) private sector inefficiency arising from the NEP largely failed. This was partly because successful privatization required the effective management of rents, yet privatization per se did not enhance the state's political capacity to enforce the rules and conditionality integral for the success of any subsidy programme.

This allows us to explain why the completion of LRT System 3 was considerably delayed and the project scaled down without penalties (when the concessionaire ran out of money) as the concessionaire was closely associated with the Prime Minister and Finance Minister. As for LRT System 2 and MAS, the owners were closely related to UMNO, and in particular, Daim, possibly even acting as proxies. This may explain why the government failed to intervene earlier in the case of MAS, and why its owner and LRT System 2

*Table 3.08* Malaysian case studies: Challenges

| | *IWK* | *LRT* | *MAS* | *Proton* |
|---|---|---|---|---|
| *Background* | Sewerage needs | Traffic congestion | Capital expansion | Fragmented auto industry |
| *Objectives* | Expand coverage, improve service and efficiency | Capital works, private incentives | Finance airline expansion, raise efficiency | Accelerate technology transfer |
| *Industry challenges* | High capital costs, public unwillingness to pay | High capital costs, low revenue, price caps | High capital costs, uncertain operating revenue, cyclical demand | High capital costs, product/ production technologies, economies of scale |
| *Specific challenges* | Information, regulation, cost covering tariffs, tariff enforcement | State coordination of system integration and transport policy | Financial structuring, loss-making domestic sector | Technology acquisition, local content |
| *Performance indicators* | System coverage, refurbishment and capital works, service delivery, environmental standards, local technology | Financing, delivery, financial performance, traffic volume | Operational efficiency, financial performance | Financial performance, production capacity, exports, protection, technology transfer, local content |
| *Performance* | Exceeded takeover targets but failed to meet coverage, service, capital investment and environment targets | Financing relied on state loans; STAR, PUTRA met delivery targets; operating revenue too low (STAR, PUTRA); increasing traffic congestion | Some improvement in operational efficiency but still inefficient by regional standards; financial position deteriorated badly | Improved financial performance but ongoing protection; production and exports increased but below targets; some technology transfer; increased local content at higher cost |
| *Ex ante failure* | Privatization design, institutional framework, tariffs | Privatization design, system integration, transport policy | Privatization design, previous management decisions, present government policies | Project viability, regulatory framework |
| *Ex post failure* | Failure to enforce payment of tariffs | Failure to integrate system | Failure to restructure debt and intervene earlier | Failure to enforce conditional learning rents |

concessionaire were rewarded through generous buy-out terms, rather than penalized for failure after the government took over the enterprises. The government's ex post capacity to correct mistakes or enforce discipline was further constrained by national interests, where the economic importance of each project/enterprise introduced a further moral hazard, making it unlikely the government would not intervene in the event of failure. Privatization here did not provide for an 'arm's length' relationship as the government continued to have a vested interest. At the same time, the government was also unable to easily replace non-performing private owners or concessionaires because of the personalized nature of the patron–client relationship and the limited pool of available entrepreneurs.

What we can conclude from the discussion in this and the preceding chapters then is that the conditions for successful privatization will depend on the political context. This will necessitate looking at the state's institutional and political capacity, and the compatibility of current and proposed institutional arrangements with the existing balance of power in society. This political economy approach provides a useful analytical framework in contrast to conventional institutional recommendations which tend to ignore the political context and hence fail to identify important political constraints facing the state's management of subsidies which are central to successful privatization. While the actual details will differ from country to country, depending on the historical and political circumstances, institutional endowments, social relations, etc, the most important condition for successful privatization in the context of developing countries is the state's ex post political capacity to correct ex ante mistakes by implementing policy and enforcing discipline in relation to the management of subsidies.

# 4 Universal access and private provision

## Malaysia's national sewerage system

The provision of water and sanitation services has traditionally been publicly provided to ensure universal access. This has entailed affordable charges, which usually means tariff levels which cannot cover the cost of service provision, let alone service expansion, particularly in developing countries. These financial constraints have resulted in the underinvestment of water and sanitation systems, with consequences for service quality and coverage. As a result, the choice facing developing countries is usually between public provision and universal access (but at the cost of increasingly poor service delivery and coverage), or private provision with higher charges (to finance service improvements and expand coverage). Privatization will therefore depend on the ability of the private operator to charge cost-covering tariffs, or more specifically, the public's willingness to pay higher charges. This will ultimately depend on the state's political capacity to enforce an appropriate tariff structure. If higher charges are not politically viable, or if universal access remains a priority, then the state will have to subsidize operations to attract private participation and ensure the project is commercially viable. The success of privatization in this context will depend on the state's institutional and political capacity to manage any subsidy regime.

These issues are all at the heart of Malaysia's privatized national sewerage system. The failure of the private concessionaire to meet system coverage, capital investment, refurbishment and environmental targets can be explained by the state's ex ante and ex post failures. Ex ante failure related to the government's failure to account for information problems when privatizing the sewerage system. The ability of the private concessionaire to undertake capital expansion depended on the commercial viability of the project, namely whether revenues were sufficient to cover capital and operating expenses. This in turn depended on sufficient information to determine current costs and tariff levels. However, there was insufficient information on costs and public willingness to pay. Poor data on the condition of assets and current performance raised operating costs and affected the concessionaire's ability to meet service, capital investment and environmental targets. Nonetheless, privatization proceeded because it arguably provided opportunities for monopoly rents from compulsory sewerage charges and a large capital works programme, as well as high share prices on the stock market (through the control of a publicly listed company) and profits from 'capital gains' which partly accounted for a series of ownership changes. In this sense, the ex ante failure to account for information constraints was in part the result of changes in social relations and patron–client networks. The original and subsequent concessionaires were all aligned to sections of the political leadership, and each was prepared to pay a premium for a controlling stake in Indah Water Konsortium (IWK), the private concessionaire, despite the problems of increasing costs and reduced revenues following downward tariff revisions.

Rather than subsidize the operator to keep sewerage charges low, the government chose to structure tariffs so that industry and business heavily cross-subsidized household customers, but without first determining the political viability of this tariff structure. This led to opposition from both household and commercial/industrial customers, resulting in several tariff revisions. The inability to enforce this tariff structure was a reflection of the government's ex post failure, and this further affected the concessionaire's financial performance and ability to finance capital expansion. However, despite these tariff revisions, IWK was still considered commercially viable provided there were no bill collection problems. This was not the case, and the continued non-payment of bills by both household and commercial/industrial customers resulted in serious cash flow problems and the concessionaire's inability to continue operations. IWK's failure was therefore ultimately the result of the state's ex post failure to impose credible subsidization strategies and, crucially, to enforce the payment of tariffs.

This political (rather than information or institutional) failure underlines the basic fact that the operation of any private sector activity requires an underlying state enforcement of rights and contracts that cannot be taken for granted in developing countries, even those with apparently 'hard states' like Malaysia. Successful privatization in this case thus depends foremost on the state's ex post (political) capacity to enforce policy. This case study also highlights the difficulties of implementing cost-covering tariffs for essential services, especially in developing countries. Such tariffs often cannot be determined through simple cost-benefit analysis (even with sufficient information) and will instead have to be negotiated or set by the government at a level which is economically viable and politically acceptable. As this will be unlikely to cover costs and provide a reasonable rate of return for the concessionaire, it will require operational subsidies and ongoing state intervention in the form of regulation.

This chapter is structured as follows. The next section examines the challenges faced by the privatization of sewerage treatment systems. This is followed by a background to the privatization and subsequent renationalization of the national sewerage system, and evaluation of performance in terms of delivery (the number of sewerage systems taken over, service provision, maintenance, capital works, effluent quality) and other objectives (local technology, Malay ownership). The next section examines the government's ex ante and ex post failures which affected IWK's performance, looking at information, institutional and political failure. The concluding section summarizes the main causes of IWK's failure and important conditions for successful privatization.

## Challenges

Public sector inefficiencies, and the increasing and considerable cost of water and sanitation infrastructure, are the two main reasons for privatization. Large infrastructure projects such as water supply and sewage treatment are hampered by inefficient operations and the lack of adequate funds (to operate and maintain existing facilities, and to build new systems). In addition, the cost of development of each cubic metre of water for the next generation of projects has been estimated at two to three times higher than the previous generation, and low- and medium-income countries are expected to spend up to 1 per cent of GDP (US$50 billion a year) on water and sanitation services by 2010 (Biswas 2000). The possible inefficiency of the public sector is particularly serious in this context. Public sector water and wastewater utilities were found to be operating below acceptable levels of performance with poor management (antiquated management techniques, poorly trained and motivated managers and staff, unattractive salaries, regular political interference in management practices and decision-making process) and low productivity (overstaffing), while inadequate pricing and inefficient billing and bill collection systems prevented utilities from raising financial resources needed for maintaining and operating adequately, and prevented the generation of much-needed funds for investing in system rehabilitation and expansion (World Bank 1994; Stottmann 2000; Biswas 2000).

Privatization is thus seen to offer developing countries the chance to:

1. acquire technical and managerial expertise and better technologies to improve economic efficiency in both operational performance and use of capital investment;
2. inject investment capital into the sector or gain access to private capital markets;
3. insulate the sector from short-term political intervention in utility operations and limit opportunities for intervention by powerful groups; and
4. turn around or restructure failing public enterprises (Biswas 2000).

The ability and willingness of the operator to improve efficiency and undertake capital investment will, however, depend on the incentive structure of the concession and a regulatory framework to distribute the benefits between the concessionaire (in the form of profits) and consumers (through lower prices and better services). Under a well-structured contract, profitability will depend on how much the operator can reduce costs while still meeting the performance standards set out in the concession agreement. The private sector must feel the deal is financially feasible, especially if it is expected to invest in system rehabilitation or expansion. High profits here will make it easier for the concessionaire to invest in capital works but may not provide incentives to improve operational efficiency. A regulatory framework is thus needed to preserve incentives by enforcing targets for performance (service coverage, quality) and capital investment, as well as adjust tariffs and arbitrate disputes.

Central to the system's commercial viability is the issue of sewerage charges which should cover operating costs and provide a reasonable return on capital if the operator is to have the incentives to remain efficient and undertake capital expansion. The setting of tariffs is both a technical and political process. It requires a detailed knowledge of the utility's current operational and maintenance costs; current tariff levels and the efficiency of revenue collection; current and projected demand for sewerage services; capital costs of improvements and annual expenditures necessary to maintain service levels; availability of funding for service improvements through grants, equity and loans; and additional operational costs for system expansion, as well as likely efficiency gains that the private operator might achieve. However, while high profits can facilitate capital investment, this will in part depend on whether cost-covering tariffs are publicly acceptable, especially in developing countries. Because sewerage charges are generally very sensitive, a key challenge is in determining an acceptable tariff level in terms of what consumers are willing to pay, as misjudging consumer demand may contribute to poor sanitation system design and performance (e.g. see Correia 1998). The main challenge facing governments is thus to balance economic and political requirements by determining appropriate tariff levels necessary to preserve private sector incentives while accounting for political sensitivities and public willingness to pay. The setting of tariffs must therefore also take political considerations into account while ensuring the viability of the utility.

Assessment of sanitation demand can be conducted through a variety of methods, although these can be costly and unreliable, involving complex, multi-faceted issues. It is important to also have mechanisms to raise public awareness and form public opinion, for example through regular media reports about drinking water quality, environmental water quality and risks of pollution, and the cost of water supply and sewerage (Kraemer 1998). However, awareness and support for sewerage treatment will also depend on consumer ability and willingness to pay, especially in developing countries where income levels are low. Here, the government has two options. It can deal with the political sensitivities surrounding sewerage charges by keeping tariff levels artificially low (and hence, politically acceptable), or it can implement cost-covering tariffs. The first option may be more desirable, especially after prolonged system neglect and the absence of explicit tariff charges, as in the Malaysian case. This will require subsidizing the operator and some form of incentive regulation. The second will depend on the political capacity to enforce the payment of tariffs, especially if there is public opposition to this.

In either case, privatization will require the government continue to play a central role, and in reality, acceptable sewerage charges are usually below the cost of service provision. This is important, especially as sewage treatment costs more than the provision of clean water because more capital equipment is needed to clean dirty water than to clean river water. Yet drinking water is often subsidized in developing countries for political reasons, as is the case in Malaysia, making it even harder to introduce sewerage charges which are potentially higher than water rates. The high cost of sewerage treatment has also required continued state assistance, with grants playing an important part in financing capital investment, even in developed countries. Government grants comprised over 40 per cent of capital investment in wastewater treatment in Germany and France, and were also significant in the Netherlands and Portugal (Correia 1998). This indicates the difficulties of operating sewerage services on a purely commercial basis.

Furthermore, as public health aspects of sewerage treatment require universal coverage, costs will vary across regions, depending on population levels and density. As such, sewerage services – and thus tariff levels – will be cheaper in larger, highly populated urban centres compared to smaller towns or rural areas. Because it is politically difficult to have different tariff charges, especially as this will be seen as disadvantaging certain (poorer) segments of the population, the government has to either subsidize operations, or tariffs have to be cross-subsidized. In the case of Malaysia, the government failed to impose a credible subsidization strategy needed to address the challenges related to the determination of tariffs and enforcement of payment. It chose to keep tariff levels low by charging much higher rates for commercial/industrial users in order to cross-subsidize household customers, yet these rates were rejected by both groups of customers. More crucially, the government lacked the political capacity to enforce payment of tariffs, even after several downward revisions.

## Background

The privatization of Malaysia's sewerage system needs to be understood within the context of the country's sewerage needs following three decades of neglect and underfunding. This was due to low priorities for sewerage development (compared to water supplies) and an unwillingness on the part of most local (municipal) government authorities to finance capital expenditure through higher user charges. The allocation of funds for sewerage development consistently and substantially lagged behind that for water supplies. Only US$330 million was allocated to sewerage services by the federal government between 1976 and 1995 compared to US$3,089 million to develop water infrastructure (Lum 1994). On top of this, and as previously mentioned, wastewater is more expensive to treat than drinking water. As a result, coverage was low, and poor effluent quality from untreated sewage led to water pollution and health risks. Only 3.4 per cent of the country's population was served by central sewerage systems in 1970, mainly in large urban centres, barely increasing to 5 per cent in 1990, compared to 100 per cent of urban and 66 per cent of rural populations with access to safe water supplies. Eighty per cent of sewage treatment plants (STPs) did not meet Department of Environment (DOE) effluent discharge standards. River and water quality deteriorated between 1 and 2 per cent every year, with 72 per cent of rivers polluted in the 1980s and early 1990s largely due to untreated sewage (*Business Times*, 2 March 1996).

Low coverage was due to attitudes to sewage treatment, and institutional and resource constraints. Safe water has been perceived as a basic need and prerequisite for development, and the pace of economic development was seen as sustainable without a corresponding development of sewerage infrastructure. The Local Government Act 1974 enabled local authorities to recover capital costs for the development of sewerage infrastructure through a 5 per cent charge on the assessed annual value of properties, and charge for operating costs for sewerage services. But despite feasibility studies suggesting this was financially viable, most state authorities perceived this to be too expensive for consumers (Lum 1994).

The water and sewerage system was also characterized by the lack of a single agency entrusted with overall responsibility for planning and management. As a public health concern, sewerage services came under the purview of both federal and state authorities. Jurisdiction and administration came under local municipal authorities, although a variety of other authorities were also involved, including Jabatan Kerja Raya[1] (JKR, Public Works Department), the Ministry of Housing and Local Development, Ministry of Health and DOE.[2] Federal ministries provided support but as they had only an advisory status with local authorities, policies were not always adhered to.

Prior to privatization, the federal government invited proposals for the private financing of infrastructure projects, and one local authority had signed a memorandum of understanding to accept a privatization offer, with another two in the process of doing so (Lum 1994). IWK's proposal to take over 48 major local authorities was accepted by the federal government on condition that it also took over sewerage services from the remaining 95 smaller local authorities, with a common tariff nationwide to enable cross-subsidization from richer to poorer sectors to make sewerage services affordable (Lum 1994). The proposal was initiated in 1991 by North West Water (NWW), a UK-based water supply and sewage treatment company, through its country manager, David Chew, whose job was to develop business in Malaysia[3] which initially involved finding local partners willing to take a majority stake. Chew came up with the privatization proposal in consultation with Vincent Tan's Berjaya Group[4] to enable NWW to progress with the project in Malaysia.[5]

IWK was incorporated on 25 January 1991[6] with a nominal paid-up capital of RM2. The consortium was led by the Berjaya Group, through Berjaya Industrial (20 per cent), with the other shareholders being NWW (25 per cent), Lembaga Tabung Angkatan Tentera (LTAT, Armed Forces Savings Board) (20 per cent), the Royal Malaysian Police Investment Cooperative (20 per cent) and AIMS Worldwide[7] (15 per cent). IWK was awarded a 28-year concession in 1993 to manage, operate and maintain a nationwide sewerage system previously administered separately by the 143 local authorities. Ownership of all public sewerage system assets would revert back to the federal government free of charge at the end of the concession period in 2020. Privatization aimed to:

1 improve service and quality through enhanced efficiency;
2 expand coverage through new capital investment to increase the number of households directly connected to centralized sewerage services;
3 develop and promote low cost, indigenous sewerage treatment technology for export; and
4 develop Malay entrepreneurial capacity through the ownership and management of assets.

The privatization was characterized by several changes of ownership and management following public unwillingness to pay and three tariff revisions. Tariff revisions and continued customer refusal to pay led to cash flow problems which affected the concessionaire's ability to meet operational and capital commitments. On 4 February 1999 the government became a special shareholder and on 23 June 2000 the Ministry of Finance (MoF) paid RM192.5 million in cash to Prime Utilities Bhd (PUB, the most recent owner of IWK) for its entire stake in IWK.

## Performance

IWK commenced operations in May 1995. Under the concession agreement, it had to meet coverage, capital investment and service targets, as well as environmental and performance standards set by the Director General of Sewerage Services (DGSS) and the DOE. Its performance can be measured by examining whether it met the terms of the concession agreement in relation to: 1, system coverage; 2, refurbishment and capital works; 3, service delivery; 4, environmental standards; 5, the development of indigenous technology; and 6, New Economic Policy (NEP) objectives, namely the Malay ownership and management of assets. We find that IWK exceeded targets for taking over sewage treatment plants (STPs), but failed to meet overall coverage, capital investment, service and environment targets (Table 4.01). It also failed to develop local technology or Malay managerial expertise.

*Table 4.01* IWK: Performance summary, 1994–2000

| *Concession targets* | | *Target (year)* | *Actual (year)* |
|---|---|---|---|
| System coverage | Number of local authorities | 143 | 84 |
| | STPs | 1,500 | 6,457 |
| | Sewer pipes | 2,200 | 9,236 |
| Refurbishment | — | — | RM181 million (1995–2000) |
| Capital works | Coverage | RM600 million (1998–2002) | RM145.2 million (1997–2001) |

*Note:* STPs = sewerage treatment plants.

### *System coverage*

IWK was to take over sewerage services maintained by 143 local authorities within two years from the federal government. However, by 2000, the federal government's Department of Sewerage Services (DSS) only managed to take over, and pass over to IWK, sewerage services of 84 local authorities, thus failing to meet overall coverage targets (National Audit Department, Malaysia 2000; Sewerage Services Department, Malaysia 2001). The concession agreement also required IWK to take over 1,500 STPs and 2,200 km of sewer pipes. IWK exceeded this figure, taking over 6,457 STPs, 9,236 km of sewer pipes, and 906,785 septic tanks, along with 277 network and pump stations between 1995 and 2000, providing sewerage services to 12.42 million people (Table 4.02).

IWK had to improve coverage for connected sewerage services and septic tank use in 48 (Category A) major towns and 96 (Category B) smaller towns over six phases between 1994 and 2022 (Table 4.03). By the end of 2000, nine million people were connected (about 45 per cent of the total population) and 4.5 million served by septic tanks (22.5 per cent of total population) (Sewerage Services Department, Malaysia 2001). This is an improvement of 72.8 and 66.6 per cent respectively (compared to around a total of 7.6 million people served by the 144 local authorities in 1996)[8] but remained below 2002 targets of 63.8 and 29.0 per cent coverage for Categories A and B towns (Prime Utilities 1996).

### *Refurbishment and capital works*

The capital works programme targeted 84.3 per cent sewerage connection and 15.7 per cent septic tank coverage in 48 major towns, and 29.5 and 70.5 per cent coverage respectively in 96 smaller towns by the end of 28 years at an estimated cost of RM6.06 billion over six phases (Table 4.03) (Sewerage Services Department, Malaysia 1998). IWK was required to plan and undertake an infrastructure programme in six phases, which included constructing

*Table 4.02* IWK: Sewerage systems operated and maintained, 1994–2000

| | *Network pipelines (km)*[1] | *Network pump stations* | *Public STPs* | *Septic tanks*[2] | *Population: connected*[3] | *Population: septic tanks*[4] | *Total pop served* |
|---|---|---|---|---|---|---|---|
| 1994 | 2,317 | 74 | 1,043 | 302,800 | 2,448,700 | 1,514,000 | 3,962,700 |
| 1995 | 3,567 | 116 | 3,239 | 749,182 | 3,783,220 | 3,745,910 | 7,529,130 |
| 1996 | 5,921 | 160 | 4,068 | 836.306 | 6,235,900 | 4,181,530 | 10,417,430 |
| 1997 | 7,052 | 180 | 4,539 | 736,797 | 7,416,490 | 3,683,985 | 11,100,475 |
| 1998 | 7,868 | 209 | 5,571 | 776,602 | 7,544,180 | 3,883,010 | 11,427,190 |
| 1999 | 8,589 | 245 | 6.081 | 822,638 | 8,311,070 | 4,113,190 | 12,424,260 |
| 2000 | 9,236 | 277 | 6,457 | 906,785 | 8,996,028 | 4,533,925 | 13,529,953 |
| 1994–2000 change | 74.9% | 73.3% | 83.8% | 66.6% | 72.8% | 66.6% | 70.7% |

*Source:* Adapted from Sewerage Services Department, Malaysia (1998, 2001a).
*Notes:*
1 Pipeline data updated from Asset Database; estimates by DSS where data unavailable.
2 Septic tank figures inaccurate in 1994–96 and adjusted in 1997 and 1998 following surveys.
3 Estimates where data unavailable.
4 Population using septic tanks assumed to be five times the number of septic tanks.

new STPs in areas identified by the government; refurbishing and upgrading existing STPs; connecting existing septic tank users to a centralized sewage treatment system through the construction of 15,000 km of new pipes; and constructing 40 modern mechanical centralized sludge treatment plants in designated locations over 15 years (National Audit Department, Malaysia 2000).

Under the concession agreement, IWK was to spend RM800 million on refurbishment and capital works for Phase 1, and a total of RM5.2 billion for Phases 2–6 from 1997 to 2022 (Lum 1994: 11). Phase 1 (1994–97) of the capital works programme involved:

*Table 4.03* IWK: Sewerage coverage targets, 1997–2022

| | *Category A (48 major towns)* | | *Category B (96 smaller towns)* | |
|---|---|---|---|---|
| *End of phase* | *Connected %* | *Septic tanks %* | *Connected %* | *Septic tanks %* |
| Phase 1 (1997) | – | — | — | — |
| Phase 2 (2002) | 63.8 | 29.0 | 15.8 | 50.6 |
| Phase 3 (2007) | 76.2 | 19.2 | 17.8 | 50.0 |
| Phase 4 (2012) | 82.6 | 14.3 | 19.4 | 49.5 |
| Phase 5 (2017) | 84.3 | 13.0 | 24.0 | 47.2 |
| Phase 6 (2022) | 84.3 | 15.7 | 29.5 | 70.5 |

*Source:* Adapted from Sewerage Services Department, Malaysia (1998, 2001a).

- refurbishing poor and non-functioning STPs and pump stations;
- constructing new STPs for Jelutong and Bayan Baru in Penang (where untreated sewage was being released into the sea);
- undertaking sewerage connection projects in Labuan, Port Dickson and Langkawi, and twelve connected sewerage projects in Johor Baru, Kuala Lumpur, Ipoh, Seremban, Melaka, Kangar and Kuching;
- replacing all biosoil type plants; and
- constructing new sludge treatment facilities (National Audit Department, Malaysia 2000).

IWK's refurbishment and capital cost estimates were based on data provided by all local authorities for 1,500 STPs. However, it later discovered the number of STPs in fact exceeded 6,000, raising operating and capital costs. Furthermore, an estimated 80 per cent of STPs handed over by the local authorities were in a state of disrepair or disuse, requiring additional refurbishment costs, and failed to meet effluent standards.[9] A refurbishment strategy was formulated and plans drawn up to upgrade sewerage systems, with refurbishment works to improve safety and aesthetic aspects given priority to address public dissatisfaction with the condition of STPs. Refurbishment works were also carried out to restore the mechanical and electrical systems to working order.

Between 1995 and 2000, IWK spent RM181 million refurbishing 481 STPs (Prime Utilities 2000). However, 81 per cent of the 6,205 STPs had not been refurbished by 2000 (National Audit Department, Malaysia 2000). IWK also carried out a total of 38 capital projects as part of Phase 1 of its capital works programme between 1995 and 2000. The total amount committed to these projects was RM224.3 million, with 37 projects completed by 2000 at a cost of RM145.2 million, and another 11 projects worth RM99.8 million at various stages of completion (Sewerage Services Department, Malaysia 2001). This compares to the target of RM600 million in capital investment for Phase 1. IWK thus failed to carry out critical infrastructure work due under the terms of the concession, including construction of new STPs.[10]

### *Service delivery*

IWK was to desludge all septic tanks in local authority areas in accordance with a schedule to ensure compliance with the original design requirements, generally once every two years. It was estimated that on-schedule desludging would reduce the pollution load of surface water sources by more than half within two years as 99 per cent of septic tanks were found not to have been desludged since 1980[11] (Sewerage Services Department, Malaysia 1998).

IWK was expected to desludge 736,797 individual septic tanks for the operational areas between 1994 and 1997, but only carried out 324,308 first-round septic tank desludgings (44 per cent) (Sewerage Services Department, Malaysia 1998). By 2000, IWK had desludged 491,685 out of 906,785 septic tanks (54 per cent) (Sewerage Services Department, Malaysia 2001). However, an estimated 65 per cent of home owners with septic tanks did not allow IWK to undertake first-round desludging, without which the company was unable to register households for billing purposes (National Audit Department, Malaysia 2000). In addition, a total of 13,122 home owners refused to connect their septic tanks to the sewerage network constructed by IWK as they did not want to pay RM2,000–RM2,500 (depending on the distance to the sewerage network) for this service (National Audit Department, Malaysia 2000). The desludging programme could not be carried out effectively due to a lack of proper sludge disposal sites, slow approval by state governments for land applications, public objections to temporary sludge disposal sites, and public refusal of desludging services (Sewerage Services Department, Malaysia 1998).

### *Environmental standards*

STP performance is measured by its ability to meet effluent quality standards. The Environmental Quality (Sewerage and Industrial Effluents) Regulations 1979 require effluents from STPs to comply with specified discharge standards. IWK was required to carry out sampling analysis of effluent quality in accordance with the requirements of the concession agreement. It managed to meet the sampling requirements for 36 per cent of the plants within the first year after take over. The shortfall was mainly due to the poor physical condition of the plants handed over, some of which had been abandoned for years. Samples could not be taken from such plants since the outlets had either been buried or could not be traced. However, a year after takeover and refurbishment works, IWK managed to take the required number of samples from 88.7 per cent of the plants.

The concession agreement also required IWK to analyse samples for biochemical oxygen demand (BOD), suspended solids (SS), pH, ammoniacal nitrogen, and oil and grease. Most of the STPs were able to comply with pH and oil and grease standards, but compliance rates for SS and BOD were low. This was because a large number of treatment plants (72 per cent in 1997) were either communal septic tanks or Imhoff tanks, which were not designed to comply with these standards. According to IWK, 80 per cent of its 8,000 plants in 1999 had not reached the required (BOD) standards mainly due to lack of local expertise, which led to a reliance on unsuitable foreign-designed systems (*New Straits Times*, 15 September 1999).

By 2000, 86.1 per cent of plants maintained by IWK were small plants serving populations of less than 2,000 each, with a large number of these still being communal septic tanks and Imhoff tanks which had difficulties complying with discharge standards. Furthermore, some sewerage systems, most notably in Georgetown, Penang, had no treatment system, with untreated sewage discharged through a marine outfall. The failure to undertake capital works in Penang resulted in an estimated 78 and 44 million litres of raw sewage being released into the sea daily in Jelutong and Bayan Baru respectively (National Audit Department, Malaysia 2000). According to the Ministry of Science, Technology and Environment, despite improvements since 1997, water quality in Malaysia remained poor, with high levels of *E. coli* detected in the sea, indicating discharge of untreated sewage (*Water & Environment International,* March 2000, 9 [66]).

Less than 17 per cent of the 5,409 STPs operated by IWK in 1998 complied with the discharge standards (Table 4.04). The remaining 83.5 per cent of treatment plants were given contravention licences while they were being upgraded.[12] The DOE reported 13,398 cases of environmental pollution attributed to sewage discharges by households (42.3 per cent), industry (37.5 per cent), livestock (16.7 per cent) and agriculture (3.5 per cent) (National Audit Department, Malaysia 2000). As a result of not meeting environmental standards, IWK was issued with RM158.7 million worth of fines by the DOE between 1994 and April 1998. However, IWK was given an exemption by the MoF and only had to pay RM56.9 million (National Audit Department, Malaysia 2000).

### *Technology*

Privatization was expected to promote the adaptation of imported technology for local needs and to develop low-cost Malaysian technology for sewerage systems for export to developing countries. By IWK's own admission, the failure of the company's STPs to meet environmental standards was due to a lack of expertise, and the inappropriateness of imported technology for local conditions (*New Straits Times*, 15 September 1999). Privatization failed to initiate development of appropriate local technology and did not even address local sewage treatment requirements.

### *Malay ownership*

The privatization of the sewerage system was an opportunity to further the NEP's 'restructuring' (to reduce ethnic disparities) as well as redistribution

*Table 4.04* IWK: Sewerage treatment plants meeting effluent standards, 1999–2000

| *Location* | *Year* | *Total plants* | *Total plants tested* | *Number meeting A standard (%)* | *Number meeting B standard (%)* |
|---|---|---|---|---|---|
| Catchment areas | 1999 | 973 | 805 | 6 (1) | |
| Others | 1999 | 5,049 | 4,077 | | 1,101 (27) |
| Catchment areas | 2000 | 995 | 617 | 11 (2) | |
| Others | 2000 | 5,215 | 3,659 | | 1,493 (41) |

*Source:* Adapted from National Audit Department, Malaysia (2000).

objectives by: 1, developing Malay entrepreneurial capacity through a Malay vendor scheme, and; 2, through ownership and management of assets. The participation of Malay contractors in IWK's refurbishment/capital works programmes as well as operations and maintenance averaged only 37 per cent (Prime Utilities 1998). While privatization offered the opportunity for Malay ownership of assets, it was characterized by several changes of ownership and management following each tariff revision.

Shortly after commencing operations in 1993, IWK was acquired by publicly listed Berjaya South Island (another Berjaya Group company) in November 1995 for RM450 million through a share swap. Berjaya South Island later changed its name to Prime Utilities Bhd (PUB). A condition of the sale was that PUB was guaranteed IWK's pre-tax profit for 1997–99 ('secured financial years') of not less than RM105 million for each financial year[13] (Prime Utilities 1999: 45). Profit guarantee agreements following each sale were introduced by the Securities Commission in an effort to ensure that profit projections were realistic, with the seller having to compensate the buyer in the form of payment of the profit shortfall by instalments or by way of issuance of new securities (see Securities Commission, Malaysia 1999b).

In August 1996, Wan Adli Wan Ibrahim (Berjaya Group's executive director on the board of PUB) acquired 19.01 per cent of PUB (through Transwater Corporation Bhd) for RM228.16 million at RM20 per share. Transwater later increased its interest in PUB to 26.53 per cent. A Second Profit Guarantee Agreement of RM105 million a year, with the same conditions, was signed on 28 August 1997 for 1999–2001 following divestment by certain parties and revisions made to the sewerage concession requested by the government (Prime Utilities 1999). On 15 September 1997, Idris Hydraulic Bhd acquired a 32 per cent controlling stake in PUB for RM370 million cash.[14] Of the 32 per cent PUB stake acquired by Idris Hydraulic, 10 per cent (six million shares) was purchased from Ilham Desiran Sdn Bhd (a wholly owned subsidiary of Transwater, controlled by Wan Adli) for RM142.5 million at RM23.75 per share; 19 per cent at RM20 per share, with the remaining 3 per cent bought on the open market. The purchase price represented a 'hefty premium' based on PUB's price of RM14.50 on 15 September 1997 (*The Star*, 16 September 1997). The succession of ownership changes suggests that Malay ownership was only short term with little apparent gain in management experience.

## Problems

IWK's failure to meet coverage, capital investment and environment targets was due to the government's ex ante and ex post failures. Ex ante failure was the failure to account for information and institutional problems. Poor data on the quantity and quality of assets to be taken over increased operational costs and affected service provision. There was also insufficient information on the utility's operating costs to determine appropriate tariff levels. Rather than subsidizing the operator to keep tariff levels low, the government sought to do this through cross-subsidies (by charging commercial/industrial customers substantially higher rates). The government should have been aware of these problems, many of which were already present before privatization, including potential public opposition to higher charges (see Lum 1994). As a result, commercial/industrial customers refused to pay the substantial tariff increase needed to subsidize households, and household customers also refused to pay the new rates.

This led to three downward tariff revisions which crucially did not improve the bill collection, leading to serious cash flow problems which affected operations, capital investment and ultimately, the operator's financial viability. This was compounded by the government's unwillingness to provide promised funding for capital expansion. (According to a former IWK director, the government had promised funding for capital expansion in return for lower tariffs, but was perhaps worried that this may have been used to cover operational losses.[15])

Related to this is the question why privatization proceeded and why the company continued to attract new buyers despite ex ante information and ongoing problems. One possible reason is the belief that the concession of a public utility would provide guaranteed revenue, and that the state would ensure the company's commercial viability. In this sense, the ex ante failure to account for information decisions were in part the result of political considerations related to the interests of (potential) buyers, all of whom were closely aligned to sections of the political leadership. However, it was the government's ex post failure to impose credible subsidization strategies and enforce the payment of tariffs (rather than ex ante failure related to information and institutional problems) that ultimately led to IWK's financial failure. Insufficient information affected the determination of both tariff levels (leading to several tariff revisions) and consumer willingness to pay. Nonetheless, the company would have remained commercially viable, despite the tariff revisions, provided it could collect tariff payments. The fact that it could not collect bills, and the *ad hoc* way in which tariffs were determined and revised, was a reflection of both institutional and political failure. Here, the government failed to legislate against the non-payment of sewerage charges, and even when it did so later, was unable to enforce payment.

## *Ex ante failure*

### *Tariff structure*

There was insufficient information on assets and hence operational costs in order to determine appropriate tariff levels. It is also unclear whether IWK was to take over from 143 or 144 local authorities.[16] IWK's original proposal involved a financial model of revenue streams based on a tariff structure with periodic tariff rate increases and assumed annual growth in customer numbers as well as capital and operating costs for the provision of sewerage services to meet this demand. If the rate of growth of customers exceeded the assumed growth, or the inflation rate for costs turned out to be lower than assumed, then IWK would stand to make more profits, and vice versa (Lum 1994). However, projecting growth in customer numbers, particularly those arising from new housing developments (for which IWK would not be required to incur capital costs, but for which it would gain from increased revenues by providing sewerage services), was difficult, and the government faced the burden of meeting the shortfall in the event of non-realization of revenue projections. The internal rate of return was eventually fixed at 14–18 per cent to ensure the project's continued viability, with flexibility to vary tariff rates periodically, taking into account audited revenues and cost reviews by consultants as to reasonableness.[17] The government would also provide a RM478 million soft loan to help the concessionaire keep charges to customers bearable (Lum 1994).

IWK's initial financial forecasts were based on the original tariff rates and estimates of its customer base and assets to be taken over. However, the tariff rates could not have been determined by the likely number of customers or operating costs given incomplete information on these. IWK's estimates of STPs (carried out by a team of university students hired to interview local authorities to establish the number and condition of treatment plants) proved to be incorrect due to poor record-keeping by the local authorities[18] (*The Sun*, 12 December 1996; *New Straits Times*, 10 August 1999).

It was only over a two- to three-year period during IWK's rolling programme of taking over from local authorities that it discovered there were three times the number of plants it had originally accounted for, with barely 20 per cent of these functioning as local authorities often had no budgets to operate STPs (*Far Eastern Economic Review*, 27 September 2001). The remaining 80 per cent of plants were in a state of disrepair or disuse, and required additional refurbishment costs. (Additional costs were also incurred from having to take on a lot more staff than necessary from some local authorities as stipulated in privatization contracts.[19]) IWK also did not have its own customer database, and its initial charges were based on households receiving water bills from the various state government Departments of Water Works, on which IWK's sewerage charges were tagged (*Business Times*, 11 February 1997). Charging on the basis of water consumption was seen as a reasonable basis to estimate revenue provided there was access to water bills. This, however, proved problematic, with some state water companies refusing to provide data on water consumption figures for free.[20]

Without sufficient information on the operations and refurbishment costs of the sewerage assets to be taken over, the proposed tariff rates appear to have been based on a study commissioned by IWK on the willingness of customers to pay monthly charges if improvements were carried out by a private company. According to the DGSS, the Frank Small survey found that 76 per cent were willing to pay RM5 a month, 50 per cent were willing to pay

RM10 a month, and 25 per cent were willing to pay RM20 a month, with 76 per cent believing that payment for sewerage treatment was justified (Lum 1994).

Tariffs were commonly applied across the country to provide a cross-subsidy from large to smaller urban centres where the unit capital and operating costs were higher (Sewerage Services Department, Malaysia 1998). As a result, tariff rates were based on different principles. The household rate was calculated from the annual assessed value of a property (i.e. the monthly basic charge) and actual water usage (i.e. monthly usage charge by cubic metres of water used), with separate rates for connected services and septic tank services. The government decided on RM5 per household as an acceptable monthly household sewerage charge, but to reduce the burden on lower income groups, the household tariff structure was based on the assessed value of the premises and water consumption. Tariff charges were then set between a minimum of RM2 a month (for lower income groups) and a maximum of RM10 a month, regardless of water consumption.

Higher rates for commercial/industrial customers – estimated to contribute 50–60 per cent of IWK's total turnover – were then needed to recover the balance of capital and operating costs (*Malaysian Business*, 16 June 1995). After much negotiation, the rate agreed for the first five years was set at about the middle of the range for commercial/industrial water supplies, i.e. RM1.20/cubic metre for connected customers, and RM0.90/cubic metre for septic tanks (Tables 4.05 and 4.06) (Lum 1994). This represented 125 per cent of the water bill in order to subsidize household users.[21]

Industry was assumed to treat its own industrial wastewater, only discharging household wastewater into public sewers or septic tanks. Charges for discharge of untreated or pre-treated industrial wastewater into public sewers were to be negotiated on a case-by-case basis (Sewerage Services Department, Malaysia 1998). Commercial/industrial rates were based on the number of occupants per day (for hotels), property size (for offices and shopping complexes) and production volume (for manufacturers). The public

*Table 4.05* IWK: Original sewerage charges (household customers), 1994

| Category of assessed value | Monthly basic charge (RM) | | Monthly usage charge (RM/m³) | |
|---|---|---|---|---|
| | Connected | Septic tank | Connected | Septic tank |
| Up to RM600 | 2.00 | 2.00 | n/a | n/a |
| RM601–RM1,000 | 1.00 | 0.68 | 0.14 | 0.07 |
| RM1,001–RM3,000 | 2.11 | 1.43 | 0.14 | 0.07 |
| RM3,001–RM10,000 | 5.32 | 3.61 | 0.14 | 0.07 |
| Above RM10,000 | 10.00 | 10.00 | 10.00 | n/a |

*Source:* Adapted from Sewerage Services Department, Malaysia (1998).

*Note:* The minimum monthly sewerage charge is RM2.00, the maximum is RM10.00.

*Table 4.06* IWK: Original monthly sewerage charges (non-household customers), 1994

| *Type of user* | *Monthly usage charge (RM/m$^3$)* |
|---|---|
| Commercial (connected) | 1.20 |
| Commercial (septic tank) | 0.90 |
| Industrial (connected) | 1.20 |
| Industrial (septic tank) | 0.90 |

*Source:* Adapted from Sewerage Services Department, Malaysia (1998).
*Note:* The minimum monthly sewerage charge is RM9.00.

sector was also billed differently, with charges for the army and the police based on the number of serving personnel per day and dependent on the size of the camp. In reality, there was multi-level, multi-tier cross-subsidization, with industry subsidizing household consumers and larger towns subsidizing smaller towns. On the island of Penang, the large number of hotels subsidized other areas where IWK operated at a loss. By opting for self-financing, the government probably sought to keep tariffs affordable for household consumers without having to subsidize operations, thereby avoiding the complexities involved in monitoring performance.

### *Willingness to pay*

Assumptions about consumer willingness to pay the proposed tariff rates appear to have been based on IWK's commissioned survey. However, it is unclear what the sample size was or what survey methodology was employed. Respondents could evidently pick more than one answer given that the total choices expressed exceeded 100 per cent. While 76 per cent of domestic households were willing to pay RM5.00, 84 per cent were willing to pay RM2.50 and 89 per cent were willing to pay RM2.00 (see Lum 1994). The percentage of businesses prepared to pay sewerage charges based on their water bills is also unclear. While the DSS blamed IWK for not ensuring public acceptability of the 'user pays' principle, it was also the federal government's responsibility to do so (see National Audit Department, Malaysia 2000).

IWK's commercial viability ultimately depended on consumer willingness to pay, and the non-payment of tariffs was partly due to government failure to account for this. The federal government apparently accepted the survey results despite the previous reluctance of state governments to finance sewerage improvements through higher charges for fear of public opposition. Perhaps not surprisingly, the initial tariff structure met with opposition from household customers whom the government hoped to cross-subsidize. More crucially, commercial/industrial customers rejected the substantial tariff increases needed to cross-subsidize households. Subsequent rejections of revised tariff rates suggest that fundamental opposition to the 'user pays' principle remained.

Opposition from household customers to the first round of sewerage bills centred on disparities in rates for the same usage, and on whether all water consumed was discharged into sewers. There were strong objections to the 'exorbitant fees' and having to pay more for a service which had previously not been separately billed (*Business Times*, 11 February 1997), particularly as there was no corresponding reduction in council rates.[22] Questions were also raised about the legality of charging for services not yet rendered, with customers perceiving no benefit from the charges or desludging services (e.g. see *Business Times*, 11 February 1997).

The 200 per cent increase in sewerage charges for the commercial sector compared with previous Kuala Lumpur City Hall (DBKL) charges was seen as too drastic, unjustified and contributing to inflation (Lum 1994). The strongest opposition came from business groups, whose monthly bill increases ranged from RM100 (e.g. for coffee shops) to RM24,000 for a five-star hotel. Increases in sewerage charges occurred at the same time as IWK sought to finance its capital works programme through a public flotation. This required high profit projections to secure a premium share price upon listing at the same time as the company was trying to convince the public to pay sewerage charges. This undermined public willingness to pay charges to what was supposedly going to be a highly profitable company.[23]

### *Institutional failure*

To facilitate privatization, the government implemented legislative and institutional changes to consolidate laws and introduce a regulatory authority. However, there were inadequacies in both legislation and regulatory structure, and overall responsibility was still not clearly designated. The regulatory authority was not independent, being subordinate to the Minister of Housing and Local Government, and it was not entirely clear which ministry or department was ultimately responsible. For example, the new IWK management appointed in August 1996 worked closely with the Ministry of Housing and Local Government, Ministry of Finance (MoF), Economic Planning Unit (EPU) and other relevant departments on a comprehensive review of sewerage services. The results were announced by the Prime Minister, with subsequent details of the review provided by the Minister of Housing and Local Government (Prime Utilities 1997).

It was not clear who determined tariffs or how these could be revised, nor was there an appeals system. While Section 9 (i) of the Sewerage Services Act (SSA) 1993 states that the DGSS has powers to promote the interests of customers with respect to 'the prices to be charged for the services', the power to impose charges lies with the Minister who 'may from time to time by regulations prescribe, either separately or as a consolidated rate, sewerage charges, fees or levy' (Section 30). According to the concessionaire, the DGSS may have prepared the recommendation and been involved in negotiations, but it was the politicians who made decisions.[24] (The number of ministers making announcements relating to the industry may have been a reflection of this.)

Regulatory performance was affected by institutional weaknesses, namely resource constraints, initial reluctance to legislate penalties for non-payment of sewerage charges and failure to accurately gauge public willingness to pay. The role of the regulatory authority was assessed by the National Audit Department (2000), which found no programme for monitoring the 2,600 STPs operated by the private sector, or enforcement, with the DSS only acting on complaints. Furthermore, there were no performance indicators for IWK and monitoring was based on monthly reports supplied by the concessionaire[25] (National Audit Department, Malaysia 2000).

There was no programme for monitoring effluent quality for STPs, with IWK itself testing effluent quality in over 6,000 STPs, and the DSS merely accepting these results without independent verification. Plant inspections were conducted by IWK staff without supervision by the DSS, and two private companies were found to be operating STPs without licence. The failure of the DSS to obtain court orders for 13,122 home owners who refused to connect their septic tanks to a central sewerage system (as authorized by Section 24 of the SSA 1993) suggests that enforcement was a problem (Malaysia 2002). The DSS also allowed three factories to discharge industrial effluent into the public sewerage systems without testing the quality of the effluent, while another nine factories did so without written approval. A large part of the regulatory problems was due to understaffing,[26] and lack of skilled technical staff, with 20 of 57 positions in the DSS yet to be filled by 2000. The National Audit Department (2000) recommended more financial and human resources for the DSS to be effective. However, the inability of IWK to meet service delivery targets and environmental standards was not due to information or institutional (regulatory) failure, but rather, to the company's cash flow problems from the non-payment of sewerage charges.

### *Political factors*

Despite these ex ante failures, privatization proceeded because it was also motivated by political considerations related to initial profit projections as well as opportunities for monopoly rents for a group of businessmen closely connected to sections of the political leadership. In this sense, the ex ante failure to account for information constraints was in part constrained by political considerations related to the choice of candidates. Privatization was driven by the commercial interests of North West Water (the overseas partner who initiated the project) in collaboration with powerful domestic interests, initially Vincent Tan (a beneficiary of several lucrative privatizations and closely associated with the Prime Minister and Finance Minister), and later fuelled by a group of Malay businessmen who believed they could make easy money through a publicly listed monopoly.

The privatization was initially regarded as a viable and even highly profitable project, and IWK's prospects rated highly, with its discounted cash flow estimated at at least RM3 billion, revenue at RM34–RM50 billion, and operating costs at RM18 billion over the 28-year concession period, based on the initial tariff rates and an average turnover growth of 10 per cent (*The Edge*, October 1994, *Malaysian Business*, 16 June 1995). Tariff revisions were expected to affect revenue by between 5 per cent (for a finite period) and 25 per cent (over the 25 year concession period). Nonetheless, most analysts estimated a return on investment of 25–30 per cent, and there was continued optimism about IWK's prospects (see *Malaysian Business*, 16 June 1995; *Business Times*, 11 February 1997, 15 November 1997). The control of IWK thus provided opportunities for monopoly rents, and its acquisition by Berjaya South Island aimed to transform that company (an investment-holding company whose main subsidiary's principal activity was garment manufacturing) into a major utility group managing one of the world's largest privatized sewerage projects.

The succession of ownership changes that followed subsequent tariff revisions were arguably in part motivated by profit guarantees as well as 'capital gains' profits from each sale, and the possibility of further profits from the large capital works programme and high share prices on the stock market. Although profit guarantees were not without problems,[27] buyers were nonetheless willing to pay a premium over the market price because of expected profits and also because control of a publicly listed company provided opportunities for 'signalling' to secure more bank credit on better terms (e.g. see Jomo 2002). This can be seen from the profits made from each sale (Table 4.07), and the fact that none of IWK's owners had relevant experience. IWK's five original owners made an estimated RM350 million in extraordinary gains from the sale to PUB (*Malaysian Business*, 16 June 1995), while the sale of Transwater's entire stake in PUB to Idris Hydraulic provided Wan Adli with a nominal profit of RM27.6 million (*The Star*, 18 September 1997). The first sale of IWK to PUB enabled Vincent Tan to acquire control of another listed company while retaining his interest in IWK (Prime Utilities 1995, 1996; Gomez and Jomo 1997). Although Berjaya South Island's profits (through its main business of garment manufacturing) were declining, the company's share price increased from RM4.52 to RM32 following news of the proposed purchase (*The Edge*, October 1994). Berjaya Group received RM860 million cash for the sale of IWK to Angsana Embun (*New Straits Times*, 26 August 1996). The share price of Transwater, IWK's third owner, also rose substantially following its purchase of IWK.

With the exception of Vincent Tan, the original concessionaire, all the ownership changes were between Malays who were also closely related to the leadership of UMNO. Ahmad Sebi Bakar, a substantial shareholder in PUB, was a close associate of Finance Minister Daim (Gomez and Jomo 1997;

*Table 4.07* IWK: Ownership changes and share prices

| *Owner* | *Berjaya* | *Prime Utilities (B. Sth Island)* | *Prime Utilities (Transwater)* | *Idris Hydraulic* | *Ministry of Finance* |
|---|---|---|---|---|---|
| Majority shareholder | Vincent Tan | Ahmad Sebi | Wan Adli | Ishak Ismail | Ministry of Finance |
| Share price paid (RM) | — | 15.00 | 20.00–24.93 | 20.00–23.75 | 1.92 |
| Date of purchase | Jan 1991 | Nov 1995 | Aug 1996–Dec 1997 | Sept 1997 | June 2000 |
| Total price (RM million) | — | 540 | 302.9 | 142.5 | 192.54 |
| Stake (%) | 20 | 100 | 26 | 32 | 100 |
| Profit/(loss) from sale (RM million) | 17.5* | 138.2** | 27.6 | (80.9) | — |

*Source:* Adapted from *The Star* (31 October 1996, 16 September 1997, 18 September 1997); *New Straits Times* (31 January 1997); Prime Utilities (1996); Cheong (1995, cited in Gomez and Jomo, 1997).

*Notes:* Berjaya South Island later became Prime Utilities Bhd (PUB). PUB was later bought by Transwater. * Vincent Tan's 20 per cent of the RM350 million made by IWK's original owners from the sale to PUB. ** Based on the 20 per cent sale to Transwater.

Gomez 2002c). Tan, the other substantial shareholder in PUB, was himself a close associate of Prime Minister Mahathir (Prime Utilities 1996). Idris Hydraulic's majority shareholder Ishak Ismail was a close ally of Deputy Prime Minister Anwar Ibrahim and executive committee member of UMNO's Permatang Pauh division (headed by Anwar before his dismissal). Anwar was reported to have 'tapped Ishak for "national service" in late 1997' following two previous changes in ownership (*Far Eastern Economic Review*, 25 March 1999).

However, not all the new owners got paid,[28] and this could be related to their relationships with the UMNO leadership. The main loser appears to have been Ishak Ismail, affiliated with Anwar, and the last private owner of IWK. Ishak had sacked Aminuddin Rouse (IWK director and deputy executive chairman, and the nephew of Prime Minister Mahathir's wife) in mid-January 1999. A few weeks later the government exercised its special share and became a special shareholder in IWK (having provided support loans totalling RM925 million). This entitled the government to nominate two representatives to the board, and more active and direct participation in the management of IWK (Prime Utilities 1999). Aminuddin was appointed executive chairman and one of two government representatives on the board on 8 February 1999. On 27 March 2000, PUB proposed to sell its stake in IWK (of 100 million shares) to the MoF for RM192.54 million cash (or RM1.92 per share) and to rescind IWK's profit guarantee agreement of

RM84 million per annum[29] for the financial years 1999–2001. On 23 June 2000, the MoF completed its purchase of IWK for RM192.54 million cash. Based on his 32 per cent stake in IWK, Ishak would have received RM61.6 million (i.e. a loss of RM80.9 million).

### *Ex post failure*

#### *Tariff revisions*

The downward tariff revisions and continued non-payment of sewerage charges underlines the government's ex post political failure to enforce payment. There were three tariff reviews (November 1996, April–June 1998 and September 1999), followed by revisions (January 1997, July 1998 and October 1999) and discounts (1997, 1998, 1999). The concession period was subsequently extended three times, following each tariff revision (1995–2022, with provisions for tariff revisions every three years after the first five years to adjust for inflation; 1996–2024; and 1998–2034) (*Malaysian Business*, 16 June 1995) (Table 4.08).

In August 1995, following widespread opposition, the government offered discounts of 40, 30 and 20 per cent respectively for the first, second and third years for all non-household customers. The government was to compensate IWK with RM300 million for losses resulting from these discounts. However, when billing was extended to the state of Perak in October 1995, accumulation of arrears (for charges for the period commencing from the original takeover date) led to more public dissatisfaction. In May 1996, the government initiated a tariff review exercise following further public complaints about rates, and in October 1996, ordered IWK to stop billing or collecting payment pending a review. The review exercise addressed issues related to billing, charges and services, as well as financing the development and management of a modern and efficient sewerage system (Sewerage Services Department, Malaysia 1998).

On 20 November 1996, the Prime Minister announced that IWK was to write off RM180 million in unpaid sewerage charges and, in return, would be provided with an additional RM450 million soft loan. The government also announced new sewerage rates effective from 1 January 1997 based on the principles of affordability and equitability, with businesses, industry and government offices paying more to subsidize lower-income home owners.

The first revision of rates not only reduced monthly charges, but also changed the basis of evaluation. Household customers (including government quarters) were charged fixed monthly rates from RM2 to RM8 (depending on type of premise), and were exempted from water usage charges. Commercial customers were levied a basic charge based on the annual value of the property[30] plus RM0.65 per cubic metre of water usage exceeding 100 cubic metres a month. Industrial customers were charged a flat rate based on the number of employees (Table 4.09).

*Table 4.08* IWK: Tariff and ownership changes

| | *1995* | *1996* | *1997* | *1998* | *1999* | *2000* |
|---|---|---|---|---|---|---|
| Tariff review | | 21 November | | April–June | September | |
| Tariff revision | | | 1 January | 1 July | 1 October | |
| Tariff reduction | | | household, commercial, industrial | 30% commercial | 5–20% commercial | |
| Govt loans (RM million) | | | | 433.7 | 503.8 | 545.4 |
| Concession extension | Until 2022 | Two years to 2024 | | 10 years to 2034 | | |
| Ownership | PUB (Ahmad Sebi) | PUB (Wan Adli) | I. Hydraulic (Ishak Ismail) | I. Hydraulic (Ishak Ismail) | I. Hydraulic (MoF) | MoF |
| Date | November | August | September | | | |

*Source:* Adapted from Prime Utilities (1995–2000); various newspapers.

*Table 4.09* IWK: Tariff revisions, 1995–1999

| | *1996* | *1997* | *1998* | *1999* |
|---|---|---|---|---|
| Tariff review | 21 Nov | | April–June | September |
| Tariff revision | | 1 January | 1 July | 1 October |
| Tariff reduction | | household, commercial, industrial | 30% commercial | 5–20% commercial |

*Source:* Adapted from Prime Utilities (1995–2000); various newspapers.

On 5 April 1998, the government agreed to further reduce tariffs by 30 and 40 per cent for the commercial sector following complaints, and IWK reduced commercial tariffs for the second time on 1 July 1998 by 30 per cent. In exchange, IWK was granted further financial assistance for the next two financial years, a further soft loan of RM500 million, and an extension of its concession by 10 years to 31 December 2034. On 16 September 1999, the government announced a third reduction in sewerage charges, of between 5 and 20 per cent, for commercial properties, with effect from 1 October 1999. These tariff revisions were mainly for the commercial sector following a backlash against cross-subsidization.[31]

The tariff revisions and bill collection problems had a negative impact on IWK's balance sheet and were reflected in IWK's actual and projected collection and profit figures (see Table 4.11, on p. 103). The tariff review in May 1996 led to the write-off of RM256.3 million in unpaid bills for 1997 and was reflected in parent company PUB's RM241.3 million loss for the year, in addition to RM367.9 million in bills written off from May 1994 to October 1996 (see Table 4.10, on p. 102). The first tariff revision on 1 January 1997 was estimated by PUB to have resulted in a RM42.5 million loss of potential pre-tax profits (*The Sun*, 12 December 1996). Commercial tariff rates were reduced by 30 per cent in July 1998 and by a further 5–20 per cent in October 1999, resulting in a revenue shortfall of RM103.7 million (National Audit Department, Malaysia 2000). The 30 per cent reduction of commercial tariffs in 1998 also accounted for a 12 per cent drop in PUB's turnover and RM25 million loss in 1999. However, these losses were not sufficient to cause the company to fail. Rather, IWK's biggest problem was the non-payment of bills.

### *Non-payment of sewerage charges*

The most serious problem for IWK was the absence of penalties for non-payment of sewerage charges. The non-payment of tariffs was partly the result of the government's unwillingness to legislate penalties, but primarily due to its inability to enforce payment of tariffs. Even after legislation, enforcement was weak, undermining revenue collection. Continued opposition even after downward tariff revisions and IWK's RM6 million public awareness campaign (*The Sun*, 9 October 1997, *New Straits Times*, 10 October 1998) suggested an ongoing unwillingness to pay. The National Audit Department (2000) recommended that the government raise public awareness about the importance of sewerage services to increase willingness to pay, and also review sewerage charges with the possibility of including them in water bills or as part of local council assessment rates.

While the downward revision of tariffs affected IWK, the company ran out of money when businesses, including hotels in Kuala Lumpur, refused to pay (Table 4.10). At one point, IWK was only collecting 15 per cent of what it was billing on a monthly basis.[32] In 1998, only 37 per cent of consumers (including 30 per cent of 73,000 commercial customers) had settled their bills, leaving IWK with RM92.7 million (RM45 million from the commercial sector) in outstanding payments. In 1999, commercial users accounted for RM72 million of the RM121 million in arrears.[33] IWK also faced difficulties collecting RM144.3 million in household tariffs in 2000 due to public opposition (National Audit Department, Malaysia 2000).

IWK's cash flow problems were compounded by the government's failure to provide the promised loans for capital investment.[34] The government offered IWK cash as long as the company wrote off unpaid bills and refunded those who had paid when IWK needed all the money it could get.[35] As a result, IWK's operating revenue was insufficient to cover its operating costs, with the company registering a RM32.2 million loss for the financial year ended April 2000 (Table 4.11), and an accumulated loss of RM332.9 million.

Despite the lack of information on customer numbers and assets, IWK was generally expected to cover its operating costs based on the proposed tariff structure and the original number of plants, provided there was 100 per cent collection.[36] Instead, operational viability was undermined by tariff revisions, and the failure of the government to provide promised loans. By 2000, IWK was no longer considered a viable business, even with 100 per cent

*Table 4.10* IWK: Losses from tariff revisions and non-payment of bills, 1996–2000

| *Year* | *Tariff Revision (RM million)* | *Unpaid Bills (RM million)* |
|---|---|---|
| 1996 | 367.9** | |
| 1997 | 256.3 | |
| 1998 | | 92.7 |
| 1999 | 103.7* | 121.0 |
| 2000 | | 144.3 |

*Notes:* *1998–99 revenue shortfall (National Audit Department, Malaysia 2000); **1994–96 bills written off (National Audit Department, Malaysia 2000).

*Table 4.11* IWK: Financial performance (RM million), 1995–2000

| | *1995* | *1996* | *1997* | *1998* | *1999* | *2000* |
|---|---|---|---|---|---|---|
| Turnover | 79.4 | 138.9 | 133.3 | 169.6 | 149.0 | 163.1 |
| Profit projected* | | | 120.4 | 112.0 | 99.3 | 177.3 |
| Profit revised* | | | (175.0) | 91.1 | 126.5 | 134.8 |
| Profit before tax | 10.2 | (5.9) | (246.2) | 5.6 | (25.0) | (32.2) |
| Collection projected | n/a | n/a | 75.0 | 328.0 | n/a | n/a |
| Collection outstanding | | | 256.0 (written-off) | 92.7 | 121.0 | 145.0 |
| Collection actual | | 0 | 107.7 | 66.7 | 56.4 | – |
| Cash flow operations | | (58.5) | 17.4 | 8.0 | (83.1) | 26.0 |
| Current liabilities | 35.38 | 62.76 | 262.5 | 260.1 | 197.7 | 200.9 |
| Long-term debt | 3.9 | 101.9 | 167.6 | 468.6 | 548.9 | 606.0 |
| Debt-equity | 1.30 | 1.02 | 1.68 | 4.69 | 5.49 | 6.06 |
| Current ratio | 2.8 | 2.77 | 0.31 | 1.06 | 0.98 | 0.68 |

*Source:* Adapted from Companies Commission of Malaysia; Prime Utilities (1996–2000), various newspapers; *projected and revised profits by Prime Utilities, cited in *Business Times*, 11 February 1997.
*Note:* Brackets ( ) = losses.

bill collection, without a doubling of tariffs.[37] The government's commissioning of an independent study of sewerage services around 1998–99 indicated official recognition that the project was becoming less viable (Prime Utilities 1998; *Business Times*, 9 October 1998; *The Sun*, 17 September 1999).

## Conclusion

In this chapter we examined the performance of IWK, looking at why the government privatized the national sewerage system, why privatization failed, and what is needed to make privatization work. Privatization was clearly motivated by the need to invest in the country's sewerage system which had been seriously neglected and under-funded. However, the choice of concessionaires shows that political considerations were also involved, with privatization providing opportunities for monopoly rents from compulsory sewerage charges and a large capital works programme, as well as high share prices on the stock market and profits from 'capital gains' (as reflected in the number of ownership changes and profits made from each sale). The success of the privatization depended on a tariff structure which allowed the concessionaire to cover operational costs, undertake capital investment, and earn sufficient returns to make a profit. However, tariffs for essential services such as sewerage treatment are politically sensitive, as highlighted by the continued public opposition despite several revisions. This has generally prevented the implementation of cost-covering tariffs, necessitating subsidies and incentive regulation.

The Malaysian government was aware of the sensitivities here (especially given the previous reluctance of state governments to increase sewerage charges in order to finance capital expansion) and sought to keep tariffs low for household customers through cross-subsidies from commercial/industrial customers. This was ostensibly to ensure the project was self-financing but possibly also because the state lacked the experience and technical ability to deal with the complexities of subsidies and incentive regulation. The success of this strategy depended on the correct determination of tariff levels economically and politically to ensure that the operator could earn sufficient returns and that customers were willing to pay this. As it turned out, both household and commercial/industrial customers opposed the new sewerage charges, even after several tariff revisions, resulting in the subsequent financial problems and renationalization of IWK.

The failure of IWK was thus the result of the government's ex ante and ex post failures. In the former, the government proceeded with the privatization despite the absence of information to determine assets, asset condition and tariff levels, and without properly accounting for public willingness to pay sewerage charges. This led to the concessionaire having to take over more STPs than agreed, increasing operational and capital costs, particularly as many plants were in poor condition. On top of this, downward tariff revisions reduced revenues. These factors adversely affected the concessionaire's ability to meet coverage, capital investment and environment targets, and prompted the subsequent changes in ownership. However, despite this, the privatization was seen to be commercially viable, as reflected in the premium paid by each new owner.

Instead, IWK's inability to continue financing operations and capital investment was ultimately due to its cash flow problems arising from the non-payment of sewerage charges. This was the result of the government's ex post (political) failure to enforce the payment of tariffs. Privatization did not improve the financing or operational efficiency of the national sewerage system because the government did not have the institutional capacity to design a credible subsidization programme, and more critically, the political capacity to enforce legislation and payment necessary to ensure its commercial success, or even discipline many politicians (including those in government) who continued to undermine IWK's credibility and encourage non-payment (*New Straits Times*, 24 March 1998).

This brings us to our final question: What is needed for privatization to work? Clearly, the main condition for the successful privatization of sewerage services was the government's political capacity to design and implement a credible cross-subsidization strategy, and in particular, to enforce the payment of tariffs. Contrary to public choice arguments that privatization insulates the sector from short-term political intervention in utility operations and limits opportunities for intervention by powerful groups (e.g. see Biswas 2000), political capacity is needed to enforce tariff payments if the privatization of sewerage services is to succeed. In this case, 'restrictive pricing policies' (i.e. non-cost covering tariffs) are not so much about short-term gains but rather a reflection of political constraints. A key lesson here is that sewerage charges have to be politically determined, which will often preclude cost-covering tariffs. This will then necessitate subsidies which will in turn entail ongoing state intervention in the form of regulation to preserve incentives.

# 5 The myth of privatized urban rail

## Kuala Lumpur Light Rail Transit

Contrary to privatization theory, urban rail systems have relied largely on public funds, either in the form of grants and subsidies, or loans through state-owned or international (development) financial institutions. Furthermore, urban rail privatization is fraught with difficulties because railways and metro systems cannot generate the revenues from fares to cover the full costs of their infrastructure, train operations and investment, as well as provide a return on capital. This has necessitated substantial subsidies, partly also to limit (politically sensitive) fare increases, and to help finance capital expansion. As these subsidies will affect the structure of risks and incentives, privatization per se is unlikely to address issues of financing and efficiency.

There are several possible reasons then why privatization may proceed even though it cannot address problems inherent in urban rail provision. Firstly, the government may actually believe that privatization can work. Secondly, it potentially benefits all parties, providing construction rents for the concessionaire and profits for banks, while at the same time allowing the government to have infrastructure projects (privately) financed. This was the case in Malaysia, where privatization aimed to facilitate the construction of Kuala Lumpur's Light Rail Transit (LRT) to address growing traffic congestion. However, privatization also allowed for resources to be allocated, through patron–client networks, to parties closely associated with segments of the political leadership. This political consideration shaped the nature of the privatization which was consistent with the preference of domestic capitalists for construction-based projects (discussed in Chapter 3). This can explain why the government chose to privatize both construction and operations to the same concessionaire, thereby providing the opportunities for monopoly rents from construction (reflected in higher cost per kilometre compared to similar systems in the region). However, this also resulted in a huge debt burden arising from capital expenditure, and which could not be sustained given the problems mentioned above, creating a moral hazard which further reinforced the attractiveness of short-term profits from construction over long-term profits from operations.

Failure here was partly due to the government's ex ante failure to properly determine project viability, and to structure the privatization to avoid creating a moral hazard. However, as ex ante mistakes are inevitable because of information and political constraints, it was more important for the government to be able to implement ex post measures to ensure the project's commercial viability by promoting system integration necessary to increase passenger numbers. Here, the failure of privatization was ultimately due to the government's ex post political failure. The government was unable to force the concessionaires and private developers to accept route alignment and the physical integration of stations necessary for system integration; it could not streamline bus operations and prevent private bus operators from plying LRT routes; it failed to restrict parking in the city and regulate parking charges; and it failed to restrict private cars in the city centre. In short, the government lacked the institutional and political capacity to plan and coordinate a successful urban rail system, needing to renationalize the LRT in order to make the necessary changes to better integrate the system.

The experiences of the UK, Singapore and Bangkok demonstrate that successful (urban) rail provision depends on effective regulation and government coordination of investment and policies to integrate different modes of transport. This requires the institutional capacity to identify an appropriate level of subsidy, and political capacity to enforce cost reductions and capital investment within this subsidy level. More crucially, having committed to what was arguably a commercially unviable privatization, the government needed to implement measures to at least ensure a second-best outcome. This will depend on its political capacity to enforce the regulation, coordinate the investment and implement the policies necessary. It is not the privatization in itself that will lead to success but rather the effective and insulated intervention of the state in financing and coordinating these processes and in monitoring performance.

This chapter is structured as follows. The next section examines the challenges faced by the privatization of urban rail systems. This is followed by a background to the privatization and subsequent renationalization of the Kuala Lumpur LRT. We then evaluate the performance of the three LRT systems in terms of financing, delivery, financial performance and impact on traffic volume (congestion). The following section examines the government's ex ante and ex post failures which affected performance, looking at information, institutional and political failure. We conclude by summarizing the main causes of the LRT's failure and important conditions for successful privatization.

## Challenges

Rail privatization is argued to finance capital investment and provide incentives to improve efficiency. Evidence however shows that the private sector has had difficulty financing (urban) rail systems and improving efficiency. This is because the rail industry is characterized by high capital costs and low farebox ratios (the ratio of fares to operating costs) which are compounded by insufficient ridership. Privatization cannot resolve the conflict between publicly acceptable fares, and the need to cover costs and provide a return on investment. As such, privatized railways have been largely financed by public funds in order to keep fares low and carry out capital investment. This has in turn undermined incentives for efficiency and strengthened the importance of regulation. Rather than the fragmentation which follows privatization, viable urban rail systems require coordination and integration, and are thus dependent on the government's institutional and political capacity to plan and coordinate investment, and implement policy.

### *High capital costs*

Capital investment is needed to build as well as expand networks, not just to meet projected passenger growth but also to increase ridership through sufficient network coverage. Privatization is meant to finance much-needed capital expansion by mobilizing private funds. However, rail operators have generally relied on substantial subsidies and grants to meet the cost of capital investment and the private sector has been unable or unwilling to finance rail development, with only three private sector urban rail schemes committed before the 1997–98 Asian financial crisis (two in Kuala Lumpur and one in Bangkok) (Shoji 2001; Shaoul 2004). Instead, the privatization of rail systems has been largely financed by public funds, usually through state-owned or international financial and development institutions. The substantial capital cost is the reason why many cities underwrite the cost of infrastructure provision (e.g. by building new lines, boosting capacity and procuring assets such as rolling stock).

Over 80 per cent of debt financing for Bangkok's Skytrain came from state-owned or international (development or financial) institutions[1] and the state financed the construction of tunnels and stations of Bangkok's Metro underground urban rail system. The privatization of British Rail involved the separation of infrastructure maintenance and investment to Railtrack, and operations to some 25 train operating companies (TOCs). Railtrack received £1 billion from the European Investment Bank (EIB) and Kreditanstalt für Wiederaufbau (KfW) (the German development bank) (Whitehouse 2003). In addition, the government wrote off a £1.6 billion debt burden before privatization, provided £225 million of debt relief on flotation, and underpriced shares, all to ensure the private owner could earn the appropriate rate of return without resorting to higher fares (Shaoul 2004). Between 1986 and 1994, public funds provided 52–72 per cent of finances for railways in Europe (Shaoul 2004). Even in Japan, where urban railways tend to pay for operating and infrastructure costs, there are special subsidies for subway and infrastructure construction (Shoji 2001).

Privatization also did not improve capital investment or efficiency here. The operator of Bangkok's Skytrain was unable to expand network coverage necessary to increase ridership due to debt problems, while Railtrack's total investment over four years (to March 2000) was less than required and went largely into station refurbishments and leasing shop lots in stations rather than network expansion (see Shaoul 2004). Railtrack was also unable to meet deadlines and cost estimates, with the upgrade of the West Coast Main Line (the most important trunk rail route in the UK) two years behind schedule and expected to cost four times the original £2.5 billion estimate (Shaoul 2004; United Kingdom 2006). The privatization of British Rail also increased subsidies by £300 million and required a further £5 billion in public investment to maintain the network (Harris 1999; Terry 2001b). Total subsidies for the 25 private TOCs following privatization were 'higher than British Rail ever received' (Shaoul 2004: 32–33). Despite these grants and subsidies, Railtrack's debt increased from £701 million (just before privatization in 1996) to over £3.9 billion in 2001 (Shaoul 2004). TOCs, on the other hand, made no profits in the first two years after privatization and the same operating margins (2 per cent) after that, mainly due to considerably higher subsidies (Shaoul 2004). Service provision, meanwhile, deteriorated after privatization, with declining punctuality and increasing customer complaints (Bagwell 2004).

### *Low farebox ratios*

Fares have not traditionally covered operating costs (let alone capital investment) in urban rail systems (Cox 1997; Halcrow Consultants 1999), with the exception of Hong Kong and Singapore (both city states), and several Japanese operators. The average farebox ratios for European urban rail systems in 1991 was 49 per cent (Shoji 2001). This is because fares are usually too low (and higher fares politically sensitive), and ridership is constrained by network coverage and existing transport policies, including automobile use. Fares have only covered 30–40 per cent of operating costs in the US and 55 per cent in the UK (Hakim *et al.* 1996b) while farebox ratios have deteriorated (Bly *et al.* 1979; Allen 1982, both cited in Shoji 2001). Low ridership levels and high operating costs have required operational and capital subsidies as well as the state underwriting capital costs (Halcrow Consultants 1999; Shoji 2001).

One way to increase farebox ratios is through higher fares based on the 'user pays' principle as is partly the case in some Japanese cities (Shoji 2001). However, in reality, universal service obligations (and political concerns) preclude this option, and contrary to privatization theory, rail fares cannot be economically determined. As rail is a high fixed-cost industry, it largely charges customers differential rates per service at the point of use as it does not provide a comprehensive and universal service, unlike utilities. This means that in the absence of adequate demand, full-cost pricing per service is self-defeating (Shaoul 2004). Railways and metro systems cannot generate the revenues from fares to cover the full costs of their infrastructure, train operations and investment, as well as making a rate of return on capital employed. In the context of private finance, this means subsidizing the providers of finance which can undermine incentives for improving efficiency (Shaoul 2004).

Government debt relief and grants to prevent higher fares following British Rail's privatization reflects the political sensitivities surrounding this issue even in industrialized countries (see Shaoul 2004). Instead, fares are often negotiated (e.g. Bangkok and Kuala Lumpur) or set by the government (e.g. Singapore and Manila), and subsidies are required to keep these affordable. Higher fares also further jeopardize ridership given the already low passenger numbers. Even in densely populated Asian cities with higher ridership intensity, operators in less densely populated areas (e.g. in Japan) have received increasing subsidies (Shoji 2001). Furthermore, successful rail operators have relied on diversification, with non-rail business providing just under half the revenue of major Japanese rail operators and over 60 per cent of the revenue of minor operators in 1995 (Shoji 2001). Even with a very high daily ridership of 370,000, income from property development was an important source of revenue for Kowloon–Canton Railway's Light Rail Division[2] in Hong Kong (Light Rail Transit Association 1997; Kowloon–Canton Railway Corporation 2003).

### *State coordination and capacity*

The problems of high capital costs and low farebox ratios inherent in urban rail systems have necessitated government grants and operational subsidies. In addition, successful urban rail systems also need to be part of wider transport policies. Both these depend on the government's ability to structure incentives and enforce conditions, as well as coordinate investment and integrate transport systems. The failure of Railtrack illustrates the difficulties of managing subsidies and structuring incentives, with industry fragmentation, increasing transaction costs and overheads leading to cost-cutting measures (e.g. contracting out) to earn returns on capital. This affected coordination and coherence (not to mention safety), making 'planning, implementation and accountability in the industry difficult, if not impossible' (Shaoul 2004: 32). On the other hand, awarding a BOT contract to the same company may address the problem of fragmentation but introduces a moral hazard whereby the concessionaire may choose to earn rents through construction rather than profits from operations, especially as farebox ratios are unable to cover operating and capital expenses. This can undermine incentives and is the reason that many governments choose to underwrite the cost of infrastructure. More crucially, the UK government was unable to enforce sanctions against Railtrack for its failure to improve passenger train performance and meet its investment programme set out in the Network Licence (Whitehouse 2003). Underlying this was the government's lack of political capacity to implement the necessary policies and enforce discipline.

Bangkok's experience further illustrates the problem of political failure and is particularly illuminating given the remarkable similarities with Kuala

Lumpur's LRT. Both systems were privatized through build-operate-own (BOO)/build-operate-transfer (BOT) concessions and based on grossly inflated passenger projections, presumably to enhance project viability in order to secure financing. This meant that ridership was insufficient to cover operating costs, let alone meet interest payments (not to mention repay the principal loan or invest in further expansion). Rather than being economically determined, fares had to be negotiated, and none of the operators were able to charge fares which they felt were necessary to recoup their investments. However, the lower fares did not increase passenger numbers sufficiently to make up for the shortfall in revenue. This was compounded by line integration problems (e.g. the lack of a common ticketing system and poor feeder bus services), inadequate network coverage (in the case of Bangkok), and inconsistent price regulations (and subsidies) across different modes of transportation (making it much cheaper to travel by bus). Underlying these problems was the political failure of both governments to implement credible subsidization policies, plan and coordinate investment and system integration, and enforce an integrated transport policy in the context of the private provision of urban rail. The failure to do this led to renationalization.

## Background

Kuala Lumpur's LRT system comprises two LRT lines and a monorail. This was part of long-term government plans for an integrated transport system to address increasing traffic congestion and projected growth around Kuala Lumpur through the construction of a privately financed urban rail system. Plans for an LRT were first commissioned in a 1970s study of mass rapid transit systems in 30 cities around the world which concluded that the project was feasible and profitable in conjunction with land development projects (see Townsend 2003). This was followed up with a Master Plan Transportation Study, carried out between 1979 and 1981. In 1984, the government approved two LRT lines, and the 1984 Kuala Lumpur Structure Plan by Kuala Lumpur City Hall (DBKL) recommended a rail system and a single public transport agency (under the Ministry of the Federal Territory). DBKL also identified a corridor, sector coverage (targeting growth areas), ridership, population projections and a related land use strategy.[3] The LRT system was subsequently delayed by the 1986 recession and fiscal constraints, with several proposals turned down due to cost.[4] In 1987, another study was conducted as part of the Klang Valley Transportation Plan.

In 1991, the government revived plans to introduce a 'one-system public transport' in the city based on studies by the Ministry of Transport, Economic Planning Unit (EPU) and DBKL (*New Straits Times*, 15 July 1991). This was to include two LRT lines and a monorail with feeder bus service, and full integration with other city public transport, including buses and a dual-track railway service. City buses were to be given new routes (to complement, and not compete with, the LRT), and DBKL was to merge bus companies into a conglomerate for a more efficient public transport system. Between 1990 and 1993, three light rail corridors were identified and concessions were awarded, without open tender, to three private operators on a BOO basis in line with the government's privatization policy. System 1 was awarded to Sistem Transit Aliran Ringgan (STAR), System 2 to Projek Usahasama Transit Ringan Automatik (PUTRA) and System 3 to Kuala Lumpur Monorail (KL Monorail).

### *Privatization*

#### *System 1 (STAR)*

In 1990, TaylorWoodrow (a UK-based company involved in housing, property development, construction and engineering) put in a bid for System 1 and won the right to progress the work and to secure funding, design and construction of the project following the failure of previous bids.[5] Taylor-Woodrow then formed a consortium with German rail manufacturer Adtranz[6] and created the operating company STAR on 13 November 1991 to build and operate the 27-km route. Two 60-year concession agreements were signed with STAR, the first on 22 December 1992 for Phase 1 (worth RM1.28 billion),[7] and the second for Phase 2 (Sections A and B) on 26 June 1995 (worth RM2.1 billion). The design, supply and construction contract worth RM1.65 billion was signed with Kuala Lumpur Transit Group (KLTG), a joint-venture between Taylor Woodrow (construction) and Bombardier/Adtranz (rail systems) on 17 July 1995.

Construction was completed on schedule and within budget, with revenue operations starting on 16 December 1996 (Phase 1, 12 km) and July 1998 (Phase 2, 11.8 km), in time for the 1998 Commonwealth Games in Kuala Lumpur. The 3.2 km northern extension was completed in December 1998, increasing the total route to 27 km. Operations were the responsibility of STAR and KLTG handed over the project to STAR once it was built. TaylorWoodrow-Adtranz also subsequently reduced its equity in STAR, which then effectively became a state-owned entity, with state institutional investors owning 50 per cent of equity.

#### *System 2 (PUTRA)*

System 2 was proposed as part of a traffic study by the University of Malaya in 1993 and, later, as part of the Klang Draft Structure Plan in 1994 (*New Straits Times*, 30 November 1993; *Malay Mail*, 6 June 1994). However, the EPU was reported to have already solicited privatization bids for System 2 in September 1993 from the Renong Group and MMC Group (*New Straits Times*, 19 October 1993). PUTRA was incorporated on 15 February 1994 by Renong, a major conglomerate linked to the ruling Malay party UMNO (see Gomez 1991) which had been a previous recipient of several major privatization contracts. The 60-year concession agreement for System 2 was awarded to PUTRA on 7 August 1995. The project was estimated to cost RM4.35 billion but later revised to RM5.4 billion, with a projected date of completion of April 1998 (Phase 1) and early 1999 (Phase 2) (*New Straits Times*, 4 May 1995; *Business Times*, 8 August 1995; *The Edge*, 12 May 1997, 13 July 1998, 26 August 1996). Construction began in September 1995 and was completed on time and below budget, with revenue operations commencing on 1 September 1998 (Phase 1) and 1 June 1999 (Phase 2).

### *System 3 (KL Monorail)*

The monorail project was originally proposed by Hitachi Corporation of Japan in the 1980s but rejected due to cost. In 1992, a consortium led by Singapore contractor Lum Chang Holdings was reported to have secured the RM900 million monorail project (*Business Times*, 6 January 1992, 26 February 1992; *Malay Mail*, 13 April 1992, 30 December 1993; *New Straits Times*, 6 December 1994). However, the project was subsequently awarded to Kuala Lumpur People Rapid Transit (later renamed Kuala Lumpur Monorail) on 29 October 1996, as part of Kuala Lumpur Linear City, an ambitious RM10 billion transport and mixed development project which was later deferred. Both projects were proposed by David Chew in 1994 (*The Edge*, 26 August 1996), who was also behind the privatization of the national sewerage system. He subsequently bought over KL Monorail from Vincent Tan. The 30-year BOT concession was awarded on 26 April 1997 for KL Monorail to 'develop, design, construct, finance, manage, operate and maintain the Kuala Lumpur monorail' over a 16-km route with completion originally scheduled for mid-1998 (in time for the Commonwealth Games in Kuala Lumpur) (*The Edge*, 2 October 1995). However, this was later rescheduled to mid-2000 and KL Monorail negotiated to revise the concession agreement and shorten the original route by half. Despite this, the project was considerably delayed, with operations commencing only on 23 August 2003.

## ***Renationalization***

All three concessionaires faced financial difficulties. STAR and PUTRA had problems servicing their loans and financing rolling stock. KL Monorail ran out of money following the 1997 Asian financial crisis and only resumed construction after obtaining another loan (*Far Eastern Economic Review*, 18 August 2000; Hilmi 2003). Following insufficient operational revenue arising from low passenger numbers and mounting debt problems barely a year after commencement of full operations for Systems 1 and 2 in 1998, the government announced it was to issue RM2.5 billion of bonds to settle the loans of STAR (along with KTMB, the mainline rail operator) and RM4.5

billion zero coupons[8] for the debts of STAR (RM2.2 billion) and PUTRA (RM2 billion). Up to RM8 billion in government bonds were also to be issued to swap against the group debts of Renong, PUTRA's parent company,[9] while KL Monorail was provided with a RM300 million soft loan in 1999. By early 1999, the government began looking at merging STAR and PUTRA, and in December 2000, announced it was taking over both operations and leasing them back to the private sector. In November 2001, the Ministry of Finance (MoF) purchased the outstanding debts of STAR and PUTRA totalling RM5.5 billion via the issuance of RM5.5 billion fixed rate serial guaranteed bonds to the lenders of both companies. It took over all assets and operations in April and May 2002. System 3 remained privately owned.

## Performance

The main aim of the LRT was to improve Kuala Lumpur's public transport network and reduce traffic congestion by facilitating private finance, delivery and operations. Its performance can be gauged in terms of: 1, financing (including the share of private and public funds); 2, delivery (construction cost, deadlines, fares); 3, financial performance (including ridership and revenue); and 4, impact on traffic volume. Privatization was not wholly successful in raising private capital as state loans were central to the financing of all three projects. In terms of delivery, only Systems 1 and 2 were completed on time, while System 3 was substantially delayed and its scope reduced. All three projects cost less than Bangkok's Skytrain, but were more expensive per kilometre than the Singapore MRT and LRT lines, especially when accounting for track topography (i.e. percentage of elevation and tunnels). Fares for Systems 1 and 2 were comparatively low but System 3 had the highest fares per kilometre. All three operators faced financial difficulties upon commencement of operations. Finally, the LRT system did not appear to reduce traffic congestion although this was in part related to wider failings in the public transport system and public transport policy.

### *Financing*

State loans were central to the financing of all three privatizations, and it is also unlikely that the projects would have been financed without implicit government support and backing which helped the concessionaires secure commercial loans. Table 5.01 provides a summary of private versus public financing of Systems 1, 2 and 3.

#### *System 1 (STAR)*

System 1 was to have been financed with RM600 million by shareholders, RM2.2 billion in commercial loan and guarantee facilities, and RM1.35

*Table 5.01* Kuala Lumpur LRT: Financing (RM million)

| | *System 1* | | *System 2* | | *System 3* | |
|---|---|---|---|---|---|---|
| | *Projected* | *Actual* | *Projected* | *Actual* | *Projected* | *Actual* |
| Total financing | 4,150 | 4,085 | — | 4,700 | 1,047 | 1,180 |
| Private equity | 600 (14.5%) | — | — | 1,200 (25.5%) | 127 (12.1%) | 260 (22%) |
| Commercial loans | 2,200 (53.0%) | 1,580 (38.7%) | — | 2,000 (42.6%) | — | — |
| Government loans | 700 (32.5%) | 2,505 (61.3%) | — | 1,500 (31.9%) | 920 (87.9%) | 920 (78%) |

*Source:* Adapted from *New Straits Times* (24 October 1996); *Business Times* (24 October 1996, 13 November 1996); *The Edge* (26 August 1996, 13 July 1998, 15 January 2001; 5 June 2001).

billion in government support loans (*The Edge*, 26 August 1996). This total of RM4.15 billion amounted to 14.5 per cent equity, 53.0 per cent commercial loans, and 32.5 per cent government loans. However, between 1993 and 1998, System 1 was funded, in two separate stages for Phase 1 (1993) and Phase 2 (1995) with RM1.58 billion in commercial loans and RM2.51 billion in various government loans.[10] This means that over 60 per cent of the financing for System 1 came from public funds (see Table 5.01). This is perhaps not surprising given that STAR was essentially a state-owned company, especially after TaylorWoodrow-Adtranz reduced its 30 per cent equity, with state institutional investors owning 50 per cent of equity.[11] This also indicates that the private sector (TaylorWoodrow in particular) was unwilling to be involved beyond the construction stage, suggesting that it was mainly interested in this part of the project. In addition, state loans were also important for providing financing at favourable interest rates and generous conditions, including 10–15 year interest-free grace periods and 30-year loan maturity (e.g. see JICA 1997, 1998a).

### *System 2 (PUTRA)*

Funding for System 2 was to come from commercial banks and to be largely sourced locally (*Business Times*, 8 August 1995). In total, PUTRA was financed through RM300 million equity, RM900 million shareholders' advances, RM2 billion commercial loans, and RM1.5 billion government support loans. This total of RM4.7 billion comprised 25.5 per cent equity, 42.6 per cent commercial loans, and 31.9 per cent government loans (see Table 5.01). Additionally, government backing was crucial in helping secure commercial loans, in particular for PUTRA's parent company Renong, which became highly leveraged in order to finance the project[12] (*Business Times*, 29 May 2001). PUTRA's average interest rate (8.86 per cent) was lower than STAR's (10.25 per cent) and the company was also subject to lower interest rates on government soft loans (6 per cent) compared to STAR (8 per cent) and more favourable loan periods (e.g. see *The Edge*, 17 November 1997; JICA 1998a; JICA 1997).

### *System 3 (KL Monorail)*

System 3 was to be privately financed through RM600 million in authorized capital, RM127 million paid-up capital and RM920 million in government support loans (*Business Times*, 9 September 2002). This total of RM1.05 billion amounted to 12 per cent private equity and 88 per cent public funds. Under its listing exercise, KL Monorail's promoters increased their paid-up capital from RM127 to RM260 million. The project was eventually financed with RM260 million in private equity (22 per cent) and RM920 million in government loans (78 per cent) (see Table 5.01). Government support loans included RM300 million[13] and an interest-free RM620 million infrastructure loan.

### *Delivery*

Delivery can be gauged in terms of construction (projected and actual costs, regional comparisons of cost per kilometre, projected and actual completion dates) and operations (fares per kilometre). Systems 1 and 2 were completed on time but System 3 was substantially delayed and its scope reduced.

#### *Construction*

System 1 as a whole was officially launched on 11 July 1998 with operations commencing on 6 December 1998, one month ahead of the concession agreement. Construction for System 2 began in September 1995 and was completed before the deadlines of April 1998 (Phase 1) and early 1999 (Phase 2), and below budget, with revenue operations commencing shortly after. System 3 was originally scheduled for completion in mid-1998 but was later rescheduled for the end of 1999 (Section 1) and the start of 2000 (Section 2), and again for mid-2000 (JICA 1998; *The Edge*, 10 February 1997; *Far Eastern Economic Review*, 18 August 2000). Following the 1997–98 Asian financial crisis, KL Monorail entered into a Revised Concession Agreement on 30 April 2000 to reschedule the project and reduce its scope. This led to the project being scaled down from the original RM2.1 billion to RM1.17 billion, and the route shortened from 16 km to 8.6 km, with completion rescheduled to December 2001, trial runs in January 2002 and operations in the first half of 2002 (*The Edge*, 4 December 2000). Actual operations only commenced on 23 August 2003.

STAR and PUTRA completed construction within or below the projected cost – RM3.5 billion for System 1 (or US$34.1 million per km) and RM4.35 billion for System 2 (US$39.5 million per km) (Table 5.02). The higher cost of System 2 was due to 79 per cent of its route being elevated and 15 per cent underground. In comparison, only 35 per cent of System 1's route was elevated, with the rest built at-grade (on ground level) and utilizing existing (disused) rail tracks. System 3 was eventually completed at a cost of RM1.169 billion (US$37.1 million per km), which, being entirely elevated, was more expensive than System 1 but not significantly cheaper than System 2 despite its simpler technology and reported savings from locally designed and built trains (see *The Edge*, 15 January 2001). The final cost was also significantly higher than the 1995 estimate of RM840 million. In short, KL Monorail only completed half the route for more than half the cost, and in twice the time.

In terms of regional performance, all three systems were cheaper to build compared to Bangkok's Skytrain but more expensive per kilometre compared to Singapore's MRT and LRT lines, even those built around the same time (i.e. after 1996) (Table 5.03). (It is worth noting that the Skytrain is

*Table 5.02* Kuala Lumpur urban rail: Breakdown of construction costs (RM million)

| | *Stage* | *Distance (km)* | *1995 cost estimate** | *1997 cost estimate*** | *Final cost'* |
|---|---|---|---|---|---|
| *System 1* | Phase 1 | 12 | 1,200 | 1,761 | 1,270 |
| | Phase 2 | 15 | — | 2,061 | 2,230 |
| *System 2* | | | | | |
| | Section 1 | 14.1 | — | 1,872 | |
| | Section 2 | 14.9 | 4,350 | 2,695 | 4,350 (Sections 1+2) |
| *System 3* | Section 1+2 | 16 | 2,100 | — | — |
| | Section 1 | 8.6 | 840 | 1,169 | 1,169 |

*Source:* Adapted from STAR and PUTRA; JICA 1998a; *BKWPPLK March 1998; **JICA 1997.

exceptionally expensive by any standards, while Bangkok's Metro subway system, though the most expensive system, is nonetheless comparable with Singapore's NEL MRT which is similarly built entirely underground.) Systems 1 and 3 in particular had the highest costs, especially given the absence of tunnels, System 1's predominantly 'at-grade' track, and System 3's simpler monorail construction.

System 3, at US$37.1 million per kilometre, compares very poorly against similar elevated LRT lines in Singapore (which range from US$15.9 to US$24.2 million per kilometre) and Manila (US$34.3 million per kilometre). System 2's track is broadly comparable with the MRT (North South and East West Lines), with both having about the same percentage of elevated track (79 versus 75 per cent). However, despite the MRT's higher percentage of tunnels (28 per cent versus Systems 2's 15 per cent), its cost per kilometre is lower (US$36 million versus US$39.5 million per kilometre) (Table 5.03). The evidence here is consistent with the general acknowledgment within the industry that construction rents are significant and widespread, with the costs of construction projects in Malaysia widely known to be inflated.[14]

### *Operations (fares)*

Systems 1 and 2 had fares comparable with the region, with System 3 having the highest fares (Table 5.04). Fares were based on proposals by operators to meet operations and maintenance cost, and for returns based on proposed profit margins[15] but which depended on government approval.[16] The concession agreement specified a fare table until the end of the concession period and operators needed to give notice for upward fare reviews which had to be agreed by the government.[17] However, the government did not favour yearly increases, preferring fare reviews every three to five years instead. Fares for System 1 (US$0.03 per km) and System 2 (US$0.02 per km) were comparable

*Table 5.03* Regional urban rail systems: Selected indicators

| | *System 1* | *System 2* | *System 3* | *MRT* (NS+ EW Lines)* | *Singapore LRT (3 lines)* | *Bangkok Skytrain* | *Bangkok Metro* |
|---|---|---|---|---|---|---|---|
| Operator | STAR | PUTRA | KL Monorail | SMRT | SMRT & SBS | BTSC | BMCL |
| Length (km) | 27 | 29 | 8.6 | 83 | 7.8–10.7 | 23.5 | 21 |
| Elevated (km) | 9.5 | 22.8 | 8.6 | 62.3 | 7.8–10.7 | 23.5 | 0 |
| Underground (km) | 0 | 4.4 | 0 | 23.3 | 0 | 0 | 21 |
| At grade (km) | 17.5 | 2.3 | 0 | 3.8 | 0 | 0 | 0 |
| Start/completion | 1994/1998 | 1995/1998 | 1997/2003 | 1983/1990, 1996 | 1996/98<br>2000/03<br>2000/04 | 1996/<br>1999 | 1999/2004 |
| Delivery | On time | On time | Late | n/a | n/a | On time | Late |
| First operations | 6 Dec 1998 | 1 Sept 1998 | 23 Aug 2003 | 7 Nov 1987 | Nov 1999<br>Jan 2003<br>Jan 2005 | 5 Dec 1999 | 3 July 2004 |
| Projected cost (billion) | RM3.38 | RM4.6 | RM0.84<br>RM1.17 | — | — | US$1.2–US$1.4 | — |
| Actual cost (billion) | RM3.5 | RM4.4 | RM1.2 | S$6.2 | S$0.29–S$0.35 | US$1.5–US$1.7 | US$2.8–<br>US$3.5 |
| Cost per km (US$ million) | 34.1 | 39.5 | 37.1 | 35.9–36.1 | 15.9–24.2 | 59.1 | 133.3 –166.7 |

*Notes:* *Singapore. Cost per km will be affected by length of route elevation and tunnels. Conversion to US$ based on the average monthly exchange rates for the period of construction calculated on Pacific Exchange Rates <http://fx.sauder.ubc.ca>.

with the MRT (North South and East West lines) (US$0.02 per km) and cheaper than Singapore's LRT (US$0.05–US$0.07 per km). However, it should be noted that this comparison was after PUTRA's fares were reduced by over 60 per cent. At US$0.08 per kilometre, System 3's fares were the most expensive.

### *Financial performance*

The success or failure of privatization is ultimately reflected in the concessionaires' financial performance. All three concessionaires faced financial difficulties shortly upon commencing operations, and in November 2001, the MoF purchased the outstanding debts of STAR and PUTRA totalling RM5.5 billion and took over all assets and operations by May 2002. KL Monorail was unable to finance System 3, needing to scale down and delay the project, and secure more loans, including RM300 million from the government (*Far Eastern Economic Review*, 18 August 2000; Hilmi 2003).

Financial problems were the result of low revenues largely due to financial projections being based on grossly overoptimistic ridership projections. STAR's projections to recoup investments within 15 years and for operating profits by 2000 were based on ridership forecasts of between 80,000 and 170,000 passengers per day. In 1997 STAR carried between 46,000 and 65,000 passengers a day. STAR's projected daily ridership for 1999 was 165,000–170,000 (10–12 per cent of the population in the catchment area), but actual passengers numbers were 65,000 in 1999 and still only 80,000–92,000, just 30 per cent of its capacity in 2003.[18] PUTRA's projected daily ridership was 360,000 a day (or 14.5 per cent of the population in the catchment area), while actual ridership was 12,000 in July 1999. This increased to 125,000 in August 2000 as a result of a 60 per cent fare reduction in July 1999. Ridership in 2003 was 150,000–160,000 a day,[19] still less than half original projections. KL Monorail projected 60,000–80,000 passengers daily in its first year of operations, increasing by 5–8 per cent thereafter. This was later revised to 85,900 passengers daily for 2002 and 181,200 by 2008. Actual ridership figures for 2003 were around 11,000 a day, increasing to around 39,000 in August 2004 (Table 5.05). Despite the large discrepancy between projected

*Table 5.04* Urban rail systems: Regional fares (US$), 2003

| | *STAR* | *PUTRA* | *Monorail* | *MRT (NS+EW Lines)* | *Singapore LRT (3 lines)* | *Bangkok Skytrain* | *Bangkok Metro* |
|---|---|---|---|---|---|---|---|
| Length (km) | 27 | 29 | 8.6 | 83 | 7.8–10.7 | 23.5 | 21 |
| Fare per km | 0.03 | 0.02 | 0.08 | 0.02 | 0.05–0.07 | 0.04 | 0.04 |

*Notes:* Conversion to US$ based on the average monthly exchange rates in 2003–4 calculated on Pacific Exchange Rates <http://fx.sauder.ubc.ca>.

*Table 5.05* Kuala Lumpur LRT: Projected and actual daily ridership

| *Operator* | *Projected* | *Actual (year)* |
|---|---|---|
| STAR | 80,000–170,000<br>(projection in 1997)<br>165,000–170,000<br>(projected for 1999) | 46,500 (1997)<br>65,000 (end 1997)<br>65,000 (1999)<br>80,000–92,000 (2003) |
| PUTRA | 360,000<br>(projection in 1997) | 12,000 (1999)<br>125,000 (2000)<br>150,000–160,000 (2003) |
| KL Monorail | 60,000–80,000<br>(projection in 2000)<br>85,900<br>(projection for 2002)<br>181,200<br>(projection for 2008) | <br><br>11,000 (2003)<br>39,000 (2004) |

*Source:* Adapted from *The Edge* (26 August 1996, 12 May 1997, 13 July 1998, 19 July 1999, 6 December 2000, 15 January 2001, 20 September 2004); *New Straits Times* (1 January 1997; 31 December 1997, 2 July 1999); *Malay Mail* (20 December 1997).

and actual ridership, these overoptimistic estimates may still have been insufficient for a viable internal financial rate of return (Table 5.06).

The internal rate of return was 14–16 per cent for STAR and 11 per cent for PUTRA. However, STAR's high debt–equity ratio of 4.8:1 and low farebox ratio of 0.44 meant that it was unable to service its loan and meet operating expenditure (Halcrow Consultants 1999; *The Edge*, 19 July 1999). The company began losing money upon commencing commercial operations in December 1996, and was unable to repay the interest on its RM2.1 billion in bank loans and RM685 million in government support loans since it started operations[20] (*The Edge*, 17 April 2001) (see Table 5.07). Three months after the start of Phase 1, STAR looked into restructuring its debt and subsequently requested assistance from the state Corporate Debt Restructuring Committee (CDRC). STAR was taken over by Danaharta (the state asset management company) on 1 January 2002, and issued a court order to wind

*Table 5.06* Kuala Lumpur LRT: Daily ridership estimates and actual numbers needed

| *Operator (year)* | *Estimated* | *Needed* | *Shortage* |
|---|---|---|---|
| STAR (2000) | 200,507 | 356,185 | 155,678 |
| STAR (2010) | 255,108 | 482,666 | 227,558 |
| PUTRA (2000) | 162,126 | 374,533 | 212,407 |
| PUTRA (2010) | 227,625 | 554,557 | 326,932 |
| KL Monorail (2000) | 99,555 | 102,545 | 2,990 |
| KL Monorail (2010) | 195,011 | 200,862 | 5,851 |

*Source:* Adapted from JICA 1998b.

*Table 5.07* STAR: Profit and loss (RM million)

| | *1993* | *1994* | *1995* | *1996* | *1997* | *1998* | *1999* | *2000* |
|---|---|---|---|---|---|---|---|---|
| Turnover | — | — | — | 1,709.0 | 34.7 | 35.2 | 40.0 | 0 |
| Operating revenue | — | — | — | — | — | — | — | 59.2 |
| Profit/(loss) before tax | 914.0 | 2,269.0 | (5,181.5) | (14,957.0) | (75.5) | (134.4) | (245.9) | (236.6) |

*Source:* Adapted from Companies Commission of Malaysia.

up on 17 May 2002. The company had assets worth RM3.1 billion and debts of RM3.6 billion.

PUTRA expected to recover the RM4.35 billion cost of System 2 in 21 years from operations alone. However, its performance was similarly affected by its debt load and low farebox ratio of 0.22 (Halcrow Consultants 1999). PUTRA's revenues were almost 30 per cent lower than STAR's, despite operating a more lucrative route, while its operating costs were 73 per cent higher, resulting in an operating loss 164 per cent higher than STAR's. Failure to reach its projected ridership reduced PUTRA's ability to service its debt obligations, putting it under financial stress as soon as operations commenced (Ratings Agency Malaysia, cited in *The Edge*, 13 July 1998) (see Table 5.08). In November 1999, PUTRA announced it was defaulting on interest payments to service its US$526 million construction loan and subsequently requested CDRC assistance.[21]

KL Monorail expected to become profitable by 2007 with a projected average annual net profit of RM82 million (RM561 million revenue) for 2007–10, increasing to RM1.66 billion (RM3.03 billion revenue) for 2011–20, RM3.69 billion (RM5.72 billion revenue) for 2021–30, and RM4.41 billion (RM6.18 billion revenue) for 2031–40 (*The Edge*, 21 April 2003). Earlier projections and actual results suggest that this is unlikely and the company recorded increasing losses (Table 5.09), with its commercial viability dependent on the approval of a debt-restructuring proposal, further loans and operational profits.[22] However, according to the company's auditors, 'there is uncertainty on the ability of [KL Monorail] to achieve profitable operations in the foreseeable future'.[23]

*Table 5.08* PUTRA: Profit and loss (RM million)

| | *1999* | *2000* | *2001* |
|---|---|---|---|
| Turnover | 6.5 | 43.1 | 71.3 |
| Operating revenue | | | 71.3 |
| Operating costs | 45.5 | (80.4) | (115.5) |
| Profit/(loss) before tax | (38.8) | (126.8) | (614.6) |

*Source:* Adapted from Companies Commission of Malaysia.

*Table 5.09* KL Monorail: Profit and loss (RM '000)

| | *1997* | *1998* | *1999* | *2000* | *2001* | *2004* | *2005*** | *2006*** |
|---|---|---|---|---|---|---|---|---|
| Projected* revenue | — | — | — | — | — | 36,000.0 | 70,000.0 | 105,000.0 |
| Turnover/ revenue | — | — | — | — | 734.9 | 15,080.0 | 32,535.0 | 38,618.0 |
| Projected* profit/(loss) | | | | | | (42,000.0) | (37,000.0) | (8,000.0) |
| Profit/(loss) before tax | (43.2) | (227.6) | 13.9 | 121.1 | 409.9 | (46,240.0) | (75,936.0) | (80,646.0) |

*Source*. Adapted from Companies Commission of Malaysia; * *The Edge*, 21 April 2003; ** KL Infrastructure Group (2006).

### *Traffic volume*

The daily traffic volume in Kuala Lumpur was expected to be reduced by a minimum of 25 per cent by the end of 1999 when all the traffic mitigation factors were in place. These included the LRT system, high-occupancy vehicle lanes, a review of parking charges, KTMB commuter trains and the amalgamation of eight bus companies into two. However, unlike Singapore which has the capacity to monitor and track traffic growth, assessing any reduction in traffic volume in Kuala Lumpur, especially attributable to the LRT system, is difficult. Nonetheless, the number of registered vehicles in the city clearly indicates increasing car ownership, while declining average speeds over the past 10 years suggests increasing traffic congestion, even four years after the commencement of LRT operations (JICA 1998). This is supported by ongoing media reports and regular government-commissioned studies on traffic congestion, with traffic conditions expected to remain susceptible to chronic congestion in the foreseeable future without drastic measures (*Business Times*, 5 October 1998). The LRT system thus did not facilitate a modal shift in transport use, although this also depended on an integrated public transport network and the implementation of complementary policies. It is the failure of the government to implement these measures which we now turn to.

## Problems

The Malaysian government was aware of the need for an integrated and coordinated public transport system. Its failure to implement this (and the traffic demand management methods discussed above), unlike Singapore, reveals the lack of institutional and political capacity. However, it is the government's political failure that is most striking, and the main reason why privatization failed. The failure of the LRT occurred on two levels. First, the government failed to ensure that the project and privatization were commercially viable (i.e. ex ante failure). This was partly related to information problems, although the evidence on construction costs indicates that the privatization was very likely driven by short-term interests in search of construction rents rather than operational profit. Underlying this were patron–client networks that shaped the choice of project (i.e. infrastructure construction) and how this was allocated.

Second, having committed to the project, the government failed to then implement the necessary policies to maximize the LRT's commercial viability, despite awareness of the problems and solutions. There is clear evidence of this ex post failure to correct mistakes. The government could not plan the route optimally because it was unable to override commercial interests who refused access to space for stations to be built. It was unable to force the operators of Systems 1 and 2 to integrate their routes and provide common stations and ticketing systems. It failed to merge bus companies and prevent bus operators from plying LRT routes. It could not regulate parking fares or introduce a 'congestion' charge necessary to encourage a modal shift from private to public transport. And it was unable to pass the necessary legislation to centralize transport planning and authority.

### *Ex ante failure*

The privatization of the LRT system could have proceeded for several reasons. The government could have believed that the project was viable given the international consensus in favour of privatization, and lobbying by foreign and local commercial interests. Failure here could have then been due to the government lacking the necessary information to make the correct decision. Conversely, privatization also potentially offered opportunities for monopoly rents from construction to parties close to the political leadership and would have been partly politically motivated. In this case, ex ante failure would have been related to political considerations which constrained the government's decision. The concessions for Systems 2 and 3 were awarded, without open tender, to individuals closely linked to segments of the political leadership, and the nature of the project was consistent with Malaysia's pattern of privatization, focusing on infrastructure construction. (System 1 remained state-owned.)

By awarding the concessions for construction and operations to the same company in each case, the government may have also sought to ensure the project was self-financing. However, this led to a moral hazard problem, where profits could be made either up front (from construction) or spread through the concession period (in the form of operating surpluses). From our previous discussion, we have seen that the project was flawed, based on unrealistic passenger projections which were arguably used to secure project approval (and financing). This created a large and potentially unpayable debt burden and led to a moral hazard problem where short-term profits from construction became more attractive, particularly as there was no chance of ever recouping costs let alone making profits (see Halcrow Consultants 1999). The long concession period also reduced risks and incentives as businesses do not plan 30 to 60 years ahead (Fayard 1999; Halcrow Consultants 1999).

The evidence suggests that the concessionaires may not have been interested in actual operations, and may have expected state assistance given the importance of the project. TaylorWoodrow, as a construction company, was arguably more interested in the construction rather than operations of System 1, and reduced its stake in STAR upon securing the concession (despite government efforts to get it to increase its equity share),[24] leaving operations to state agencies which controlled the consortium. PUTRA on the other hand, was owned by Renong, UMNO's holding company, and was relieved of the project and its debts when the government renationalized the LRT system. KL Monorail was able to reduce its capital commitment and extend its concession period without penalties. The company continued to operate the monorail but at a loss and with substantial government loans.

The higher cost of construction for all three projects when compared with similar systems in Singapore and Manila suggests that privatization offered the possibility of monopoly rents during construction. The large discrepancies between projected and actual ridership figures further suggest that inflated forecasts served to secure project approval and financing, and that the privatization of the LRT system was in fact not commercially viable without much larger subsidies (see *The Edge*, 13 July 1998). While there is a strong tendency for rail costs to be underestimated (e.g. see Flyvbjerg *et al.* 2002), project approval can also be secured where inflated construction costs are disguised by over-optimistic revenue forecasts. The close relationship between patron and client could also explain why the government did not discipline the operator of System 3 (KL Monorail) despite its failure to carry out the agreed capital investment or meet deadlines. The government also paid more for System 2 (which was owned by an UMNO-related company) than System 1 (state-owned) despite the former having a much higher debt.

### *Ex post failure*

Having failed to determine that the privatization was viable before proceeding, the government more crucially failed to then promote commercial viability. The implementation of any ex post policies would have differential benefits and costs, and successful implementation would require state capacity to override attempts by potential losers to veto the suggested changes. These failures could have partly been due to institutional fragmentation, but from media reports we have seen that the government was aware of the problems affecting the performance of the LRT and sought to address these by: 1, physically integrating the LRT system; 2, streamlining bus operations and integrating the public transport system; and 3, managing traffic. However, its ability to implement the necessary policies here was constrained by private sector obstructionism, including the refusal of the LRT operators to cooperate, and by institutional fragmentation. Evidence of ex post failure can be found in the government's inability to integrate the LRT system, streamline bus operations and reduce the use of cars. This suggests that the failure was more clearly due to the government's lack of (ex post) political capacity to enforce policy, and especially to override political resistance.

### *Failure to integrate the system*

Successful LRT operations depended on government policies to promote integration between the different LRT lines. This included route alignment, access to stations, fare structure and common ticketing, and physical interface. The government identified corridors and mapped out areas that needed coverage, but failed to plan and integrate the individual LRT lines, and the LRT system as part of the wider public transport network. Crucial decisions were left to the individual concessionaires[25] and there was no requirement or even encouragement for the operators to work together (Halcrow Consultants 1999). As a result, route alignment and station locations were not optimal, fares and ticketing were not standardized, physical interface between separate lines was poor, and the public transport network as a whole was not integrated. All these factors contributed to low ridership.

Route alignment was compromised by space and cost constraints, with System 1 built on existing old rail tracks rather than through densely populated areas,[26] resulting in lower passenger numbers compared to System 2. System 2 was delayed by land acquisition problems and many of its stations were isolated. Part of its route was affected by the refusal of the developer of Mid-Valley Mega Mall, a major shopping centre, to accommodate a station. Similarly, KL Monorail's final station had to be built some 150 m from the main rail hub connecting all three LRT lines with the commuter rail network, because the owners of the adjacent land refused access.[27]

Poor physical integration was compounded by the different concession and construction periods, and the lack of cooperation among concessionaires and other commercial interests. Both STAR and PUTRA proceeded independently and refused to cooperate in terms of common stations and ticketing. In the end, the government had to allow the common stations to be constructed independently, physically connecting these later.[28] The proposed consolidation of the ticketing and fares systems, joint maintenance of facilities and the placing of all operators under one company, made little headway as operators would not cooperate, and the government was unable to enforce this. According to STAR CEO Zainal Abdul Ghani, operators were 'pulling in different directions' due to a failure to understand their respective roles in 'the bigger picture' (*The Edge*, December 2001). An example of this was KL Monorail's fares which were more expensive than LRT fares even though the monorail was to function as a 'downtown people mover' (see City Hall Kuala Lumpur, undated). This further undermined cumulative system effects.[29]

*Failure to streamline bus operations*

As rail coverage is naturally limited to a catchment area of 600-metre radius, the LRT system must rely partly on an efficient feeder bus service to increase ridership. Stations were serviced by a flat fare (RM0.50) feeder bus with a projected 15-minute (peak) and 20-minute (off-peak) interval. However, the service proved unreliable and was unprofitable for the contracted bus companies, leading to its eventual discontinuation and takeover by the LRT operators themselves.[30]

The LRT system also needed an efficient and complementary bus service which functioned as a dispersal system. However, the existing public transport system was characterized by poor integration between modes and the absence of a coherent network, with parallel bus services competing directly against LRT routes rather than acting as feeder services to LRT stations (Halcrow Consultants 1999). Buses also operated on flat fares (which were tightly regulated) compared to distance-based fares on the LRT, making it much cheaper to travel by bus than by LRT.

The government sought to streamline and integrate bus operations, and restructure fares to encourage interchange into the LRT system. However, its proposed merger of the 14 bus companies was delayed because of the political influence of bus company owners.[31] Even after the government finally got the majority of bus companies to merge into two consortiums (inner and outer city), their commercial viability was undermined by the continued operations of independent bus operators plying parallel routes amounting to an estimated 30 per cent of total passenger kilometres (Halcrow Consultants 1999).

*Failure to reduce car use*

Passenger numbers on the LRT largely depended on government policies to induce a modal shift from private to public transport use, and original demand forecasts for the LRT were based on government and DBKL plans to 'aggressively' pursue certain policies to promote the use of public transport.[32] Discussions on restricting cars centred on introducing area road pricing (ARP, a form of 'congestion' charge), promoting high-occupancy vehicles (HOVs), restricting parking spaces and reviewing parking charges. However, the government was unable to introduce the necessary legislation, relying instead on cooperation from the public and businesses. As a result, these measures were never implemented, with government policies largely incoherent and characterized by institutional fragmentation. The voluntary car pooling campaign failed repeatedly as the government was unwilling or unable to enforce its HOV policy, first mooted in 1994. Similarly, the introduction of ARP was not implemented despite being raised as early as 1991.[33] This was expected to restrict car trips to 1997 levels, increase the public transport share of daily passenger trips to 24.2 per cent (2000), 25.4 per cent (2010) and 28.9 per cent (2020), and improve the LRT operators' financial performance (although these figures were based on higher than actual ridership) (Rosli and Ooi 1993; JICA 1998b).

To work, ARP needed to be complemented by increased parking charges in the city and urban development control, as well as traffic guidance systems (JICA 1998b). The government sought to introduce these measures by phasing out all roadside parking to discourage single-occupancy vehicles (1994 and 1996), increasing parking fees in the city centre (1995, 1996, 1997) and reducing parking areas, including freezing approvals for new high-rise buildings in the city centre and reducing cheap or free parking spaces in existing and new buildings. However, the government found it difficult to implement these due to existing local by-laws[34] and opposition by the building and national car industries, parking operators, businesses and interest groups (see *Business Times*, 1 May 1997, 17 January 2001; *New Straits Times*, 26 January 1998, 17 January 2001). The government was even unable to promote 'park and ride' facilities at LRT stations as it was more lucrative for car park operators to be located in the city.

Instead, conflicting solutions were often proposed, partly driven by a preference for road construction that also characterized much of Malaysia's privatization programme. Traffic congestion also increased in the absence of urban development control, particularly as new housing and commercial projects were developed without accompanying public transport infrastructure. In the absence of urban planning, the government's three-pronged public transport strategy for Kuala Lumpur involving the bus, the LRT and commuter rail services was seen to be insufficient to offset the additional demand on the transport system generated by new commercial developments in the city.[35]

### *Institutional fragmentation*

Incoherent and conflicting transport policies were also the result of institutional fragmentation. In 1993, urban transport policy in Kuala Lumpur involved 10 ministries, 12 federal agencies and seven local agencies overseeing planning, financing, implementation, fares, operations, regulation and enforcement. The absence of a single agency responsible for administering all aspects of transportation comprehensively resulted in delays in the decision-making process.[36] Despite proposals for a single body with overall responsibility for transport policy in 1984 and 1995, this was never established.[37] The absence of a central transport authority and laws also complicated the introduction of ARP as it was unclear who would receive revenues collected.[38] Instead, institutional changes after 1986 increased the powers of the EPU but without really centralizing authority.

In 1986, the Ministry of Transport was responsible for formulating policies relating to land, sea and air transport, and for coordinating all planning activities as well as ensuring the implementation of development programmes and projects of the departments and statutory bodies under it. The Ministry of Public Enterprises through the Road Transport Licensing Board (LPPJ) determined policies related to applications for operating licences, fares, routes, etc. The EPU had one representative out of the seven members on the LPPJ council. The Ministry of Works was responsible for infrastructure construction, improvement and maintenance. This was undertaken through the Planning Research Development Unit (BPPP – planning of federal roads), state Public Works Department (JKR – planning of state roads), and Malaysian Highway Authority (LLM – planning of toll expressways). Proposals for public transport projects in the Klang Valley could also originate from the local (Selangor) state government, Ministry of the Federal Territory, and DBKL. Within Kuala Lumpur, DBKL also shared traffic control and surveillance responsibilities with the Road Transport Department (JPJ).

Authority for the regulation of the development and operation of public road transport (granted by Part V of the Road Transport Ordinance [RTO] 1958 Amended) provides JPJ and the Ministry of Transport with the task of administration and enforcement of the RTO and subsidiary legislation so as to ensure road safety in the regulation and control of commercial transport use. However, overall implementation of the RTO also comes under the purview of the LPPJ, traffic branch of the police, the Ministry of Environment, JKR and local government authorities. Crucially, neither the Ministry of Transport nor the Ministry of Public Enterprises were given the outright responsibility for assuring that public transport services were adequate. Furthermore, while the roles of LPPJ and JPJ are separate, this division of authority was not always efficient. While public road transport was controlled by LPPJ and JPJ, rail was directly regulated by the respective department under the Ministry of Transport, i.e. Malayan Railways (KTMB), which was the sole operator of railway services in the Klang Valley and its management was under the jurisdiction of the Railway Ordinance 1948.

By 1994, planning for all modes of transport including traffic control was the responsibility of the EPU. Local governments carried out planning, design, construction and maintenance of smaller projects, and implementation of general plans and big projects (e.g. railways) already determined and financed by the federal government. The Ministry of Transport oversaw all transport modes, the Ministry of Works concentrated on road matters only, and the Ministry of Entrepreneur Development was responsible for buses and taxis.

However, this did not reduce overlap and duplication, leading to some conflicting policies or programmes[39] with a lack of clarity about roles and responsibilities,[40] including which body was responsible for government targets for transport modes quoted by STAR and PUTRA as the basis of their demand forecasts (Halcrow Consultants 1999). The institutional framework for urban rail remained highly fragmented, being divided between the EPU, DBKL and local governments (planning); EPU and MoF (financing); MoT, Department of Rail and Railway Asset Corporation (implementation); Cabinet and EPU (fares); and MoT (regulation) (Halcrow Consultants 1999).

The absence of a central authority was due to the government's lack of political capacity to override the competing interests of various departments. As existing law did not provide sole authority to a single department, departments and ministries were unwilling and under no legal obligation to give up existing powers. This was further complicated by the sharing of portfolios among the ruling coalition's component parties, with no one party willing to give up authority. In this context, DBKL's 1984 proposal for a single transport agency came from one ministry with no authority. Even the MoF's Special Task Force on Public Transportation, formed in 2001 by the federal government in the absence of a central authority, relied on persuasion and networks rather than enforcement.[41]

In contrast, Singapore's urban rail network is financed by the government through the Land Transport Authority (LTA) and run by two companies, based on an initial 10-year license. The Singapore Mass Rapid Transit (SMRT) Corporation (62.3 per cent state-owned) operates two urban rail lines, two light rail services, rail operations and maintenance, and bus and taxi services. The private SBS Transit runs a bus service and one urban and one light rail line. Fares are regulated by the Public Transport Council and integrated by the LTA through an integrated fare system. This integrated operations enabled SMRT to earn an average annual pre-tax profit of S$118 million (1999–2001), with its MRT rail system registering an average annual pre-tax profit of S$113 million (1999–2003) on an average daily ridership of 1.03 million (1999–2003) across four integrated networks (SMRT Corporation 2001–4). The commercial viability of the MRT was due to the government underwriting the cost of infrastructure construction, which allowed the company to operate without the burden of debt servicing. The LTA continues to finance the expansion of the rail network to accommodate passenger growth from new housing developments.

More crucially, the MRT was undertaken as part of an integrated transport policy. But unlike the UK, Malaysia and Thailand, the Singapore government had the political capacity to develop the necessary institutions and policies, supported by relevant laws which it was able to enforce as part of an integrated transport policy covering different modes of transport. Policy was implemented through the LTA which had the regulatory powers to: plan, design, construct, manage and maintain roads (through the Street Works Act); plan, design, construct, manage, operate, maintain and regulate the railway (the Rapid Transit Systems Act); and provide parking places for motor vehicles, and license and regulate the use of parking places (the Parking Places Act). This enabled the government to limit automobile traffic using price mechanisms (auctions or certificate of entitlement, heavy taxes on car ownership, road use and parking charges) and maximize public mobility through the use of public and non-motorized transport and taxis.

## Conclusion

Privatization does not address the considerable financing and system coordination requirements of urban rail systems. The sector is characterized by very high capital costs and low farebox ratios which have made it difficult for operators to finance capital expenditure, cover operating costs and earn a return on investment. In addition, fares often need to be kept low due to the political sensitivity of high fares and thus cannot cover costs. High fares will also potentially reduce passenger numbers. The inability of the private sector to provide affordable fares and at the same time finance capital expansion has necessitated state subsidies. This in turn will require ongoing state intervention to monitor and regulate performance. The state will also need to coordinate capital investment and operations to promote system integration, and to integrate urban rail systems with the wider public transport network in order to improve coverage and hence, passenger numbers.

The main economic objective of the LRT was to improve Kuala Lumpur's public transport network and reduce traffic congestion. Privatization aimed to facilitate the private finance, delivery and operation of the system. While the private sector helped finance the LRT, public funds were central to all three privatizations, contributing between 32 and 78 per cent of financing. In terms of delivery, Systems 1 and 2 were completed on time but System 3 was substantially delayed and its scope considerably reduced. All three projects were more expensive per kilometre than comparable lines in Singapore and Manila, in particular System 3. Fares for Systems 1 and 2 were comparatively low but System 3 had the highest fares per kilometre in the region. The concessionaires of Systems 1 and 2 faced financial difficulties upon commencement of operations and were unable to service interest payments on their loans. System 3, while still privately owned and operated, faces increasing financial difficulties following mounting losses, and its commercial viability will depend on debt restructuring, further loans and operational profits which seem unlikely in the foreseeable future. Finally, the LRT system did not appear to reduce traffic congestion although, as discussed, this was in part related to wider failings in the public transport system and public transport policy.

The privatization of the LRT was characterized by both ex ante and ex post failures in terms of our definitions. Despite the problems inherent in urban rail systems, the privatization proceeded because it was partly motivated by political considerations. These in turn affected decisions related to the type of privatization, resulting in the government's ex ante failure to ensure project viability and preserve incentives. Privatization allowed resources to be allocated to parties close to segments of the political leadership, and the nature of the privatization was consistent with the preferences of local capitalists, centring on infrastructure construction. Rather than underwrite capital costs to allow the private operator to focus on operational efficiency without a debt burden (as is the case in Singapore), the government awarded the concessions for construction and operations to the same operator in each case. This created opportunities for short-term rents from construction but also led to a moral hazard where this became more attractive than long-term profits arising from operational efficiency.

This is supported by the comparative evidence of construction costs in the region. The attractiveness of profits from construction as opposed to operations may also have provided STAR and PUTRA with a strong motivation to complete construction on time. This ex ante failure to properly structure incentives created a huge debt burden resulting in the financial problems of the concessionaires for Systems 1 and 2. This was compounded by revenue projections based on grossly inflated and unrealistic passenger numbers (for all three systems) which were partly based on government policies to promote public transport, but arguably also to secure project approval and financing. As a result, the concessionaires for Systems 1 and 2 were unable to service interest payments on loans.

However, as ex ante decisions were in part constrained by imperfect information and political considerations, the success of the LRT system then depended on the government implementing policies to integrate the public transport network thereby increasing passenger numbers and improving the project's commercial viability. From the evidence, we know that the government was aware of what policies were needed ex post, but was unable to implement these. The government failed to physically integrate the LRT system, streamline bus operations and integrate the public transport system, and restrict cars in the city. It could not enforce conditionalities on the concessionaires, override private-sector recalcitrance and obstructionism, and centralize planning and authority in order to implement a coherent transport policy. Instead, state intervention was marked by institutional fragmentation (itself the outcome of political factors) and the absence of a coherent transport policy. This indicates that the government's ex post failure was due to political, rather than institutional, factors and underlines the importance of the state's political capacity to enforce system integration as the most important condition for successful urban rail operations. This problem is unlikely to be addressed by privatization for the reasons already discussed.

# 6 Perverse incentives

## Malaysia Airlines

Privatization offers the possibility of financing an airline's capital expansion and improving efficiency. However, the airline industry is characterized by substantial and increasing capital costs, low profit margins, and periodic downturns. This has led to regular bankruptcies and mergers, and necessitated state subsidies and bail-outs because of the economic cost of failure. In this context, the benefits of private ownership are less clear cut as it does not necessarily provide a more credible promise for the state not to intervene. Furthermore, the substantial capital costs are often beyond the financial capacity of the private sector, necessitating some form of state financial assistance or implicit guarantee of commercial loans as has been the case historically. This potentially undermines incentives as risks are shared. Furthermore, national airlines are prestigious and usually created and maintained for political reasons. This introduces a moral hazard where the government has a vested interest in the viability of the airline, and privatization does not necessarily promote a more 'arm's length' relationship between government and enterprise in this case.

The privatization of Malaysia Airlines[1] (MAS) aimed to help finance the airline's expansion plans. However, privatization was arguably not 'feasible' in terms of 'attractiveness to the private sector' given the significant industry challenges, MAS's low profitability and institutional constraints arising from its role as national carrier. It was also not feasible for the government because the substantial capital costs involved were prohibitive for any potential private investor. Why then did privatization proceed? On the one hand, it appeared to have been motivated by political considerations related to state efforts to promote Malay entrepreneurs. The candidate was also closely associated with the political leadership, in particular Finance Minister Daim Zainudin, suggesting that the privatization decision was shaped by political factors related to intra-party rivalry within UMNO.

On the other hand, recent evidence suggests that the sale may have been related to government attempts to cover substantial foreign exchange losses by Bank Negara Malaysia (BNM), the central bank, by raising much needed funds on the private financial markets.[2] According to the owner, he was 'instructed' to purchase a controlling stake in MAS in the 'national interest' (see *The Sun*, 6 July 2006). This would partly explain why MAS was sold at RM8 per share when this was only worth RM3.50, with commercial banks likely to have been 'instructed' to lend the money.[3] It may also explain why the government paid RM8 per share upon renationalization when shares were worth only RM3.80, and despite already having a controlling stake in the airline.

In either scenario, the outcome was the same. Ex ante failure to properly structure incentives affected performance. Privatization improved productivity in certain areas, but MAS remained inefficient by regional standards. This ongoing inefficiency compared to its regional competitors, and its debt burden, had a negative impact on the airline's financial performance, and the government was forced to intervene when the new owner, faced with mounting company and personal debts, was unable to continue financing the airline. While it remains unclear what actually motivated privatization, the central issue is why the government, despite being aware, was unable to address problems that arose from ex ante failures to properly structure incentives.

Regardless of whether the candidate was the actual owner or merely a nominee or agent of the government, privatization did not significantly change the institutional relationship between the airline and the state. Management decisions were generally constrained by the state, and the government continued to have a say in major decisions, although the new owner appeared to have some autonomy over certain decisions (including those related to the airline's contracts with third party companies). As an agent, the owner would have had few incentives to improve efficiency. The purchase structure of the airline and subsequent fleet expansion also placed a huge debt burden on the new owner which was unsustainable and acted as a further disincentive, particularly given the problems inherent in the airline industry. These factors, independently or in combination, arguably created perverse incentives for the pursuit of short-term profits (in this case, through the third-party purchase of aircraft and the creation of separate cargo and catering divisions)[4] (e.g. see *New Straits Times*, 25 February 2002).

The near bankruptcy and subsequent renationalization of MAS thus had a series of contributing factors that can be classified as ex ante and ex post failures of government. In the former category, the choice of candidate was poor (regardless of government motivation), and the government failed to ensure that the financial structure of the privatization was viable, or account for the substantial capital demands and cyclical nature of the industry. In the latter category, it failed to correct this ex ante failure, including addressing problems related to previous government policies (which affected MAS) and monitoring and disciplining the new owner, despite being aware of problems fairly early on. Here, successful privatization would have required that the government structure the purchase of the airline viably, or implement corrective measures by providing operational subsidies (especially as domestic fares were regulated), monitor performance and enforce conditionality.

Both types of failures were in part related to the nature of resource allocation through patron–client networks, and the legacy of previous state capital accumulation strategies discussed in Chapter 3. The choice of candidate was consistent with ongoing state attempts to create a class of Malay industrialists who were also closely associated with (and loyal to) segments of the political leadership. However, the new owner did not have the financial and managerial capacity, having based his corporate expansion on the takeover of existing profitable enterprises through his political connections (e.g. see Gomez and Jomo 1997). This compromised his ability to finance and run the airline. His close association with the political leadership and the national importance of the airline also led to a moral hazard, where the government was unlikely to allow it to fail, but was also unable to intervene earlier to enforce discipline (or replace the owner) and prevent the airline's financial deterioration.

This chapter is structured as follows. The next section will provide a discussion of the challenges faced by the airline industry, how privatization addresses these, and the challenges posed specifically by MAS (including government objectives). This is followed with an overview of MAS, its privatization and renationalization. We then evaluate the operational and financial performance of MAS in relation to its immediate regional competitors, accounting for the effects of the Asian financial crisis. The following section identifies the main problems in terms of ex ante and ex post failures. The final section summarizes the main findings and concludes.

## Challenges

The aim of privatizing airlines is to finance capital expansion and enhance operational efficiency. However, the airline industry is characterized by low profit margins, high indebtedness, rising capital costs and overcapacity, with state subsidies and bail-outs common features, especially in recent years. The airline business model is also highly risky, being capital-intensive and highly leveraged, with a high controlling premium of around 30 per cent. Profitability is cyclical, with high profits attracting excessive entry and fare competition, followed by a period of losses and restructuring. Airlines thus need high margins and a guaranteed uptake (passenger load), but demand is susceptible to the industry's cyclical nature and external shocks, resulting in problems if not failures.

Historically, airlines have only been able to make profits on their operations in favourable circumstances and the industry has only been marginally profitable between 1960 and 1990 (Davies 1964; Doganis 1991). Even in 1984–89, the most successful period in airline history, operating profit only averaged about 4–6 per cent (at its peak), and dropped to 1–2 per cent after interest and non-operating items were included (Doganis 1991). Operating margins were further reduced after taking into account operating revenues, expenses, profit and loss. High capital costs and low profit margins led to airline debt. The significant difference between operating results and profits after tax

*Table 6.01* International airlines: Revenue and expenditure, 1990–1999 (current US$ million)

| | *Total operating revenue* | *Total operating expenditure* | *Operating result* | *Operating result/ operating revenue* | *Profit after tax* | *Profit/ operating revenue* | *Operating revenue/ operating expenditure* |
|---|---|---|---|---|---|---|---|
| 1990 | 199,500 | 201,000 | (1,500) | (0.8) | (4,500) | (2.3) | 99.3 |
| 1991 | 205,500 | 201,100 | 4,400 | 2.1 | (3,500) | (1.7) | 102.2 |
| 1992 | 217,800 | 219,600 | (1,800) | (0.8) | (7,900) | (3.6) | 99.2 |
| 1993 | 226,000 | 223,700 | 2,300 | 1.0 | (4,400) | (1.9) | 101.0 |
| 1994 | 247,400 | 239,000 | 8,400 | 3.4 | (100) | (0.0) | 103.5 |
| 1995 | 267,000 | 253,500 | 13,500 | 5.1 | 4,500 | 1.7 | 105.3 |
| 1996 | 282,500 | 270,200 | 12,300 | 4.4 | 5,300 | 1.9 | 104.6 |
| 1997 | 291,000 | 274,700 | 16,300 | 5.6 | 8,550 | 2.9 | 105.9 |
| 1998 | 295,500 | 279,600 | 15,900 | 5.4 | 8,200 | 2.8 | 105.7 |
| 1999 | 306,500 | 294,000 | 12,500 | 4.1 | 8,500 | 2.8 | 104.3 |

*Source:* Adapted from ICAO (1992–99).
*Note:* ( ) = loss.

for the industry as a whole in 1990–99 indicates a huge non-operating (fixed) cost, i.e. aircraft purchases (Table 6.01). Profit was only 2.9 per cent of operating revenue in the best year (1997), and averaged 0.26 per cent for the whole period.

While the financial performance of Asia Pacific airlines was generally better than the industry average, apart from 1997–98, both operating results and profits as a percentage of operating revenue were still very low, at 5.4 and 3.1 per cent respectively, for the most profitable period in 1995 (Table 6.02).

*Table 6.02* Asia Pacific airlines: Revenue and expenditure, 1990–1999 (current US$ million)

| | *Total operating revenue* | *Total operating expenditure* | *Operating result* | *Operating result/ operating revenue* | *Profit after tax* | *Profit/ operating revenue* | *Operating revenue/ operating expenditure* |
|---|---|---|---|---|---|---|---|
| 1990 | 38,800 | 37,200 | 1,600 | 4.1 | 1,700 | 4.4 | 104.3 |
| 1991 | n/a | n/a | n/a | n/a | n/a | n/a | n/a |
| 1992 | 47,200 | 45,650 | 1,550 | 3.3 | 1,000 | 2.1 | 103.4 |
| 1993 | 52,400 | 51,200 | 1,200 | 2.3 | 50 | 0.1 | 102.3 |
| 1994 | 61,000 | 58,300 | 2,700 | 4.4 | 1,600 | 2.6 | 104.6 |
| 1995 | 69,000 | 65,300 | 3,700 | 5.4 | 2,150 | 3.1 | 105.7 |
| 1996 | 68,000 | 64,850 | 3,150 | 4.6 | 1,700 | 2.5 | 104.9 |
| 1997 | 65,800 | 63,100 | 2,700 | 4.1 | (750) | (1.2) | 104.3 |
| 1998 | 60,180 | 58,300 | 1,880 | 3.1 | 320 | 0.5 | 103.2 |
| 1999 | 64,800 | 61,800 | 3,000 | 4.6 | 1,900 | | 104.9 |

*Source:* Adapted from ICAO (1992–99).
*Note:* ( ) = loss.

The industry is further characterized by short-run marginal costs close to zero, encouraging airlines to sell remaining seats at virtually any price above the very low marginal cost of carrying an additional passenger. Price instability is aggravated by the tendency of new entrants to aggressively try to capture market share, and financially weak or subsidized (often national) carriers to generate sufficient cash flow by undercutting existing tariffs (Doganis 1991). The high cost of exit has also jeopardized the profits of efficient airlines as loss-making or inefficient airlines continue to operate with substantial subsidies. Besides direct payments, indirect government support may involve rescheduling debts, cross-subsidies, as well as undercutting existing fares in order to generate sufficient cash flow to meet daily payments (Doganis 1991). Subsidies have been made available either as a support for an adolescent industry, or for political and prestige reasons (Davies 1964).

Although new technology reduced operating costs per capacity tonne-kilometre, it also drastically raised capital costs. The cost of a new aircraft increased from US$2 million (for a 200-seater Boeing 707 or 250-seater Douglas DC-8 in the mid-1950s) to US$45 million (for a 265-seater Airbus A310 in 1984) and US$60 million (for the same plane in 1990). At least three European airlines suffered losses of around £8 million each in 1961 as a result of plane purchases, while US airlines merged as a means to survive (Davies 1964). Nonetheless, airlines continued to purchase new aircraft as a result of easier access to financing, facilitated by manufacturers and leasing companies, and competitive pressures, despite the industry performing poorly. The result was high levels of indebtedness among many major airlines by the early 1980s.

High capital expenditure increased the debt–equity ratios and interest repayments. A large part of current revenues is needed to finance interest payments on accumulated debts. After paying interest, International Air Transport Association (IATA) member airlines collectively lost US$5.65 billion in 1980–82 (Doganis 1991). Interest charges for the world's airlines totalled around US$4.0–4.5 billion in 1987. (To finance the estimated US$400 billion invested globally on aircraft between 1990 and 2000, airlines would have needed an operating profit before interest of 6 per cent a year which had not been achieved since 1969.) Additional earnings, not leverage alone, are key to financing the industry's needs (Mandell 1979). The growing reliance on external finance, rather than self-financing or equity capital, also contributed to very high debt–equity ratios, with many airlines under-capitalized and needing capital injections to manage interest payments and order new aircraft without bankrupting themselves (Doganis 1991).

The tendency of airlines to embark on massive fleet expansions has created overcapacity in times of sharply falling profit margins, particularly with newer, higher-capacity and faster aircraft. Airlines have historically expanded their fleets, which increased aircraft capacity without corresponding growth in passenger traffic (Davies 1964). This is largely due to the time lag between ordering (when growth rates are high) and receiving new aircraft, and the inability of airline managements to match supply (which they have considerable control over) with demand (which they have relatively little control over) (Doganis 1991). The best performing airlines tend to purchase new fleets counter-cyclically.

Airlines also have little control over externally determined input costs such as prevailing wage levels, aviation fuel prices and (airport) user charges. In particular, they are very sensitive to exogenous factors, which affect cost (e.g. aviation fuel prices) and demand (i.e. global economic conditions), with the best airlines implementing fuel price hedging policies to insulate against price volatility. Dramatic increases in fuel prices in 1978 in the face of stagnating demand and falling yields led to the 1979–83 industry crisis, while the market turnaround after 1986 was essentially due to a fall in the real price of aviation fuel and a sudden increase in demand for air services (Doganis 1991). More recently, the 1997–98 Asian financial crisis, events post-11 September 2001, and the outbreak of the SARS epidemic in 2002–3 in East Asia resulted in heavy losses for Asia Pacific airlines.

Additionally, MAS had specific problems related to historical factors, operational inefficiency and institutional constraints. Following the split with Singapore International Airlines (SIA) in 1972, SIA inherited most of the lucrative international routes and was able to develop new routes because of Singapore's position as an international hub while MAS focused on domestic routes and was left with loss-making domestic operations, no international routes, an ill-equipped fleet, and a 'less than decent' home airport (*The Star*, 10 June 1993; *The Edge*, 12 November 2000). While MAS operated in a monopolistic domestic market, it was not able to determine domestic fares due to government regulation which sought to promote national integration,[5] and no domestic fare increases were allowed between 1983 and 1990. As a result, international revenues largely subsidized the domestic sector (which provided only a quarter of total revenue in 1985 despite accounting for almost half of passenger trips).

Although MAS had seemed profitable since 1982, profits were modest and in part due to accounting practices and the sale of assets. For example, increasing the residual value of assets from 10 to 20 per cent reduced depreciation expenditure,[6] allowing MAS to show a RM16.1 million profit, as opposed to a RM65 million loss, for 1994, while the sale of seven aircraft (totalling RM337.1 million) contributed to the bulk of earnings in 1993 (*New Straits Times*, 2 June 1994). Although gains from sales are usually treated as operating profit, excluding aircraft sale figures provides a better measure of performance of airline-service operations. MAS's operating profit from 1990 to 1994 (before privatization) compared poorly with SIA and Cathay Pacific, and its paid-up capital was also well below the major airlines in the region (Malaysia Airlines 1992b).

## Background

The privatization of MAS was partly to overcome government financial constraints and meet the airline's capital expansion plans in 1984 (which would have otherwise required MAS to generate an unrealistic profit of US$30 million a year) (Doganis 1991). Partial divestiture was seen as an attractive solution to meet the airline's capital investment needs in the absence of additional equity capital from the government, and MAS was corporatized[7] in 1985 (Doganis 1991). Some equity was sold to the public and the Brunei government in September 1985 for RM180 million, but the Malaysian government retained a significant interest through the Ministry of Finance (MoF) (Gomez and Jomo 1997). The airline was publicly listed on 16 December 1985. In 1988, Bank Negara Malaysia (BNM), the central bank, acquired a 32 per cent stake in MAS from the MoF.

While divestiture of MAS shares[8] (based on a 1985 consultant's proposal) reduced the government's share from 90 to 42 per cent by November 1986, it did not really change the institutional relationship between MAS and the government (Jones and Fadil 1992). The creation of a 'golden share' allowed the government to retain control by having the right to appoint three directors, ensure repayment of capital paid up on the special share in priority over any other shareholder in the event of the company winding-up, and require MAS to redeem the special share at par at any time (Malaysia Airlines 1995). However, the government would stop guaranteeing MAS loans and credit facilities.

In December 1993, the government announced that Malaysian Helicopter Services (MHS), a publicly listed company controlled by Tajudin Ramli, would acquire the 32 per cent stake in MAS from BNM for RM1.79 billion (or RM8 per share when MAS shares were trading for RM3.50).[9] There was no open bidding, and according to Tajudin in a document filed in court in 2006, the actual sale was made to his private company, RZ Equities Sdn Bhd, to expedite the sale and bypass time-consuming approvals which MHS, as a publicly listed company, would have had to obtain; this was necessary to offset large foreign exchange losses incurred by BNM (estimated at RM16–RM32 billion) when it speculated on the sterling in 1994 (see *The Sun*, 6 July 2006).

However, rather than cash, the MAS acquisition was to involve a share swap, with BNM obtaining 112 million new RM1 MHS shares, issued at RM16 each (Gomez and Jomo 1997). After a fall in share prices, the share swap proposal involving MAS and MHS was rescinded, and RZ Equities acquired a 32 per cent stake (224 million shares) in MAS for RM1.79 billion in June 1994 (Gomez and Jomo 1997). MHS was given a one-year call option to acquire RZ Equities from Tajudin and did so in August 1994. MHS later changed its name to Naluri. Tajudin assumed control of MAS on 6 August 1994. The purchase was entirely financed by bank loans, the largest in the country, with Tajudin pledging most of his shares in Naluri and TRI and his other interests as security for the syndicated loan. With the sale, Tajudin (through DCB Merchant Nominees (Tempatan) Sdn Bhd) owned 32 per cent of MAS, while the government owned 27.2 per cent[10] and retained a 'golden share' through the MoF.

After successive losses and mounting debts between 1998 and 2000, Tajudin admitted he could no longer finance MAS. The government confirmed on 6 November 2000, after two years of speculation, that it was involved in talks to buy Tajudin's stake in MAS, and approved, in principle, the purchase of MAS on 23 November 2000 (*Asian Wall Street Journal*, 24 November 2000). On 20 December 2000, Tajudin signed an agreement to sell his share in MAS back to the MoF for RM1.79 billion, or RM8 per share, when MAS shares were trading for around RM3.80. The government was reported to have agreed on the price considering the net tangible assets of MAS and the premium for a controlling stake (*New Straits Times*, 21 December 2000) even though it paid less to the Brunei government and already owned 49.2 per cent of MAS by 12 December 2000 through various agencies.[11]

## Performance

Privatization here will be taken to refer to the period after the sale of a controlling stake to Tajudin in December 1993 as the government continued to be the majority shareholder after corporatization in 1985. MAS's performance can be measured in terms of operational efficiency (revex ratio, productivity, passenger load factor, passenger yield) and financial performance (leverage, liquidity and profitability). Although both sets of indicators were affected by the 1997–98 Asian financial crisis, we can isolate external factors in assessing the performance of MAS before and after privatization in two ways.

The first is to examine data before the Asian financial crisis, which started in the second half of 1997. As MAS's financial year ends in June, this allows us to consider data covering three years of privatization before the crisis (1994–97), with the three years prior to privatization (1990–93), excluding 1993–94 (which may be viewed as a transition year as privatization was announced at the end of 1993 and Tajudin only assumed control of MAS on 6 August 1994). Although this is a fairly brief period to assess, it does isolate, to a degree, the impact of the Asian financial crisis, and provides some indication of efficiency gains and financial performance.

Secondly, we can reduce the effects of external factors by comparing MAS's average performance in each period (as well as post-1997) with the combined average performance of its main regional competitors (referred to as MAS's 'competitors') – Singapore International Airlines (SIA), Cathay Pacific and Thai Airways. It is also important to examine trends for each of these indicators, and to locate them in the context of overall industry trends. Hence, if MAS exhibited improvements which coincided with general improvements in the industry, then these may not necessarily have been due to management decisions. This is instructive as the seriousness of MAS's financial problems only became obvious after 1997, as its competitors were recovering. This suggests that the causes of its operational and financial problems can be traced to the period before 1997.

MAS's performance is broadly consistent with the trends in the airline industry, particularly the higher than average growth in the Asia Pacific region. The global industry between 1990 and 2000 was characterized by strong growth rates in traffic and passenger kilometres, with the exception of 1991–93 and 1997–98. This growth was highest in the Asia Pacific, which was least affected by the early 1990s slump, but most severely affected by the 1997–98 crisis which began in the second half of 1997. The region, however, started recovering by 1999.

Given the nature of MAS's domestic sector, and the regulation of domestic fares, and in order to facilitate regional airline comparisons, the data mainly focuses on international flights, and as much as possible from the same industry source. (However, it is not possible to separate MAS's international and domestic data in most instances, which means that if the domestic sector was being subsidized by international revenues, the results may be biased. Among MAS's competitors, only Thai Airways operates domestic flights.) As the data has been gathered from the public domain, it is subject to some inconsistencies depending on the source and accounting year, and in the case of MAS financial reports, frequent revisions. As a rule, data from MAS's most recent financial statement will be used for earlier years. Airline comparisons will be based on International Civil Aviation Organization (ICAO) data. ICAO and IATA data for the year listed usually refers to the entire period, while data from MAS refers to the financial year until June. This discrepancy may affect MAS figures for 1997 in some instances, but not sufficiently to invalidate observations of trends and relative performance based on efficiency and financial ratios. It also allows us to compare airline performances.

### *Operating efficiency*

Operating efficiency can be measured by the revex ratio, productivity, passenger load factor and passenger yield (Table 6.03).

#### *Revex ratio*

MAS's average revex ratio (total operating revenue as a percentage of total operating expenditure) increased marginally from 100.1[12] before privatization to 102.2 after privatization. This represented a marginal improvement in relation to its competitors' combined average but still compared poorly to SIA (111.9 per cent), Cathay Pacific (112.9 per cent) and Thai Airways (114.0 per cent) after privatization. Malaysia Airlines' own data suggests a more significant improvement from 97.0 to 104.1. However, regardless of source, performance before and after privatization was generally below the Asia Pacific and world averages. This means that operationally, MAS was generally losing money and its performance after privatization was only marginally better, and even then, only for the period 1994–96. This compares unfavourably with its performance before privatization if we take into account the industry downturn in 1990–93.

### *Productivity*

Total capacity (available tonne kilometres or ATK) is measured by adding available passenger tonne kilometres (APTK) and available freight tonne kilometres (AFTK). MAS had the largest fleet, but the lowest output and ATK for international flights, and had significantly fewer (international) passenger-kilometres (passenger-km) compared to the three other Asian airlines. This was because, despite carrying the most passengers, MAS's total international passengers (4.7 million before and 6.5 million after privatization) was the lowest, and substantially less compared to SIA (8.1 million and 11.4 million) and Cathay Pacific (7.9 million and 10.2 million), contributing the lowest operating revenue of the four airlines here.

Data for MAS's total employees include domestic operations, hence it is difficult to isolate the company's labour productivity for useful comparisons with SIA and Cathay Pacific (which only operate international flights). Nonetheless, average labour productivity improved significantly after privatization from 170.6 to 315.6 ('000 ATK per employee), and from 37.8 to 61.0 per cent of its competitors' combined average, in part as a result of longer working hours after privatization. However, MAS's labour productivity remained low compared to SIA and Cathay Pacific (but higher than Thai Airways after 1995), although, as mentioned, this figure was likely to have been weighed down by domestic operations.[13]

### *Passenger load factor*

Passenger load factor is a measure of capacity utilization, derived by dividing passenger traffic (revenue passenger-km, RPK) by passenger capacity (available seat kilometres, ASK). Improvements in MAS's average passenger load factor for international flights were negligible (from 68.4 to 68.7 per cent) and consistent with the fairly constant international average of 67.6 per cent for 1991–97. MAS's average passenger load factor (as a percentage of its competitors) decreased after privatization from 99.0 to 96.9 per cent. Its passenger load factor was partly a reflection of the industry average and the company's periodic fleet expansion programmes. However, passenger load factor showed little improvement after privatization, and was higher on average for domestic flights, most notably from 1994, indicating excess capacity on international flights following the company's international fleet expansion.

*Table 6.03* Regional airlines: Average performance, 1990–1993 and 1994–1997, selected indicators

| | *MAS average* | | *Competitors average* | |
|---|---|---|---|---|
| | *1990–93* | *1994–97* | *1990–93* | *1994–97* |
| Revex ratio | 100.1C | 102.2 | 113.4 | 112.9 |
| Fleet size | 73.3 | 97.3 | 54.7 | 70.2 |
| Available tonne-km (ATK) | 2,413.1 | 4,611.6 | 6,342.0 | 9,376.5 |
| Passenger km (millions) | 11,131.9 | 20,802.9 | 27,686.6 | 38,545.2 |
| International passengers (millions) | 4.7 | 6.5 | 7.1 | 9.8 |
| Revenue (US$ million) | 997.7 | 1634.2 | 1982.9 | 2701.7 |
| Labour productivity | 170.6 | 315.6 | 451.9 | 517.3 |
| Passenger load factor | 68.4 | 68.7 | 69.1 | 70.9 |
| Passenger yield | 0.061 | 0.054 | 0.077 | 0.075 |

*Source:* Adapted from ICAO (1992–99), IATA and Malaysia Airlines data.
*Note:* C = combined data from ICAO and MAS.

Improvements in MAS's domestic passenger load factor contributed to the overall increase in total load factors after privatization.

### *Passenger yield*

Passenger yield is a measure of revenue per traffic, and derived by dividing total passenger revenue by revenue passenger-km (RPK). Total passenger-km increased by 88.1 per cent (international) and 82 per cent (total) following MAS's fleet expansion by 32.7 per cent after privatization. This fleet expansion from 134 to 138.6 per cent of its competitors' fleets allowed MAS to increase total international passenger-km from 42.4 to 57.2 per cent in relation to its competitors. However, while total international passenger-km increased substantially after privatization, passenger revenues did not increase correspondingly. As a result, average international passenger yields actually decreased from 0.061 to 0.054, reflected in a noticeable decline from 79.2 to 72.0 per cent of its regional competitors' combined average. Decreasing yields were believed to have cost MAS US$700 million a year.[14] MAS improved its output or capacity (ATK) by 97.7 per cent after privatization, which allowed it to improve its performance from 39.9 to 53.4 per cent in relation to its competitors. This was a direct function of increased fleet capacity and greater flight frequency.

### ***Financial performance***

MAS's financial performance can be measured by its leverage, liquidity and profitability.

*Leverage*

MAS's poor financial performance was partly due to operational problems, largely the result of the substantial debt and interest payments incurred from its fleet expansion. Long-term debt (LTD) increased significantly in 1993, 1994 and 1998 following new aircraft purchases (Malaysia Airlines 1994). As a result, MAS's debt and debt–equity ratios increased noticeably after 1993 indicating a serious debt problem. MAS's leverage increased, as can be seen in its average debt ratio,[15] which increased from 0.49 to 0.71. As a result, the average debt–equity ratio[16] increased from 1.02 to 2.50 after privatization (Table 6.04).

Interest also grew in the same period, especially after 1997, with operating profit and cash increasingly unable to cover interest payments, as illustrated in the decreasing interest cover and cash–interest ratios. Although the average interest cover[17] improved marginally from –0.09 to –0.07, operating profit and cash were generally insufficient to cover interest payments in 1991–97. The high average cash–interest ratio of 4.02 before privatization was largely due to a RM337 million profit from the sale of aircraft in 1993. Nonetheless, the average cash–interest ratio of 0.60 after privatization indicates that the airline was having problems meeting interest payments. Interest cover was never good to begin with and steadily deteriorated after 1994. Similarly, its current assets–interest ratio declined noticeably in the same period, indicating the company had problems meeting interest payments (Table 6.04).

*Liquidity*

Average liquidity (current ratio) was poor throughout the period and actually declined from 0.59 to 0.54 after privatization, consistent with the declining trend from 1993. Net cash flow from operating activities (including aircraft sales) minus interest payments improved after privatization. This is even more true after we remove revenue from the sale of aircraft, which reveals a negative cash flow after interest payments for 1991 and 1993 (Table 6.05).

*Profitability*

Profitability is determined by the airline's ability to generate unit revenues higher than unit costs. Low unit costs are no guarantee of profit if an airline is unable to even generate the low unit revenues necessary to cover such costs. MAS's operating profit as a percentage of operating revenue was below the international and regional average, and was very poor compared to SIA, Cathay Pacific and Thai Airways. Except for 1994, this figure deteriorated steadily until 2000. Average operating profit as a percentage of operating revenue declined from –0.07 to –0.40 after privatization, although the latter figure included the whole of 1997 (i.e. the start of the Asian financial crisis). However, while this distorts the picture before and after privatization, MAS's

*Table 6.04* MAS: Leverage ratios and debt, 1990–1997

| | *1990* | *1991* | *1992* | *1993* | *1994* | *1995* | *1996* | *1997* |
|---|---|---|---|---|---|---|---|---|
| Long-term debt (RM billion) | 1.13 | 1.23 | 1.01 | 3.04 | 5.52 | 5.18 | 5.93 | 6.12 |
| Average LTD | | | 1.60 | | | | 5.69 | |
| Debt ratio | 0.51 | 0.48 | 0.42 | 0.58 | 0.73 | 0.71 | 0.74 | 0.69 |
| Average debt ratio | | | 0.49 | | | | 0.71 | |
| Debt–equity | 1.05 | 0.94 | 0.74 | 1.37 | 2.74 | 2.46 | 2.78 | 2.25 |
| Average debt–equity ratio | | | 1.02 | | | | 2.50 | |
| Interest (RM million) | 119.5 | 115.0 | 104.7 | 103.6 | 184.4 | 327.0 | 429.7 | 403.1 |
| Interest cover | (0.29) | 1.12 | 0.37 | (1.77) | 2.30 | 0.54 | 0.38 | (1.12) |
| Average interest cover | | | (0.09) | | | | (0.07) | |
| Cash–interest ratio | 2.85 | 2.87 | 0.50 | 8.68 | 4.85 | 0.63 | 0.50 | 0.68 |
| Average cash–interest ratio | | | 4.02 | | | | 0.60 | |
| Current assets–interest ratio | 36.1 | 46.2 | 50.8 | 86.3 | 68.4 | 40.4 | 33.7 | 47.8 |
| Average cash–interest ratio | | | 54.9 | | | | 47.6 | |

*Source:* Adapted from Malaysia Airlines (1991–98).
*Notes:* Averages for 1991–93 and 1995–97. Brackets ( ) = negative.

*Table 6.05* MAS: Liquidity ratios, 1990–1997

| | *1990* | *1991* | *1992* | *1993* | *1994* | *1995* | *1996* | *1997* |
|---|---|---|---|---|---|---|---|---|
| Current ratio | 0.587 | 0.631 | 0.319 | 0.820 | 0.774 | 0.492 | 0.561 | 0.559 |
| Average current ratio | | | 0.59 | | | | 0.54 | |
| Net cash flow (operations) | n/a | 153.9 | 379.4 | 224.2 | 580.5 | 865.1 | 1,517.2 | 1,118.0 |
| Net cash flow (sale of planes) | n/a | (291.5) | 29.7 | (319.4) | 551.1 | 863.2 | 1,516.1 | 881 |
| Average net cash flow | | | (193.7) | | | | 1,086.8 | |

*Source:* Adapted from Malaysia Airlines (1991–98).
*Notes:* Averages for 1991–93 and 1995–97. Brackets ( ) = negative.

performance also declined from –0.006 to –0.036 per cent in comparison to its competitors as average returns on assets[18] declined from 33.7 to 4.0 per cent after privatization (Table 6.06).

*External factors*

The Asian financial crisis in 1997–98 had a big impact on the region's airlines, with MAS particularly badly affected as its capital requirements were financed mainly in US dollars and Japanese yen because MAS was apparently not allowed to borrow domestically to avoid 'crowding out' the Malaysian financial market.[19] Around 70 per cent of MAS's RM10.3 billion in short-term loans and fixed leases was in US dollars (at the end of September 1997), with nearly US$3 billion in dollar-denominated debt (*The Edge*, 5 January 1998; *Asiaweek*, 6 March 1998).[20] By May 1998, 81 per cent of MAS's RM10.6 billion debt was mainly in US dollars with 12 per cent in Japanese yen (*The Edge*, 8 June 1998). This high US dollar exposure meant that a RM0.10 change in the exchange rate could have affected MAS by RM40 million. A 69.5 per cent fall in profit was attributed to foreign exchange losses of RM2.1 billion (US$1=RM3.30) in 1997 (*The Edge*, 5 January 1998).

Around 43 per cent of MAS's total revenue was in ringgit, 14 per cent in US dollars, and the rest in other currencies. However, while 44 per cent of expenses was in ringgit, 28 per cent of expenses was in US dollars, including debt servicing and fuel costs.[21] Fuel and oil accounted for 14.4 per cent of operating expenses at a time when the ringgit had depreciated 35 per cent against the dollar (*Asiaweek*, 6 March 1998) but MAS did not have a fuel hedging policy. This meant that MAS had to struggle to cover interest payments, even without the impact of the crisis, as its debt burden increased substantially. This was evident in the company's attempts to restructure its

*Table 6.06* MAS: Operating profit (loss) as a percentage of operating revenue, 1990–1997 (current US$ million)

| | *MAS* | *SIA* | *Cathay Pacific* | *Thai* | *Asia average* | *World average* | *MAS average* | *Competitor average* |
|---|---|---|---|---|---|---|---|---|
| 1990 | (1.2) | 14.2 | 14.1 | 17.0 | 4.1 | (0.8) | | |
| 1991 | 3.6 | 13.9 | 16.1 | 7.2 | n/a | 2.1 | | |
| 1992 | 1.1 | 10.4 | 16.2 | 8.6 | 3.3 | (0.8) | (0.07) | 10.8 |
| 1993 | (4.9) | 8.1 | 9.3 | 7.9 | 2.3 | 1.0 | | |
| 1994 | 8.5 | 12.6 | 9.8 | 13.3 | 4.4 | 3.4 | | |
| 1995 | 3.1 | 11.7 | 15.4 | 12.9 | 5.4 | 5.1 | | |
| 1996 | 2.7 | 9.2 | 13.3 | 12.1 | 4.6 | 4.4 | (0.40) | 11.2 |
| 1997 | (7.0) | 9.0 | 6.5 | 10.6 | 4.1 | 5.6 | | |

*Source:* Adapted from ICAO (1992–99); Malaysia Airlines (1991–98), Cathay Pacific Airways (1995–98); Singapore Airlines (1997–2000); Thai Airways (1998–2000).
*Note:* Averages for 1991–93 and 1995–97.

debt as early as March 1997 (at least six months before the Asian financial crisis).

MAS was thus severely affected by the 1997 crisis, with the ringgit's depreciation requiring more capital injection to meet its loan obligations and working capital. But while the industry and its competitors began recovering after 1998, MAS's performance deteriorated badly until its renationalization in 2000. The recovery of Thai Airways, despite the baht's depreciation, suggests that there were other problems which affected MAS's performance. In July 1997, MAS was reported to have finalized plans to raise RM3.1 billion to reduce its RM6.1 billion in company loans (at US$1 = RM2.50). This was abandoned following the currency depreciation and then pegging of the ringgit (at US$1 = RM3.80) (*New Straits Times*, 22 February 2000). However, with insufficient cash flow, MAS would have been unable to survive its over-borrowing even without the impact of the 1997–98 crisis.[22]

## Problems

The data on MAS shows that its operational performance did not improve significantly after privatization while its financial position deteriorated considerably. This can be explained by two types of government failure. Ex ante failure was evident in the choice of owner, purchase structure (which created an unsustainable debt burden), and an essentially unchanged state–business relationship, all of which undermined incentives. MAS also inherited conditions and problems which had existed before privatization, including the need to service unprofitable domestic routes and previous management investment decisions. However, this does not explain why the government failed to correct these problems when they became known. Despite a continuing representation on the board, and significant powers through its 'golden share', the government failed to monitor performance or intervene even though it was aware of problems, including mismanagement, early on. This ex post failure to correct earlier mistakes was arguably a more important factor in MAS's poor performance as more timely intervention could have limited financial losses. This suggests that the government's ability to intervene was very likely constrained by political factors, in part due to the nature of patron–client relationships, in particular, the owner's close association with the Finance Minister,[23] as well as the national importance of the airline. Both these factors created a moral hazard, where the government was unlikely to allow the airline to fail, but was also unable to intervene earlier to enforce discipline or replace the owner.

### *Ex ante failure*

There were three aspects of ex ante failure: poor selection, poor purchase structure and the failure to account for the airline's inherited problems. The choice of owner necessitated the privatization be financed entirely by loans, and also affected the quality of management. The purchase structure in turn undermined incentives for efficient management by creating a huge debt burden. MAS also inherited problems, including previous management decisions, which further affected its performance and the new owner's ability to finance the airline.

### *Selection and purchase structure*

The new owner had neither the financial capacity nor the managerial experience. Tajudin was a trained accountant and former merchant banker[24] who had emerged as a major entrepreneur after acquiring a controlling stake in publicly listed Technology Resources Industries Bhd (TRI, formerly Roxy Electric Industries) in June 1990. He had no experience running an airline, although there is some indication of interest. Tajudin was reported to have proposed a second airline to the government in 1991, and MHS, a listed helicopter and air services company, purchased a 33.3 per cent stake in Netherlands-based Schreiner Aviation and 24.9 per cent of World Airways in 1993 reportedly to compete with MAS (*The Edge*, 17 July 1995). Between 1990 and 1993, TRI acquired MHS which later changed its name to Naluri. However, Tajudin's earlier corporate success was attributed to state patronage rather than business acumen, and the development of TRI into a Malay conglomerate was apparently the result of 'changes in ownership, rather than through accumulation and expansion of a company's productive investment activities' (Gomez and Jomo 1997).

MHS's fixed assets were equivalent to the cost of two Boeing 737s, but it was expected to take over an airline with a fleet of ninety-four planes (including fifty-two Boeing 737s). This affected the purchase of MAS which was based entirely on RM1.79 billion in loans (the largest in the country), without a clear 'take out' plan other than to wait for MAS shares – pledged as collateral – to appreciate. This was as much a reflection of Tajudin's limited financial capacity as it was of his political influence to secure loans. However, the poor purchase structure created an unviable debt burden, which subsequently affected the owner's ability to continue financing operations. It was also based on flawed project evaluations (with over-optimistic estimates) and easy credit from banks (*Far Eastern Economic Review*, 25 January 2001). Interest repayments, estimated at RM144–RM179 million a year (based on interest rates of 8–10 per cent) would have created disincentives to improve efficiency given the minimal likelihood of the owner recovering capital costs.

The financial problems of Tajudin's other publicly listed companies – Naluri (which owned MAS) and TRI – further affected his ability to finance MAS, with the sale of MAS seen as necessary to pay off Naluri's RM890 million debt under the government's Corporate Debt Restructuring Committee (CDRC) scheme (*Business Times*, 27 June 2000). (Tajudin reportedly wanted to sell his stake in MAS as early as 1997 [*The Edge*, 17 March 1997].) Naluri was also directly involved in the failed Air Maldives (a joint venture with the Maldives government in 1994). Tajudin was accused of acting in bad faith by pushing the commercially unviable London route, blamed for Naluri's failure to provide finance and threatened with legal action (*Far Eastern Economic Review*, 7 December 2000; *New Straits Times*, 15 August 2000).

The owner's airline inexperience was evident in the lack of yield management, untimely fleet expansion and reports of financial impropriety. These are discussed in detail below. However, as these ex ante problems could have theoretically been corrected, the quality of the government's ex post intervention becomes a more important determinant of successful privatization, particularly in the absence of more suitable candidates (i.e. with at least Tajudin's limited financial capacity, a better understanding of the airline industry, and superior management skills and connections to run the industry better).

### *Inherited problems*

The new owner inherited several problems with the airline: an unprofitable domestic sector, poor international routes and previous management decisions. As the country's national carrier, MAS was obliged to continue flying unprofitable domestic routes on government-set fares as part of its national service. MAS's domestic flights were more expensive per kilometre due to the shorter stages (distances) and contributed less revenue despite greater passenger numbers. Revenue per passenger was RM93 (domestic) and RM435.40 (international) in 1990 and RM118.90 (domestic) and RM656.90 (international) in 1998 (Malaysia Airlines 1998). Estimated losses from the domestic sector ranged between RM7 million and RM360 million a year (*The Star*, 11 August 1994; *New Straits Times*, 28 June 2000), but MAS was not allowed to raise its fares, partly due to pressure from politicians from the east Malaysian states of Sabah and Sarawak.

The domestic sector was unprofitable due to the government requirement for relatively frequent and cheap flights, with a high proportion of employees staffing counters in remote airports servicing local destinations, and a mismatched fleet which kept aircraft utilization down and imposed heavy demands on maintenance, spare parts and training (*Far Eastern Economic Review*, 8 July 1999; also see *Malaysian Business*, 1 July 1999). Losses were compounded by a high fuel bill (due to the high number of domestic flights and short sector lengths) which dragged down profits (*New Straits Times*, 17 March 1994). The continued operation of the domestic sector necessitated some form of subsidy rather than relying on cross-subsidies from MAS's international operations as this would only undermine the airline's competitiveness. The government subsequently chose to separate domestic routes from MAS's main operations, but only after its renationalization.

Historically, MAS was also disadvantaged by limited international routes, with many focused in areas of high Malaysian traffic prior to privatization (e.g. London, Hong Kong, Madras). Route expansion only occurred in the late 1980s but was hampered by a lack of interest in and scepticism about the viability of the new Kuala Lumpur International Airport (KLIA) as a hub versus Bangkok and Singapore (Paribas Capital Markets 1994; *The Edge*, 12 November 2000). The previous management also failed to enter into strategic alliances to cope with growing international competition (*Business Times*, 29 November 2000). Furthermore, air treaties and new airline routes are negotiated by governments, often for non-commercial reasons, and traffic rights were not under Tajudin's direct control (*Asiaweek*, 6 March 1998; *The Edge*, 2 January 2001). MAS also suffered big losses from several international routes (e.g. Mexico, Johannesburg, Vancouver)[25] which were largely initiated by the Prime Minister and maintained for diplomatic reasons. These routes were subsequently suspended (*The Edge*, 7 August 2000).

MAS's inefficiency was partly related to overcapacity (and fleet underutilization) following major fleet expansions in 1990–94 and 1995–96, which preceded industry downturns. It is unclear whether the major fleet expansion programme in 1995 was initiated by Tajudin given that MAS was already engaged in the expansion of its fleet to around 100 planes in a move which was described as aggressive, ambitious, but untimely (at a time of intense industry competition and fare cutting), and far outpacing demand for additional capacity (Paribas Capital Markets 1994; *Asian Wall Street Journal*, 25 May 1995). MAS made firm commitments in 1990–91 to purchase nine Boeing 747–400 (for delivery in 1991–97), twenty-six Boeing 737–400/500 (1992–95) and ten Airbus A330 (1994–96), with options for seven Boeing 747–400 (1995–99), sixteen Boeing 737–400/500 (1995–98) and six Airbus A330 (1997–98) (Malaysia Airlines 1991). On 27 March 1991, MAS signed an agreement with Boeing to purchase six Boeing 747–400 aircraft, and in 1992, confirmed orders for seventy-two aircraft in line with its fleet modernization and expansion programme (Malaysia Airlines 1992a).

In 1992, MAS took delivery of twenty-two planes[26] for approximately RM2 billion. It also signed an order on 14 May 1992 for seventeen Boeing 737–400s (for 1993–95 delivery) for RM1.6 billion. In 1993, twenty-seven new planes were added,[27] with delivery expected of another eleven Boeing 737–400/500 (in 1994–96) and two Boeing 747–400 (in 1995–97), and upgrades to the Airbus A330 (by 1995/96), with efficiency and productivity in fleet utilization expected to improve operating costs (Malaysia Airlines 1994). The seventy-two aircraft were financed with a RM1.75 billion rights issue (on 5 August 1992) and a US$120 million loan as part of MAS's fleet renewal programme which was to run to 1998 (*The Star*, 10 March 1993). By the management's own admission, the high gearing required for fleet expansion 'could constrain and erode profitability due to high interests' (Malaysia Airlines 1992b) and delivery of the sixteen aircraft was expected to jeopardize profitability in the shorter term (TA Securities 1993; *New Straits Times*, 17 March 1994).

The evidence thus suggests that MAS was already in the middle of a huge fleet renewal programme, and may have committed itself in 1992 to increase its fleet to about 100 planes by 2000 at a cost of RM9.5–RM10 billion (Barclays de Zoete Wedd 1994; Paribas Capital Markets 1994; *New Straits Times*, 28 August 1994). Given the time lag between new aircraft orders and actual deliveries (and hence payment), MAS inherited aircraft orders made by the previous management which contributed to its debt burden. Increases in long-term debt (LTD) and long-term leases (LTL) can be traced back to the new (Boeing) plane orders made in 1990–92. As a result, long-term debt tripled in 1993, while leases doubled and long-term loans nearly doubled with the delivery of twenty-eight aircraft, and all three indicators increased substantially again in 1994 which coincided with the arrival of thirteen new aircraft (Table 6.07).

### *Ex post failure*

Ex ante mistakes related to poor selection, the purchase structure and inherited problems could have been corrected. The failure to address these represented the government's ex post failure. This was characterized by the failure to monitor (which could partly be an institutional failure) and to act (which is very likely a political failure). The government failed to monitor management performance and intervene despite representation on the board, and significant powers through its 'golden share'. This may have been due to the owner's close relationship with the Finance Minister, and the small pool of available entrepreneurs which restricted the government's ability to replace the owner. This meant that privatization did not change the institutional relationship between the state and enterprise, improve efficiency by exposing MAS to market discipline (i.e. it did not increase the credibility of the state not intervening in the event of failure), or increase the state's capacity to

*Table 6.07* MAS: Debt burden (RM billion) and aircraft orders, 1990–2000

| | *Long-term debt* | *Leases* | *Short-term loans* | *Long-term leases* | *Orders [total]* | *Delivery [total]* |
|---|---|---|---|---|---|---|
| 1990 | 1.13 | 0.63 | 0.42 | 1.07 | A [10] | |
| 1991 | 1.23 | 0.59 | 0.40 | 1.17 | B [16] | |
| 1992 | 1.01 | 0.54 | 1.33 | 0.97 | C [17] | A+ [10] |
| 1993 | 3.04 | 1.33 | 0.80 | 1.71 | | ABC [28] |
| 1994 | 5.52 | 3.29 | 0.94 | 2.23 | | C [13] |
| 1995 | 5.18 | 3.23 | 1.49 | 1.95 | | C [2] |
| 1996 | 5.93 | 4.01 | 0.99 | 1.92 | D [25] | C [1] |
| 1997 | 6.12 | 3.61 | 1.07 | 2.49 | | D [7] |
| 1998 | 9.27 | 6.09 | 1.11 | 3.66 | | D [8] |
| 1999 | 8.72 | 5.32 | 1.57 | 3.40 | | D [2] |
| 2000 | 7.59 | 4.76 | 0.95 | 2.84 | | D [1] |

*Source:* Adapted from Malaysia Airlines (1991–98); Boeing Corporation (2002) <http://active.boeing.com/commercial/orders/summaries.cfm>.
*Notes:* A, B, C and D refer to orders made in 1990, 1991, 1992 and 1996 respectively. A+ denotes delivery from orders made before 1990, hence total deliveries and total orders may not tally.

discipline the owner. This ex post failure meant that the government had to renationalize MAS in order to implement corrective measures which included the separation of domestic operations and removal of the airline's debt burden.

MAS's performance raises two types of management issues. The first is about the owner's ability to manage the airline efficiently. The second relates to reports of impropriety and mismanagement. From media reports, we can determine that MAS faced problems fairly early on, and well before the onset of the Asian financial crisis in 1997–98. Concerns were raised in 1996 about MAS's performance and mounting debt, as well as the future earnings growth of MAS and TRI (both which fared poorly on the Kuala Lumpur Stock Exchange). There were also reports about management problems, MAS contracts being awarded to Tajudin's own companies, his involvement in aircraft sales and purchases through a third party, and rumours of Tajudin wanting to sell MAS to concentrate on TRI (*The Edge*, 23 December 1996, 17 March 1997). There were concerns about passenger loads, mounting debt costs and MAS's gearing at 187 per cent (for the 1995 financial year) which made it difficult to finance fleet expansion (*The Star*, 15 January 1996). Its debt–equity ratio increased from around 1.5 to 2.3 (*New Straits Times*, 7 May 1998), or from 190 per cent (1995) to 220 per cent (1997), as net debt grew from RM6.3 billion (1995) to RM8.3 billion (1997) as a result of its fleet expansion programme (PhileoAllied Securities, cited in *The Edge*, 22 January 1996).

The main management challenge in airlines is yield management – balancing greater capacity (and hence revenue) from fleet expansion with excess capacity, especially in an economic downturn. Increased capacity, in turn, requires more flight frequency and viable new routes. MAS sought to increase its capacity, the number of its international routes and flight frequency. As part of its aircraft modernization and rationalization programme, it announced plans to buy twenty-five new Boeing aircraft[28] valued at more than RM10 billion (US$3.97 billion) on 8 January 1996[29] (Malaysia Airlines 1996). The new, more fuel-efficient aircraft were also seen as vital for keeping operating costs under control. The fleet expansion may also have been undertaken to match the expected increase in international competition after completion of KLIA.

However, MAS had no yield management or financial projections for its fleet purchase and depreciation.[30] Instead, Tajudin embarked on an expansion programme for MAS 'to become the largest, most successful and most respected airline in the world' (Malaysia Airlines 1995: 15). This fleet expansion was overambitious and poorly timed, being made at the height of the economic boom in 1994–95 (and most likely based on a GDP growth forecast of 8 per cent, with continued traffic growth). The purchase increased capacity without a corresponding increase in revenue, and was made despite low profits and a modest passenger load factor, without first deciding on or establishing new routes or strategic alliances (*The Edge*, 24 December 2000,

12 November 2000). MAS's routes were limited in comparison to its direct competitors, and it remained outside the world's airline alliances including the 15-member Star Alliance, and its main competitor, Oneworld. The decision to expand the fleet was also questionable as MAS was in the middle of a (less ambitious) fleet modernization programme, having recently taken delivery of twenty-seven new-generation, fuel-efficient aircraft, which included twenty-one Boeing 737–400/500 and six Boeing 747–400, with further delivery of another eleven Boeing 737–400/500 (in 1994–96), two Boeing 747–400 (in 1995 and December 1997), and upgrades to the Airbus A330 (by 1995–96) to make its fleet the youngest in the region and possibly the world (Malaysia Airlines 1994).

As a result, although the increases in capacity and flights improved some performance indicators, financial performance deteriorated with decreasing yields (due to inefficient yield management, e.g. the poor choice of routes) and a growing debt burden. The increased debt burden and interest repayments led to over-gearing and liquidity problems with MAS unable to sufficiently cover its interest payments given its low operating revenue. The fleet expansion was thus a serious management mistake, undertaken without first establishing new routes and when profits were insufficient to justify this, resulting in low ATK and passenger load factors, indicating both under-utilization and overcapacity. However, such expansion is not atypical in the airline industry and market pressures from SIA and Cathay Pacific may have prompted MAS to upgrade and expand its fleet to remain competitive.

Tajudin also embarked on short-term cost-cutting measures at MAS which improved some productivity indicators but resulted in the deterioration of service standards and put the airline at a disadvantage in maintaining and improving long-term competitiveness (*The Edge*, 24 December 2000). Instead of implementing a fuel hedging policy, MAS chose to cut costs through a low fuel policy (denied by MAS), which violated international safety standards. This came to light following a plane crash in Sabah and investigations in the UK after an MAS aircraft's emergency landing due to low fuel reserves (*The Edge*, 24 December 2000). Tajudin's management style alienated and demoralized staff, causing considerable dislocation and leading to some 80 pilots leaving for other airlines[31] (*The Edge*, 12 November 2000). Meanwhile MAS continued to be overstaffed, with inefficiency and low productivity, and higher than average operational costs (*The Sun*, 14 June 2001; *The Edge* 2 July 2001, 10 December 2001).

Finally, Tajudin created 'viable profit centres', including MAS Catering (April 1995) and MAS Cargo (April 1996). In theory, these profit centres were meant to be more focused and hence more profitable by increasing business and revenue, despite additional costs. However, management of the various divisions was unfocused and territorial.[32] While MAS Cargo revenues increased from RM580 million (1996) to RM660.6 million (1997) (with RM8.1 million in profit), this was on the back of a record 44.6 per cent growth of cargo and air traffic in 1996 (Malaysia Airlines 1996, 1997).

Furthermore, MAS Cargo had seen steady increases in revenue before privatization, including a 42.5 per cent increase to RM376.0 million (1991) and a 23.6 per cent increase to RM464.8 million (1992) (Malaysia Airlines 1992a). Instead, aggressive expansion left the cargo and catering divisions profitless, with the effects felt after 1997 when MAS Cargo recorded its second straight year of losses of RM123.9 million on 30 September 1999 (*Asian Wall Street Journal*, 27 July 2000; *The Edge*, 21 February 2000). MAS Catering also started losing money, with pre-tax profit falling from RM19.6 million (1996) to RM13.1 million (1997) despite meal production increasing from 18,000 meals a day in 1992 to 28,000 (Malaysia Airlines 1992a, 1996, 1997).

Both divisions became subjects of police investigations from 9 January 2002 following an internal audit by the new management. A police report was lodged against Tajudin, Wan Aishah Wan Hamid (a former MAS director) and MAS Cargo vice-president Ralph Gotz for breaches of the Companies Act in failing to disclose their interests in related-party transactions. Investigations centred on management irregularities and the misappropriation of funds at MAS Cargo; business arrangements between MAS and a German-based cargo handler controlled by Tajudin; and contracts between MAS and Advanced Cargo Logistic GmbH (60 per cent owned by Naluri) to develop its European cargo hub[33] (*New Straits Times*, 25 February 2002). These contracts were believed not to have favoured MAS, resulting in MAS scaling down its commitments to minimize the adverse financial impact after its renationalization[34] (*Business Times*, 19 February 2002; *New Straits Times*, 25 February 2002).

MAS subsequently filed a civil claim against Tajudin and two others for RM174.62 million following losses at its cargo operations in Germany from 1999 to 2001, alleging breach of duties in entering into various projects and businesses with third parties in total disregard to the interest of the company. The airline also claimed that Tajudin (with his co-defendants) had conspired to cause loss and damage to the company, and sought substantial damages and an account of all secret profits/benefits. MAS also filed a suit against Naluri, MAS Golden Holidays Sdn Bhd (MGH) and MAS Hotels & Boutiques Sdn Bhd (MHB) for dishonest assistance in the breach of fiduciary duties and obligations by Tajudin, and sought damages for alleged dishonest assistance and knowing receipt, damages for alleged conspiracy and damages for alleged unlawful interference in the business of MAS and MGH.

As was the case in the other case studies, this alleged behaviour was consistent with the pursuit of short-term rents rather than long-term operational profits from efficiency gains. In this case, it may have been due to the unpayable debt burden which created perverse incentives for the owner, or the fact that the owner may only have been an agent of the government. Conversely, it may have also been shaped by the preferences of domestic capital for such rents as discussed in Chapter 3.

Privatization did not significantly alter the relationship between MAS and the state, and did not improve monitoring or increase the credibility of the state not intervening. Although 32 per cent of MAS was divested to MHS, the government retained a 27.2 per cent stake in addition to its 'golden share'. The composition of the board of directors also did not alter considerably with the change of ownership, aside from the positions of chairman and managing director. Although the size of the board was noticeably smaller by 1996–97, half the directors were the same from 1993–94, and the government had three representatives (from the Ministries of Finance, Tourism and Transport) (Malaysia Airlines 1991–98). Despite this, a former government representative admitted that the board was unaware then of questionable management decisions relating to aircraft purchases and the creation of separate cargo and catering divisions.[35]

However, while (government) board members may not have been aware of all management decisions, it is unlikely that Tajudin would have been able to make major decisions to expand MAS's fleet without government knowledge or approval. According to Tajudin, he

> was not allowed to manage MAS according to normal commercial terms but at all times reported to and abided by the decisions of the government on material matters, including . . . the re-branding, livery, disposal of assets, restructure of human resources, policies involving domestic and international routes, passenger and cargo hubs, investments, etc.
>
> (*The Sun*, 6 July 2006)

He also claimed he was not permitted to implement matters which were not approved by the government, and was not allowed to sell any of his shares in MAS on the open market.

In this case, management problems appeared to be tolerated within the context of economic growth, with Mahathir admitting that 'there may be some mismanagement' but that these were 'viable companies . . . doing relatively well' before the Asian financial crisis (*Far Eastern Economic Review*, 24 June 1998). However, it is unlikely that the government was completely unaware of the scale of the problem (MAS was almost bankrupted), but nevertheless it failed to intervene sooner. This suggests that there were political constraints to acting sooner, possibly related to the owner's relationship to the Finance Minister. Furthermore, without a pool of qualified candidates, the government was probably left with renationalization as a last resort, a process which required time.

From the measures put into place after renationalization, it is clear that the government knew what needed to be done, but appeared unable to implement these measures sooner. These included financial and operational benchmarks,[36] while incentive and disincentive payments were to be made (if MAS performed above ceiling targets) or paid by MAS (if it did not meet minimum targets) (Nomura Asian Equity Research, 29 November 2002). Most significantly, the government was finally able to address the airline's debt burden and domestic service obligations by separating MAS's balance sheet from its operations; transferring domestic operations to the government; and selling or transferring non-core assets (including aircraft assets and liabilities) (see Malaysia Airlines 2002). The timing of these ex post measures after the airline's renationalization suggests that the government was unable to implement these when MAS was privately owned.

## Conclusion

Privatization improved some aspects of MAS's operational efficiency, largely due to the increased capacity as a result of its fleet expansion. This allowed MAS to substantially increase output (ATK) and passenger-km performed, which led to some increase in its revex ratio. However, passenger loads remained largely unchanged and passenger yields actually declined due to passenger revenues increasing at a lower rate than passenger-km performed. Both figures indicate poor yield management leading to continued excess capacity.

Comparisons with its competitors indicate that despite efficiency gains after privatization, MAS was still very inefficient, largely because its performance base was much lower to begin with. (Conversely, efficiency gains after privatization can be attributed to these very low efficiency levels before 1994.) MAS also fared the worst operationally compared to its competitors and the averages for the region and world. This means that efficiency gains after privatization were insufficient to generate the necessary revenue to meet MAS's capital financing requirements. Put slightly differently, MAS's competitors were on average significantly more efficient, and on top of this, did not have the debt burden of fleet expansions.

While MAS's financial problems were largely due to its huge debt burden after privatization, this was the culmination of substantial increases in 1993, 1994 and 1998 as a result of aircraft deliveries from its fleet expansion programmes. As aircraft orders made before privatization (1990–92) were only delivered in 1992–94, this was reflected in the substantial increase in long-term debts, leases and long-term loans from 1993 to 1994 which added to MAS's debt burden after privatization. MAS's financial performance in terms of its leverage was thus not entirely due to decisions made after privatization. Conversely, given that gains in operational efficiency were largely due to increased capacity which allowed MAS to narrow the performance gap with its competitors, these must be seen as largely due to management decisions on fleet expansion made before privatization. In short, while not all improvements were due to the new owner after privatization, neither were the subsequent financial problems entirely his fault. MAS's mediocre performance in the four years (1990–93) prior to privatization coincided with a global slump, even though the Asia Pacific region was least affected by this. This means that the growth in traffic, revenue and profits following MAS's privatization in 1994 was largely due to the growth in the overall industry, particularly the higher than average growth rates in the Asia Pacific region.

MAS's poor performance can be attributed to a series of factors that can be usefully classified as ex ante and ex post failures of government. Privatization was strongly motivated by political considerations related to state efforts to promote Malay entrepreneurs and possibly government attempts to cover foreign exchange losses by BNM. In either case, ex ante decisions were constrained by political factors (namely the nature of patron–client relationships), with the choice of private owner closely associated with segments of the political leadership, in particular the Finance Minister. This also partly accounted for poorly structured incentives which affected performance. Privatization was unable to finance the airline's capital expansion programme or improve efficiency as the owner did not have the money in the first place, and was unable to improve performance sufficiently to pay for this. This was because the government failed to properly structure the airline's purchase to prevent the owner from being saddled with an unpayable debt burden in the context of inherent industry problems and cycles which it did not account for. (On the other hand, if the owner was merely an agent or nominee of the government, then he would have had even fewer incentives to improve efficiency.) In addition, MAS was expected to subsidize domestic routes and was constrained by previous management decisions. These created perverse incentives which were reflected in reports of mismanagement and financial impropriety.

More crucially, the government failed to correct these ex ante failures despite being aware of the problems. The financial restructuring of MAS after its renationalization aimed to relieve the airline of its debt burden and domestic obligations, while also introducing performance benchmarks to promote efficiency. The introduction of these measures only after MAS's renationalization suggests that the government may have lacked the political capacity to implement them earlier. This is partly because state intervention (e.g. the reallocation of property rights) is more difficult with divestiture compared to a concession, particularly where there is a limited pool of potential candidates to replace the owner with. However, the state's ex post (political) capacity to correct mistakes was also compromised by the owner's close association with the political leadership and the national importance of the airline which created a moral hazard where the government was unlikely to allow the airline to fail, but was also unwilling to discipline the owner. Here, the government's ex post failure to correct mistakes represented a bigger problem than the original ex ante failure when it privatized the airline. This once again underlines the importance of the state's political capacity to correct mistakes as the most important condition for successful privatization. The state's political capacity can in turn only be determined by locating the privatization within a country context.

# 7 Rents and industrial upgrading

## Proton

The automobile industry offers strong backward linkages with key heavy industries and manufacturing sectors, and is as such often a central part of industrialization strategies in developing countries. However, in order to move beyond the basic assembly of imported vehicles, the domestic firm will need to acquire the necessary technology to develop indigenous design and manufacturing capabilities. This task is challenging in itself but is made even more difficult in the context of late industrialization where the latecomer will be constrained by its initial inefficiency until learning takes place. Domestic firms will also find it difficult to meet the substantial capital requirements for both technology acquisition and scale economies in a mature industry. It is for these reasons that countries attempting to industrialize will need to subsidize domestic firms for learning and eventual 'catching up'. Technology acquisition is thus key to the development of a competitive domestic auto industry, but this can only take place if subsidies promote learning.

As subsidies potentially dilute incentives, these must be conditional on performance targets being met if learning and associated efficiency gains are to take place. The success of the technology acquisition process will therefore depend on the management of any explicit or implicit subsidy programme, in particular, the state's institutional capacity to design the appropriate incentive structures, and especially its political capacity to enforce conditionalities, including withdrawing subsidies if necessary. However, state support, in the form of learning rents and other subsidies, may not be enough to encourage a domestic industry given the capital requirements and risks involved, especially in the early stages, and limited entrepreneurial capacity. Domestic capitalists may be unavailable or simply unable or unwilling to invest, in which case the state may have to undertake the initial investment. In this case, incentives are further diluted due to the separation of residual control (ownership) from residual income (profits) which characterizes state-owned enterprises (SOEs).

Proton, Malaysia's national car project, was launched in 1983 as part of a state-led heavy industries programme to rationalize the car industry, promote industrialization through backward linkages, and meet ethnic redistributive objectives. As an infant industry, Proton's immediate challenge was technology acquisition necessary to develop design and production capabilities in order to produce a Malaysian car. To facilitate this process, Proton was provided with significant learning rents in the form of tax breaks for R&D, and tariff and import duty exemptions. Despite this, technological progress was slow and the company remained uncompetitive and dependent on protection. Proton's privatization in 1995 can thus be seen in terms of government attempts to increase efficiency by improving the technology acquisition process. Privatization was also consistent with government efforts to promote capital accumulation and create Malay industrialists.

This raises two key issues. If technology acquisition requires an effective rent-management strategy in this sector, then success is dependent on whether enforcement of conditionality is easier or more difficult with private ownership. Improvements from privatization can be said to come from changes in the management and regulatory structure. Privatization may provide a more tractable management structure by reducing the owner–manager–worker chain of command, thereby improving the owner's incentives (e.g. see Alchian and Demsetz 1972). It also provides an opportunity to change the state–enterprise relationship through a more effective regulatory structure. By creating an arm's length relationship between the government and the enterprise, privatization offers the potential for more credible sanctions and hence, a more effective regulatory structure by ensuring that subsidies are only temporary and contingent upon meeting performance targets.

However, these potential benefits may not be likely where political considerations determine the choice of candidate, and where the national significance of the enterprise will mean the state has a continued vested interest. It is indeed very likely that these two factors will be related, with the choice of candidate politically determined precisely because of the enterprise's importance. Secondly, even if privatization improved the government's enforcement capacity, commercial viability would still depend on the private owner's financial capacity to meet and sustain the substantial capital investment requirements for technology acquisition and large-scale production. This is an even more difficult task in the context of a mature industry characterized by low growth, overcapacity, industry consolidation and high entry barriers.

Proton's privatization was characterized by ex ante and ex post state failures. While privatization may have been 'desirable' (in terms of industrialization), it was arguably not 'feasible' (in terms of potential profitability and attractiveness to the private sector) given the high capital costs, technological challenges and industry trends. Government requirements relating to local content and Malay participation further affected Proton's competitiveness. These factors would have undermined private incentives, and the case for privatizing Proton was weak, offering only a second-best solution in terms of addressing long-term technological problems. One possible explanation for privatization then is that it offered the opportunity to earn short-term profits through a protected domestic market (along with long-term profits through improved technology and international competitiveness). Here, failure can be blamed on the government's decision to proceed with the privatization without a clear understanding of the global conditions and industry challenges, including the financial resources and time required for technology acquisition, and without designing a viable subsidization strategy with a clear time frame for protection. This was compounded by earlier state failure to secure technology transfer from Proton's Japanese partner and ensure that the project was commercially viable. This ex ante failure on the government's part appeared to have been due to leadership mistakes in approving the project in the first place, and later believing it was still viable in spite of industry trends.

However, the issue is less about whether Proton was viable to begin with but whether privatization accelerated the technology acquisition process which was key to developing a more competitive product to capture market share and facilitate economies of scale. Here, privatization was not even able to provide a second-best outcome (e.g. in terms of Proton's own modest targets) because of the government's ex post failure. The government did not have a long-term plan for the reduction and eventual removal of tariff and import duty exemptions to accelerate the process of technology upgrading, and there was no performance-related conditionality or attempt to withdraw rents. As discussed in Chapter 3, this has been a historical problem in Malaysia, in part related to ethnic and political considerations. In Proton's case, the government's disciplinary capacity was also constrained by specific aspects of patron–client relationships between the company and the political leadership due to the Prime Minister's continued personal interest in the development of a flagship auto manufacturing sector in Malaysia that gave the company national importance. This political commitment created a moral hazard and meant that privatization did not change the fundamental weaknesses in the institutional relationship between the government and enterprise.

To complicate matters, ex ante and ex post decisions were also adversely affected by ethnic considerations. The desire to promote Malay participation in the auto industry undermined proper project evaluation and, later, Proton's competitiveness, most notably through its local Vendor Development Programme (VDP) which required Proton to source components from (inefficient) Malay vendors. Proton's inefficiency arose from insufficient economies of scale. This was the result of a small domestic market, limited production capacity and limited exports. The inability to achieve economies of scale was due to technology transfer problems which compromised product design and production scale, as well as poor marketing and distribution, particularly overseas. Despite management efforts, both capacity expansion and technology acquisition involved substantially more capital and time than the new owner could afford, and which the government did not fully account for when it initiated the project or when it decided to privatize.

However, the timing of the decision to sell Proton back to the government (when Proton's domestic market share was declining, and with industry liberalization approaching), and the owner's subsequent diversification into other non-competitive sectors, suggests that the owner was unwilling to undertake the necessary capital investment and may have been attracted to Proton because of the rents from car sales in a protected domestic market. This preference was consistent with the general preference of Malaysian capital for captive rents in non-competitive sectors, as discussed in Chapter 3, and underlies the difficulties the government faced in attempting to create a dynamic capitalist class. While Proton subsequently developed its own body design and engine, and rationalized its local content programme and distribution, this occurred only after it was renationalized. Crucially, product design remained poor and uncompetitive as Proton was unable to develop the necessary technology. This again illustrates the inherent technological challenges in the industry, and the viability problems of the project, not to mention privatization. More critically, it underlines the importance of the state's disciplinary capacity in the management of necessary subsidies (in this case, learning rents) as the most important condition for successful privatization.

This chapter is structured as follows. The next section will discuss the challenges faced by the auto industry and Proton specifically. This is followed by the background to Proton's creation, privatization and renationalization. We then evaluate the performance of Proton before and after privatization, looking at its financial performance, production capacity, export and protection levels, technology acquisition, local content, and marketing and distribution. The following section identifies the main problems and causes of failure, and prioritizes the main conditions necessary for successful privatization. The final section summarizes the main findings and concludes.

## Challenges

Competitiveness in the auto industry is largely a function of economies of scale and productivity. The capacity to sell vehicles also depends on final product quality and marketing and distribution. The level of technology will determine the quality of product design and the efficiency of the production process. Marketing and distribution are also important as achieving economies of scale requires selling cars. Here, Proton faced industry-related challenges as well as challenges specific to late industrializers, along with constrains posed by wider government objectives.

### *Industry characteristics and trends*

The auto industry is characterized by requirements for substantial scale economies and capital investment, as well as increasing concentration, overcapacity and low margins. Industry data, particularly in the 1970s (when feasibility studies for Malaysia's national car project were being conducted) provides some context in which to assess challenges faced by the car industry. Estimates of economies of scale in annual passenger car production ranged from 100,000 cars per year (1959) to 600,000 (1972), with a minimum of 800,000 units for long-term viability (in the 1970s), and fairly constant returns at 700,000–1.5 million units (Maxcy and Silvertson 1959; Rhys 1972; White 1971, all cited in Bloomfield 1978). Economies of scale for engines in 1971 were around 400,000–500,000 per year, with final assembly at 200,000–300,000 units per year (Pratten 1971, cited in Bloomfield 1978). The collapse of the British auto industry in the 1990s can be traced back to the competitive disadvantage of many UK firms by 1975 because of the failure to achieve the necessary economies of scale (Central Policy Review Staff 1975, cited in Bloomfield 1978: 85–86). The high-volume and increasingly capital-intensive nature of the industry also required high levels of capacity utilization for economic and profitable operation, with severe financial consequences for underutilization of capital and production capacity.

Both scale economies and technology involve high capital costs. Early estimates of capital requirements in the US ranged from US$576 million (in the 1950s) to US$1 billion (1960s) to produce 800,000 cars per year (White 1971, cited in Bloomfield 1978), with marketing costs increasing from 31 to 46 per cent of distribution costs by 2000 (*Automotive News*, 15 October 2001). Companies also faced heavy expenditure for new model development (with shorter model life cycles of two to three years) and to meet more stringent environmental and safety standards. High capital requirements, overcapacity and low margins have historically necessitated industry rationalization with long-term trends towards mergers, strategic alliances and partnerships needed to provide technical economies of scale, capital resources for model development, more automated production, and increased marketing efforts (Bloomfield 1978; Bando 2000). Industry rationalization was also necessitated by low margins and declining profitability, partly the result of intense competition and overcapacity.

Overcapacity resulted in a big drop in profitability. Of the major car producers in 1973–87, only General Motors' net income as a percentage of net revenue averaged around 5 per cent, with Ford and Chrysler on occasion exceeding this. In general, the figure was below 5 per cent, with the last three companies registering significant, consecutive losses (Bloomfield 1991). Profits for many companies in Western Europe were small even before the oil crisis, and only Daimler and Peugeot made substantial profits and retained full profitability. Several large corporations had to be bailed out (British Leyland) while others went bankrupt (Iso, Jensen, MG Rover), changed ownership (Ferrari, Lamborghini, Aston Martin, Maserati) or merged (Citroën/Peugeot, DAF/Volvo). Overcapacity was expected to remain a problem until the end of the 1980s, possibly with as much as 25 per cent of the world's car capacity needing to be phased out for industry viability (Bloomfield 1978).

***Late-comer and specific challenges***

As an infant industry, Proton's competitiveness was further constrained by technology transfer problems and a limited domestic market size. Economies of scale requires exports, which in turn depend on technology (for product design and efficient production), marketing and distribution. The reason why production scale is not large is that the product is not competitive enough to capture a larger market share. But if it does not capture a larger market share it will not become more competitive. Here the technology acquisition strategy of the government is critical, since scale of production cannot be vast at the outset, and requires significant state assistance in the form of conditional subsidies, whether explicit or implicit, if the enterprise is to succeed. Thus, the problem of scale economies needs to be located within the context of technology acquisition.

In addition, Proton also had to meet government objectives to rationalize the local automotive industry; spearhead the development of component manufacturing industries; provide incentives for the acquisition and upgrading of technology, engineering norms and industrial skills; and promote New Economic Policy (NEP) restructuring objectives (by developing Malay participation as well as creating and sustaining employment). These were in part shaped by the political and economic imperatives discussed in Chapter 3. Specifically, a national car project allowed the government to meet the growing demands of the Malay middle class by promoting backward linkages with local component manufacture, while at the same time addressing the economic challenges of industrial upgrading. This meant that Proton had to upgrade its own technological capabilities as well as those of its local vendors to ensure that government objectives were met, and local component costs were kept low.

In return, Proton was provided with learning rents in the form of tariff and excise duty exemptions, and tax rebates for product development. Successful technology acquisition depends on the terms of technology transfer agreed with the technical partner, and the firm's 'absorptive capacity' (i.e. existing knowledge and competence, and the intensity of effort or commitment) (see Bell *et al.* 1984; Jacobsson 1993; Kim 2004). However, Proton's technology acquisition was affected by political considerations, namely NEP objectives to promote Malay (and bypass domestic Chinese) capital which compromised learning and efficiency. The haste of negotiations with Mitsubishi along with managerial constraints (inherited from the NEP) compromised technology acquisition. Proton's competitiveness was further hampered by the need to support (inefficient) local component manufacturers through technology transfers. Finally, Proton had no control over marketing and distribution. Domestic distribution, image and branding were handled by Edaran Otomobil Nasional (EON), the national distributor which was not owned by Proton. This led to coordination problems between production and distribution, conflicts of interest (e.g. Proton was unable to even determine accessory fittings and retail prices), and price increases which profited EON at the expense of Proton (*The Edge*, 12 April 1999).[1] These constraints created additional challenges for Proton as a late comer, and subsequently also affected its performance after privatization.

## Background

The origins of Proton can be traced back to the government's efforts to promote local content and greater efficiency in the 1960s through integration of a fragmented auto industry. This aimed to reduce imports, save foreign exchange, create employment, develop strong forward and backward linkages with the rest of the economy, transfer industrial technology, and increase Malay automotive participation. However, despite government measures to promote local content, efficiency and greater Malay participation, the market remained fragmented by the late 1970s, with a multiplicity of assembly plants producing low volumes of numerous makes and models due to the small market.[2] The refusal of assemblers to standardize design, material and dimensional specifications further limited economies of scale (Doner 1991). Local content was around 8–10 per cent and local component manufacture largely involved assembly of non-proprietary items (e.g. tyres, batteries, exhaust systems, paints) or imported parts, with low levels of technology (Chee and Fong 1983; Doner 1991; Tharu 1994). Malay presence in the industry was minimal, and mainly restricted to auto distribution and reconditioning, usually in the weakest firms (Doner 1991). The industry remained local Chinese-dominated, import-dependent and disappointing in terms of its contribution to industrialization. Total sales rose in 1983, but imports for the assembly sector grew faster, while the industry's (parts and assembly) contribution to total manufacturing output and GDP declined (Doner 1991).

By June 1978, problems in the auto sector, combined with stagnation and poor economic performance, led to a change in government policy, from fostering import-substitution type industries run by foreign car manufacturers, to state-led development of a Malaysian car as key to a Malay-led, second-stage import substitution (Doner 1991). This aimed to address issues related to constraints on economies of scale posed by too many assembly plants and a small domestic market; the domination of the local auto industry by joint ventures between Japanese car manufacturers and local Chinese assemblers, to the exclusion of Malay companies; and the slow progress of local production of auto parts (Bando 2000).

The Heavy Industries Corporation of Malaysia (HICOM) was created in 1980 to undertake large-scale ventures in strategic manufactures,[3] including a national car. Following unsuccessful talks with Japanese car manufacturer Daihatsu,[4] Mahathir proposed the national car project to Mitsubishi Corporation (MC) in October 1981 after his appointment as Prime Minister that year (Doner 1991). The project was approved in November 1982 and a contract was signed between HICOM and MC and its subsidiary, Mitsubishi

Motor Company (MMC), in May 1983. Proton was incorporated on 7 May 1983 as a joint-venture company between the Malaysian government through HICOM (70 per cent), MMC (15 per cent) and MC (15 per cent) to manufacture, assemble and sell motor vehicles and related products, including accessories, spare parts and other components. Mitsubishi agreed to establish an 80,000 unit capacity plant with Proton (with US$168 million in Japanese loans) to stamp, assemble, paint and test 1,300cc and 1,500cc engine cars (Doner 1991; Tharu 1994). The agreement covered 'starting dates, equity shares, training of Malaysian personnel, and new design changes every two years, with model changes every five years' (Doner 1991).

Production was to begin in 1986, with a capacity of 40,000 vehicles a year and output of 5,000 vehicles in the first year, increasing annually to 120,000 a year by the 1990s. Local content was to start at 36 per cent, with the local manufacture of engines and transmissions planned (Doner 1991; Tharu 1994). Proton launched its first car, the 1.3 litre Saga, in July 1985, almost a year ahead of schedule, and produced 8,700 cars that year. It was exempt from import duties until 1991, after which it had to pay 13 per cent import duty on CKD (completely knocked down) packs (compared with 42 per cent for non-national cars) and half the excise duty of non-national cars (depending on engine capacity) (see Table 7.01). This gave Proton cars a 24–64 per cent price advantage over non-national cars with comparable engine sizes and allowed the company to capture 65 per cent of the passenger vehicle market by 1987 and 74.2 per cent in 1993 (SalomonSmithBarney 2002; *The Sun*, 12 June 1993). A progressive duty structure also skewed industry volume towards the smaller engine segments dominated by Proton (Table 7.02).

Proton was converted into a public company on 22 November 1990 and publicly listed on the Kuala Lumpur Stock Exchange (KLSE) on 26 March 1992.[5] On 20 October 1995, Khazanah (the Ministry of Finance's investment arm) sold its 32 per cent stake in HICOM, without open tender, for an estimated RM1.72 billion (at RM5.20 per share) to Mega Consolidated

*Table 7.01* Malaysia: Passenger car tariffs, 1992–2003 (%)

| | *National* | *Non-national CKD (completely knocked down)* | *Non-national CBU (completely built up)* |
|---|---|---|---|
| Import duty* | 13 | 42 | 140–300 |
| Excise duty** | 50% of the rate for non-national car | Based on value | Based on value |
| Sales tax*** | 10 | 10 | 10 |

*Source:* Adapted from TA Securities (1996).
*Notes: *Duty on imported parts; **duty on finished product; ***sales tax is calculated at 10 per cent of (cost, insurance, freight + import duty charged). For import duty on non-national CBU, see Table 7.02.*

*Table 7.02* Malaysia: Auto industry import duty structure, 1992–2003 (%)

| *Categories* | *CKD* | *CBU* |
|---|---|---|
| Proton | 13 | n/a |
| *Non-national cars* | | |
| First 1799cc | 42 | 140 |
| 1800–1999cc | 42 | 170 |
| 2000–2499cc | 60 | 200 |
| 2500–2999cc | 70 | 250 |
| Above 3000cc | 80 | 300 |

*Source:* Adapted from Ministry of International Trade and Investment, Malaysia.

Sdn Bhd on a 'willing buyer willing seller basis'.[6] Mega Consolidated was wholly owned by Gadek Bhd, which was in turn owned by Diversified Resources Bhd (DRB), the main listed company of Yahaya Ahmad. With the acquisition of HICOM, both DRB and Mega Consolidated collectively owned 95 per cent of HICOM, and the company became DRB-HICOM.

The choice of Yahaya Ahmad was consistent with the broad features of privatization described in Chapter 3. He was politically well connected, being a personal friend of Prime Minister Mahathir and Deputy Prime Minister Anwar Ibrahim. However, he also had relevant experience, having trained as an automotive engineer in the UK, worked in the industry, and started up several automotive-related companies.[7] In 1992, Yahaya invited Mahathir to visit the plant of Automotive Manufacturers (a DRB subsidiary) which had the capacity to produce 46 different models (including Isuzu, Mitsubishi, Citroën and Tata vehicles), and offered to help Proton overcome capacity constraints[8] (*Malaysian Business*, 1 July 1993; *The Star*, 16 March 1996; *Asiaweek*, 11 April 1997). In June 1993, the government announced DRB's joint-venture with Proton through Usahasama Proton-DRB Sdn Bhd (USPD) to manufacture the Satria.

Yahaya was subsequently killed in an accident on 3 March 1997 and was replaced as chairman by Saleh Sulong, his business partner and DRB-HICOM's general manager. However, Yahaya no longer played a strategic role after the appointment of Tengku Mahaleel as Proton's managing director in 1997. Following the 1997–98 Asian financial crisis, DRB-HICOM faced financial difficulties and was unable to pay its mounting debts or finance Proton's expansion plans. The death of owner Yahaya also created some uncertainty about the future of the company. The government started purchasing shares in Proton as early as September 1997.[9] On 29 October 1998, state oil company Petronas confirmed it was considering purchasing Proton and subsequently purchased 27.2 per cent of Proton from DRB-HICOM for RM7 per share in April 2000.

## Performance

Although Proton was privatized in March 1992 following its public listing, the government remained the controlling shareholder. Privatization here therefore refers to the period after the sale of a controlling stake to Yahaya Ahmad in October 1995. Proton's performance needs to be assessed in relation to the problems the company faced prior to privatization. Specifically, privatization sought to improve efficiency and competitiveness by addressing slow technology acquisition and diseconomies of scale (low production capacity). Success here can be gauged by Proton's production capacity, export performance, protection levels, technology development and local content. Privatization also needed to address Proton's marketing and distribution as its sales performance depended on this. While Proton continued to be profitable, this was due to protection, tax exemptions, rebates and subsidies, and the company remained uncompetitive. Technology acquisition was slow and proved too costly for the private owner, and Proton failed to meet even its own targets for production capacity and export, continuing to rely on the domestic market through protection. Problems in marketing and distribution were similarly only addressed after the company's renationalization, but in any case could not compensate for the lack of competitiveness of Proton cars.

Examination of these performance indicators will focus on the two-year period immediately before (1993–94) and after privatization (1996–97) in order to exclude the effects of the Asian financial crisis from the end of 1997. As ownership and control of Proton was only transferred to Yahaya in October 1995, this year will be viewed as a transition year. This brief period necessarily restricts analysis, especially given the time needed to implement the necessary changes and the time lag between implementation and results. This is particularly so with technology transfer and local content. Furthermore, as Proton's financial year ends in March, the annual reports do not provide clear evidence of trends. As such, measures taken after privatization will be examined over a longer period (for which data is available) through a review of the longer-term impact of changes introduced by Yahaya. This is to provide a more balanced assessment of post-privatization improvements while factoring in the effects of the 1997–98 Asian financial crisis. Data is mainly sourced from SalomonSmithBarney (based on data provided by Proton). There are discrepancies between this and data published in the press, for example, but SalomonSmithBarney provides a consistent detailed data source for comparison. Selected comparisons with Hyundai, South Korea's first passenger car manufacturer, provide a benchmark given the success of that company and the Malaysian government's attempt to emulate it.

### *Financial performance*

Proton's financial performance after privatization improved in almost all areas due to a growing domestic car market, continued protection and favourable exchange rates. An increase in average turnover from RM2.7 billion (1993–94) to RM5.7 billion (1996–97) enabled Proton to increase average profits before tax (PBT) (from RM296.6 to RM741.9 million), average net profit (RM256.1 to RM548.7 million), average return on assets (ROA) (10.5 to 14.7 per cent), average return on equity (ROE) (23.9 to 29.1 per cent) and PBT margins (9.85 to 12.65 per cent) (Table 7.03). However, average net profit margins actually declined marginally from 9.8 to 9.4 per cent, while average net interest cover deteriorated from –8.35 to –25.5 per cent (Table 7.04). Furthermore, the high net profit margin (11.9 per cent) and ROA (18.5 per cent) in 1997 were not particularly significant improvements over Proton's net profit margin in 1993 (11.6 per cent) and ROA in 1992 (15.9 per cent).

Proton's improved operating profit margin was attributed to its across-the-board cost-cutting exercise in 1996–97, lower local component costs (as a result of Proton pressing local suppliers to reduce costs), higher efficiency ratios of 94 per cent, less capital works-in-progress, and high margins derived from a good model mix, and increased plant efficiency (see *Asiaweek*, 11 April 1997; *The Edge*, 10 March 1997, 30 June 1997). Yahaya claimed to have 'delayered' and 'downsized' Proton's staff 'to empower management to take responsibility and make decisions quickly' (*Business Times*, 19 August 1996), although there appeared to be no cutting of staff.[10]

However, improved operating margins were also due to the depreciation of the Japanese yen[11] by 25 per cent (1996) and 16 per cent (1997) (*The Edge*, 24 June 1996). The company also benefited from a lower effective tax rate for additional reinvestment allowances arising from higher capital expenditure in 1996 (*The Sun*, 16 July 1996). Sales growth in 2001 and 2002 was the result of the overall increase in Malaysian car sales due to lower interest rates, a RM1.25 billion government fund to finance car purchases for teachers, excise duty exemptions for hire-car operators using national cars, and generous hire purchase periods (*Malaysian Business*, 16 January 2002; *Investors Digest*, 16 February 2002; *Business Times*, 6 May 2002).

### *Production capacity*

Proton's production capacity expansion increased from an average of 12.3 per cent (1993–94) to 18.2 per cent (1996–97) (Table 7.05) and this continued to increase in 1998 before being reduced in 1999 and 2000 following the Asian financial crisis. Capacity utilization increased along with production capacity and was generally high (well above 80 per cent for 1995–2002, with the exception of 1998) and above Proton's own breakeven level (calculated at 67 per cent in 2000), although this was already high in 1994 (SalomonSmithBarney 2002).

*Table 7.03* Proton: Profitability, 1991–2000 (RM million)

| | *Turnover* | *Turnover growth* | *Profit before tax* | *PBT growth* | *Net profit* | *Net profit growth* | *Net profit margin* | *ROA-end* | *ROE-end* |
|---|---|---|---|---|---|---|---|---|---|
| 1991 | 1,786.0 | 261.5 | | 187.0 | | 10.5 | | | |
| 1992 | 2,191.8 | 22.7 | 407.9 | 56.0 | 259.4 | 38.7 | 11.8 | 15.9 | 42.2 |
| 1993 | 2,286.5 | 4.3 | 311.2 | (23.7) | 265.2 | 2.2 | 11.6 | 11.8 | 27.1 |
| 1994 | 3,087.0 | 35.0 | 282.0 | (9.4) | 246.9 | (6.9) | 8.0 | 9.2 | 20.7 |
| 1995 | 3,708.4 | 20.1 | 307.9 | 9.2 | 232.1 | (6.0) | 6.3 | 7.6 | 17.1 |
| 1996 | 5,166.7 | 39.3 | 454.6 | 47.6 | 355.9 | 53.3 | 6.9 | 10.9 | 22.5 |
| 1997 | 6,222.2 | 20.4 | 1,029.1 | 126.4 | 741.5 | 108.9 | 11.9 | 18.5 | 35.7 |
| 1998 | 6,788.5 | 9.1 | 724.6 | (29.6) | 440.6 | (40.6) | 6.5 | 8.5 | 16.9 |
| 1999 | 4,075.0 | (40.0) | 99.0 | (86.3) | 66.8 | (84.8) | 1.6 | 1.2 | 2.4 |
| 2000 | 6,496.7 | 59.4 | 141.3 | 42.8 | 70.6 | 5.6 | 1.1 | 1.3 | 2.6 |

*Source:* Adapted from Proton (2001); SalomonSmithBarney (2003).
*Notes:* PBT (profit before tax); ROA (returns on assets); ROE (returns on equity). Growth rates, net profit margin, ROA and ROE are in percentage (%). Brackets ( ) = negative or loss.

*Table 7.04* Proton: Liquidity and leverage ratios, 1991–2000

| | *Current ratio (x)* | *Quick ratio (x)* | *Gross debt (RM million)* | *Net cash (RM million)* | *Gross gearing* | *Net gearing* | *Gross interest cover* | *Net interest cover* |
|---|---|---|---|---|---|---|---|---|
| 1991 | 1.8 | 1.6 | 594.1 | (136.3) | 1.74 | 0.40 | 12.3 | 187.8 |
| 1992 | 2.0 | 1.8 | 612.8 | 305.6 | 0.69 | (0.34) | 17.3 | (14.8) |
| 1993 | 1.6 | 1.4 | 700.4 | 229.3 | 0.65 | (0.20) | 11.3 | (5.4) |
| 1994 | 1.4 | 1.2 | 800.5 | 5.9 | 0.61 | 0.00 | 8.8 | (11.3) |
| 1995 | 1.4 | 1.0 | 723.1 | 251.3 | 0.52 | (0.16) | 11.1 | (15.1) |
| 1996 | 1.6 | 0.9 | 561.9 | 77.4 | 0.32 | (0.02) | 11.7 | (38.4) |
| 1997 | 1.5 | 1.1 | 466.5 | 991.7 | 0.19 | (0.38) | 42.2 | (12.6) |
| 1998 | 1.3 | 0.8 | 655.0 | 807.9 | 0.23 | (0.28) | 17.1 | (5.4) |
| 1999 | 1.3 | 1.0 | 494.7 | 1,071.6 | 0.19 | (0.38) | 2.6 | 0.4 |
| 2000 | 1.4 | 1.1 | 607.7 | 865.8 | 0.23 | (0.21) | 3.1 | 0.5 |

*Source:* Adapted from SalomonSmithBarney (2003).
*Notes:* Brackets ( ) = negative.

However, capacity and production levels were significantly below Proton's own target for economies of scale. In 1996, Proton aimed to produce 500,000 cars by 2000 to achieve optimum efficiency scale but only managed 230,000 (*Business Times*, 31 July 1996; *The Edge*, 12 April 1999; SalomonSmith-Barney 2002). Proton's estimates for economies of scale of the Campro engine was 160,000–260,000, substantially less than the 1971 industry estimates of 400,000–500,000 (Pratten 1971, cited in Bloomfield 1978). Furthermore, doubts remained about whether Proton sold enough cars to

*Table 7.05* Proton: Production capacity, 1992–2002 ('000)

| | *Production capacity* | *Capacity increase %* | *Unit sales* | *Sales increase %* | *Utilization %* |
|---|---|---|---|---|---|
| 1991 | 120 | | 98.9 | | |
| 1992 | 120 | 0 | 118.1 | 19.4 | |
| 1993 | 123 | 2.5 | 127.2 | 7.7 | |
| 1994 | 150 | 22.0 | 131.1 | 3.1 | 87 |
| 1995 | 165 | 10.0 | 160.1 | 22.0 | 97 |
| 1996 | 205 | 24.2 | 184.4 | 24.4 | 90 |
| 1997 | 230 | 12.2 | 184.2 | (0.1) | 80 |
| 1998 | 180 | (21.7) | 109.1 | (40.8) | 61 |
| 1999 | 180 | 0 | 170.3 | 56.1 | 95 |
| 2000 | 230 | 21.7 | 195.2 | 14.6 | 85 |

*Source:* Adapted from SalomonSmithBarney (2003); 1992–94 data from *Business Times* (31 December 1993), *The Edge* (27 January 1997), *The Star* (21 June 1997).
*Note:* Unit sales may exceed production volume for any given year as sales may be from old stock.

be able to develop its own engines (*The Edge*, 24 June 2000; *Business Times*, 13 September 2000). The cost of Proton producing its own engines and transmission was considered too high given its capacity,[12] and its target remained small compared to Hyundai's annual production of 1.3 million in 1995. Excluding the effects of the 1997–98 crisis, and based on a growth rate of 10–20 per cent a year, Proton's capacity would only have increased to 240,000–340,000 by 2000, suggesting initial targets may have been too optimistic (Table 7.06).

Part of Proton's long-term plan to become more competitive was by substantially increasing production capacity by opening Proton City, a state-of-the-art plant, expected to save 20 per cent in costs by employing just-in-time (JIT) methods to cut down on stocking and space.[13] In 1999, Proton announced it was two years away from a fully automated internet-based end-to-end procurement, production and distribution system initiated in 1997 (*The Edge*, 12 April 1999). Proton City was postponed following the 1997–98 Asian financial crisis and its owner's inability to finance capacity expansion. The project was later financed by Petronas before it sold Proton to Khazanah.

## Exports

Export performance is one measure of competitiveness. Proton's exports increased by an average of 20.7 per cent (1996–97) compared to a contraction of 4.1 per cent (1993–94) (Table 7.07). However, export growth slowed substantially after 1997 and contracted after 1999, while exports as a percentage of unit sales actually declined from an average of 15.8 per cent to 14.7 per cent after privatization, indicating a growing reliance on the protected domestic market. Hyundai's capacity expansion in comparison was driven by its export markets, in particular North America, which allowed Hyundai to increase production capacity from 150,000 in 1984 to 700,000 in 1988. (Gwynne 1991).

*Table 7.06* Proton: Potential capacity*, 1996–2002 ('000)

| | *10% projected growth* | *20% projected growth* | *Actual* |
|---|---|---|---|
| 1996 | | | 165 |
| 1997 | 181.5 | 198 | 205 |
| 1998 | 199.7 | 237.6 | 230 |
| 1999 | 219.6 | 285.1 | 180 |
| 2000 | 241.6 | 342.1 | 180 |
| 2001 | 265.8 | 410.5 | 230 |
| 2002 | 292.4 | 492.6 | 240 |

*Source:* Adapted from SalomonSmithBarney (2003).
*Note:* * Based on 10–20% p.a. projected growth rates.

*Table 7.07* Proton: Exports, 1992–2002 ('000)

| | *Unit sales* | *Exports* | *Export growth %* | *Export share %* | *Export target* | *Hyundai output* | *Global output* |
|---|---|---|---|---|---|---|---|
| 1992 | 98.9 | 18.7 | | 18.9 | | 701.7 | |
| 1993 | 118.1 | 21.8 | 16.1 | 18.5 | | 774.9 | |
| 1994 | 127.2 | 16.5 | (24.3) | 13.0 | | 892.7 | |
| 1995 | 131.1 | 16.6 | 0.6 | 14.8 | | 966.3 | 36,500 |
| 1996 | 160.1 | 20.0 | 20.4 | 14.3 | | 1,037.7 | 38,700 |
| 1997 | 184.4 | 24.2 | 21.0 | 15.1 | 38.0 | 975.6 | 39,742.6 |
| 1998 | 184.1 | 27.2 | 12.3 | 17.3 | 32.0 | 586.7 | 39,396.0 |
| 1999 | 109.1 | 14.5 | (46.6) | 15.3 | 52.0–53.0 | 947.3 | 40,144.0 |
| 2000 | 170.3 | 14.5 | 0.0 | 9.3 | 125–200 | | 40,948.0 |
| 2001 | 195.2 | 8.8 | (39.3)* | 4.7 | | | |
| 2002 | 239.8 | 8.2 | (6.8)* | 3.7 | | | |

*Source:* Adapted from SalomonSmithBarney (2003); 1992–94 data from *Business Times* (31 December 1993), *The Edge* (27 January 1997), *The Star (*21 June 1997); export targets from *The Star* (8 January 1998), *New Straits Times* (19 March 1998), *Asiaweek* (11 April 1997); Hyundai production from (http://www.geocities.com/MotorCity/Speedway/4939/korea.html); global production (http://www.geocities.com/MotorCity/Speedway/4939/carprod.html£make).
*Note:* * Forecast.

Proton also failed to meet its own (often revised) export targets, both before and after privatization. In 1995, Proton's medium-term (three-to-five-year) export target was 30 per cent of production by 1998–2000 (*The Star*, 23 January 1995). After privatization, Proton's export target was 38,000 for 1997 and became even more preposterous – 125,000–200,000 for 2000 (i.e. 25–40 per cent of the planned 500,000 capacity for 2000) and 375,000 in 2003 (Table 7.07). These targets appeared to be unrealistically ambitious even without considering the effects of the 1997–98 crisis, and based on annual export growth rates of 10–50 per cent (Table 7.08).

Exports were constrained by Proton's limited product range (seven models compared to twenty-eight by Ford and thirty-eight by Toyota). However, Proton did not produce or sell enough of its existing models to be able to increase its product range without further penalties from diseconomies of scale. Even Proton's best-selling model, the Wira, was being produced in uneconomic quantities, averaging at 82,000 units a year (1995–2002) (SalomonSmithBarney 2003). Poor export performance was mainly due to over reliance on the UK market (38 per cent of total exports in 1996), and the fall in exports to the UK (from 14,900 units in 1993 to 4,600 in 1998) due to intense competition from Japanese and Korean cars (*New Straits Times*, 27 May 2000). Proton's Australian distributor also dropped the brand in 1997 as it was unable to match the reductions in Korean car prices.[14] Exports between 1986 and mid-2003 totalled 230,000 to fifty countries, but only fifteen markets remained active in 2003 (*Business Times*, 28 June 2003). Furthermore, exports were loss-making in 1999–2000, and only turned a modest

*Table 7.08* Proton: Export potential ('000), 1996–2000

| | *Target* | *10% projected growth* | *20% projected growth* | *50% projected growth* | *Actual* |
|---|---|---|---|---|---|
| 1996 | | | | | 20.0 |
| 1997 | 38.0 | 22.0 | 24.0 | 30.0 | 24.2 |
| 1998 | 32.0 | 24.2 | 28.8 | 45.0 | 27.2 |
| 1999 | 52.0–53.0 | 26.6 | 34.6 | 67.5 | 14.5 |
| 2000 | 125–200 | 29.3 | 41.5 | 101.3 | 14.5 |
| 2001 | | 32.2 | 49.8 | 158.0 | 8.8 |
| 2002 | | 35.4 | 59.8 | 228.0 | 8.2 |

*Source:* Adapted from SalomonSmithBarney (2003).
*Note:* Calculations based on the Korean Institute for Economics and Technology forecasted annual average growth rates of 48.7–51.2 per cent for South Korean automobile exports between 1984 and 1990 (*Industrial Management*, 9(6), 1987).

RM3.7 million in pre-tax profit in 2001 largely due to Proton UK breaking even (*New Straits Times*, 20 November 2001). By 2003, exports still contributed only 5–10 per cent of revenue, despite a target of 30 per cent (which was still low compared to Hyundai) (*New Straits Times*, 20 October 2003).

### *Protection*

Proton's efficiency can also be measured by ongoing protection levels, actual progress towards regional trade liberalization under the Asian Free Trade Agreement (AFTA), and projections involving lower protection levels. Under the Association of Southeast Asian Nations (ASEAN) Common Effective Preferential Tariff (CEPT, the main mechanism for the realization of AFTA), import duties for cars were expected not to exceed 20 per cent by 2003. Despite early imminent government warnings to Proton about the removal of trade barriers under AFTA, Malaysia's automotive import duty structure remained essentially unchanged since 1991.

Instead, the government announced in September 1999 that it was not ready to reduce tariffs on imported CKD and CBU units, and rejected cuts in import tariffs on automobiles and auto parts from Thailand. In early May 2000, it secured deferment for the transfer of CKD units from the temporary exclusion list to the inclusion list on 1 January 2005. Mahathir admitted that Proton would not be very competitive in an open market and the government's request for continuation of protective tariffs on auto imports until 1 January 2005 was accepted by ASEAN on 18 July 2000. The government also kept its options open in case Proton remained uncompetitive. According to the Deputy Minister of International Trade and Industry: 'If by 2005 we still feel that we need to be exempted from AFTA, we will then review the policy' (*New Straits Times*, 25 August 2000).

Even Proton's Japanese director admitted that it would not be easy to cut costs and improve the quality of locally manufactured cars in 'four short years' before AFTA in 2005, and expected Proton's market share to fall from 60 to 30 per cent (*New Straits Times*, 22 July 2000).[15] The impact of partial duties would substantially reduce the price difference between Proton and competing Japanese models while the removal of duties would make competitor models significantly cheaper (TA Securities 1996) (Table 7.09).

Proton's continued reliance on protection for its price advantage was reflected in a steady loss of market share from 74 per cent (1993) to 43–45 per cent (2003) as the government relaxed its control over new car prices, allowing distributors to cut prices (Table 7.10). By 2003, the price gap between Proton and its competitors declined considerably, with comparable models from Japanese, Korean and American manufacturers[16] selling for between RM50,000 and RM76,676 compared to RM72,811 for the Proton Waja 1.6X (the premier model of the range).

### *Technology development*

Proton attempted to increase competitiveness by reducing costs and increasing production, pushing for technology transfer to reduce its import content from 30 per cent (in 1996) to 10 per cent. Yahaya sought to overcome technology transfer problems with Mitsubishi through tie-ups with French car manufacturer Citroën, and later, Renault, and through the purchase, in October 1996, of Lotus Group International Limited, a British automotive engineering company and manufacturer of luxury sports cars. The Citroën tie-up was initiated by Yahaya with the aim of using the engine of the Citroën AX.[17] (Yahaya also owned the Citroën franchise through DRB-HICOM subsidiary, Directional.) The deal for the 10-year-old Citroën AX was attractive as it involved no further development costs, and was 50 per cent cheaper than the cost of Proton's previous small model, the Satria 1.3L.[18] However, Citroën had replaced the AX with the Saxo and was no longer interested in its development, and Proton complained about technology transfer problems (*Asiaweek*, 4 November 1997). The Tiara 1.1 (a rebadged Citroën AX) was released in 1996, but was poorly conceived, lacking features and suffering mechanical problems. Three years later, and after several generous discounts, Proton discontinued its production.

By mid-1996, Proton only had 20 per cent design competency and its acquisition of Lotus was a major step in upgrading its engineering capabilities. There were immediate benefits, reflected in the modest commercial success locally of its 'Lotus-tuned' versions of the Satria 1.8 GTi and Perdana V6 2.0 (both released in 1998), as well as potential cost savings. Lotus also contributed to the Campro engine[19] and two new models, the Waja and Gen-2. Development of the Waja began in June 1996 and the car was launched in November 2002. The Waja was Proton's first in-house design and a departure from variations of the Mitsubishi Lancer, although still based on

*Table 7.09* Proton: Impact of reduction of import and excise duties on car prices with partial duties and no duties, 1997 (RM)

| | *Price under existing rates* | *Price under Proton's rates* | *% price difference* | *Price with no duties* | *% price difference* | *Proton's existing price* |
|---|---|---|---|---|---|---|
| Nissan Sunny 1.3 | 44,190.07 | 32,562.16 | (26.3) | 26,373.42 | (40.3) | 31,433.41 (1.3) |
| Honda Civic 1.5 | 59,119.37 | 41,159.89 | (30.4) | 33,337.07 | (49.4) | 40,051.14 (1.5) |
| Toyota Corolla 1.6 | 65,608.07 | 43,472.63 | (33.7) | 35,210.25 | (52.7) | 51,777.78 (1.6) |

*Source:* Adapted from TA Securities (1996).
*Note:* ( ) = % less than Proton's price.

*Table 7.10* Proton: Domestic market share, 1993–2003 (%)

| *1993* | *1994* | *1995* | *1996* | *1997* | *1998* | *1999* | *2000* | *2001* | *2002* | *2003* |
|---|---|---|---|---|---|---|---|---|---|---|
| 74.0 | 71.0 | 61.7 | 63.9 | 64.0 | 64.0 | 54.0 | 52.1–63.4* | 63.7* | 62.0 | 43.0–45.0** |

*Source:* Adapted from *Business Times* (31 December 1993), *The Edge* (27 January 1997), *The Star* (21 June 1997) for 1994–98; Autoworld <http://www.autoworld.com.my/> for 1999–2000; * Malaysian Automotive Association (cited in *The Edge*, 23 September 2003); ** SalomonSmith-Barney (2003).

a Mitsubishi (Carisma) platform, for which Proton bought the intellectual property rights. Mitsubishi and Renault supplied engines, the latter tie-up followed the failure of the Tiara and Proton's dissatisfaction with Citroën. The Waja increased local content to 95 per cent, and savings from this model were reflected in profit margins about three times those of the Wira, while development of the Campro engine was expected to save Proton RM2,000 per car (i.e. 30 per cent in engine costs alone),[20] or RM200 million a year (10–15 per cent of costs) in royalty payments (*Business Times*, 27 September 2002).

Proton's engine management system, jointly developed with Lotus Engineering and Siemens VDO in July 2001, cost RM20 million but was estimated to reduce Proton's engineering development cost by 20–30 per cent (up to RM145 million in annual material costs) (*Business Times*, 18 January 2002; *New Straits Times*, 13 February 2002). Proton's expenditure on imported parts and materials, mainly engines and transmissions from Japan and Europe, declined from RM1.72 billion (2000) to RM1.44 billion (2001) and RM1.29 billion (2002) (*Business Times*, 28 June 2003). However, increased technical capabilities did not significantly reduce Proton's technical fees, with royalties (for engine assembly) actually increasing as a percentage of total technical fees (SalomonSmithBarney 2003), suggesting that there was insufficient technology transfer to translate into significant cost reductions.

The Proton Gen-2, developed after Proton's renationalization, was based on a variation of the Carisma platform but with Proton's own body and engine. In response to pressure to release new models to regain market share, the Gen-2 was rushed into production in 2004 and resulted in design problems and poor build quality which received some poor reviews in the UK motoring press.[21] More crucially, Proton was unable to develop the necessary variable valve timing technology for the Campro engine, or its own gearbox, having to source this from Mitsubishi. These problems illustrate the difficulties and considerable time required for technology acquisition. Technology development proceeded at a slow pace, with delivery of the Waja and Gen-2 delayed because of supply bottlenecks and new versions for production not being ready (*The Economist*, 8 May 2004). The Campro engine, originally scheduled for production by 2002, was only released in 2004 due to technical difficulties (*Business Times*, 13 September 2000, 14 June 2002; *The Economist*,

8 May 2004). Overall, Proton was still seen as inferior, uncompetitive in price and technology (due to an outmoded mass production stage with pockets of JIT practices), and with the worst-quality record in the country (*The Sun*, 25 September 1997; *Business Times*, 22 March 2002; *The Economist*, 8 May 2004). Even by 2002, Proton's competitiveness continued to be constrained by technology limitations, a lack of new products and cost, with prices expected to increase by 11 per cent (*Business Times*, 20 January 2001, 22 March 2002). Poor design and disappointing sales also led to the discontinuation of the Juara mini-van/people carrier in 2002.

### *Local content*

As most of Proton's cost savings were expected to come from lower component costs, it was important to increase local content and, at the same time, reduce its costs. Yahaya attempted to reduce the cost of local components by restructuring Proton's component manufacturing and Vendor Development Programme (VDP), and pushing vendors to expand capacity (by meeting 30 per cent export targets) and to invest in R&D (to reduce technological dependence) (*Business Times*, 19 August 1996). Proton also moved away from its previous single-source policy in 1997, requiring several companies to compete for the supply of particular parts (*New Straits Times*, 1 April 2002). Proton managed to increase local content and reduce the cost of local components after privatization, but this came from local vendors being issued with directives to comply with price reductions, rather than from efforts to improve vendor efficiency (*Asiaweek*, 11 April 1997; *The Star*, 8 February 2001). Furthermore, previously increasing local content appeared to level off (SalomonSmithBarney 2003), suggesting that further gains may not have been possible without actual efficiency improvements or technological advances.

Domestic parts manufacturers remained uncompetitive, lacking expertise and largely dependent on overseas partners for technology (e.g. see *The Edge*, 10 August 1998; Bando 2000). Many of Proton's parts and equipment continued to be inferior, in part due to vendor complacency arising from secure long-term contracts and political pressure (Bando 2000; *Business Times*, 2 January 2002), and most of Proton vendors did not possess the QS9000 certification needed to supply the major car manufacturers, with even the larger vendors continuing to depend primarily on Proton (*The Sun*, 13 September 2000; *New Straits Times*, 8 March 2002; *Business Times*, 26 June 2003). Increasing local content did not reduce Proton's costs as production of local components relied on imported material from Japan, and local component costs actually increased following the ringgit's devaluation after mid-1997 (*The Edge*, 16 September 1996; also see *Business Times*, 4 December 1998). Import content was still high at 30 per cent (Proton's target was 10 per cent), and imported Japanese parts continued to make up 30 per cent of the cost of a Proton car by late 1997, further exposing Proton to currency fluctuations (*Asiaweek*, 4 November 1997). Increasing local content also made Proton less competitive than ASEAN-assembled cars with lower local content (*New Straits Times*, 8 November 2002).

Proton sought to restructure its vendor programme by streamlining its 151 vendors into 30–40 'system suppliers' who would have to upgrade with the R&D capability to design and fabricate component systems for Proton and other manufacturers. A significant feature was the creation of second- and third-tier sub-contractors and suppliers who would supply first-tier vendors to improve efficiency and reduce costs. Proton was only able to implement a modular approach to component sourcing with the production of the Waja, where 20 'tier one' vendors acquired design and engineering capabilities for component development and verification to manufacture components in collaboration with Proton engineers (Proton 2001). However, Proton only managed a 3–4 per cent reduction in local component costs in 2003 as the loss of market share made it difficult to negotiate for lower local component costs with vendors given their smaller output.[22] Petronas was later reported to have sought government approval to source cheaper parts from overseas to lower costs after it took over Proton and AFTA offered Proton the opportunity to source components more cheaply and lower its selling price by 18 per cent (at 6 per cent per annum) (*The Edge*, 6 December 1999).

### *Marketing and distribution*

Yahaya sought to make Proton more market-oriented, focusing on marketing, price positioning and building up its market image. This involved changing EON's sales culture from one of merely taking orders to actually trying to sell cars, and improving its existing marketing strategy by reassessing and repositioning in low-profit overseas markets, rather than by exploring new ones. After privatization, Proton appointed USPD as its second national distributor (for the Tiara, Satria, Satria GTi, Wira Aeroback and Putra models). USPD was set up following DRB's joint venture to assemble the Satria with Proton. However, EON and USPD operated as separate business units, and Yahaya did not seem to address integration and coordination problems. As a result, there were inconsistencies in sales forecasts and quality, customer support, and marketing, leading to a mismatch between demand and production (by as much as eight times for the Satria GTi) (*The Edge*, 12 April 1999). Proton was still unable to determine retail prices, leading to EON remaining more profitable (*The Star*, 8 February 2001). Furthermore, EON's marketing of the car relied on similar strategies as before, and Proton continued to receive customer complaints on its cars and service levels, with many dealers only interested in selling cars but not in after-sales service (*The Star*, 28 May 2001).

It was only much later that Proton attempted to address integration and coordination problems through the acquisition of 70 per cent of USPD from

DRB-HICOM for RM297 million in 2000.[23] It refused to purchase EON (partly because EON would not agree to contribute 30 per cent to Proton's new model development costs) and instead chose to make USPD (renamed Proton Edar) its sole distributor, relegating EON to the status of 'super dealer'.[24] The purchase of USPD (and its subsequent increase in market share at the expense of EON) allowed Proton to gain control of distribution and marketing, and to bypass problems associated with EON. The new 'super dealer' arrangement also allowed Proton to combine both EON's and Proton Edar's resources, rationalize and streamline sales and after-sales service, and promote a common corporate identity (*Business Times*, 1 April 2003). Proton, through Proton Edar, determined prices, allowing it to better pitch models against the competition (*The Star*, 8 February 2001). Proton Edar also determined and installed accessories (e.g. air-conditioners, rubber mats and body stripes) which were previously very lucrative for EON. EON was allowed to maintain existing margins (which were higher than for other dealers, but lower than for Proton Edar), but its model range was restricted and it was not allowed to undercut Proton Edar's retail prices (*Business Times*, 10 April 2003, 21 August 2003). These changes were only implemented after Proton's renationalization.

Nonetheless, sales still relied on cheap financing, special promotional packages and government support. Exports continued to suffer from problems with branding, product quality, pricing, sales, after-sales service and distribution, and the company appeared unable to resolve the contradiction between selling cheap, basic cars and trying to compete in more expensive market segments (*New Straits Times*, 13 May 2000). While the acquisition of Lotus was meant to provide Proton cars with superior performance and a niche market, Proton found it difficult to shed its past image. According to its CEO Tengku Mahaleel, the Proton brand was 'somewhere at basement bargain' and 'neither here nor there . . . bought because they are cheap and there is decreasing nationalistic support' (*Business Times*, 10 January 2001, 10 August 1998). This was compounded by regular statements from the Prime Minister that Proton would concentrate on selling 'not so sophisticated cars with all the gadgets' in Asia, the Middle East and North Africa (given its inability to compete technologically) (*The Star*, 7 October 2000).

## Problems

From the available evidence, privatization did not improve Proton's performance overall. While some financial indicators improved, this was on the back of continued protection and the growth of the domestic market. Production capacity increased but was still below economies of scale and Proton's own targets. Exports increased in absolute terms until 1998 (but not as a share of total sales) and declined to pre-1992 levels after 1999. Proton continued to lose domestic market share despite ongoing protection. Underlying these problems was the slow rate of technology acquisition and failure to achieve economies of scale (production capacity). As a result, the company remained uncompetitive, relying on domestic sales, with protection levels unchanged. Proton's overall poor performance can be explained by the government's ex ante and ex post failures.

### *Ex ante failure*

Ex ante failure occurred at Proton's conception and privatization. As an infant industry, Proton's viability crucially depended on technology acquisition and learning rents. However, the haste in which the national car project was originally created led to several ex ante failures on the government's part. It failed to secure a favourable technology transfer agreement with Mitsubishi, ensure that learning rents (protection) was temporary and conditional upon meeting performance targets, and plan for exports. These ex ante failures affected Proton's learning and technology acquisition. Under these circumstances, privatization in itself was unlikely to solve Proton's main problems, at most only providing a second-best outcome, and the decision to privatize represented another ex ante failure. The government continued to underestimate the problems inherent in the auto industry (and especially an infant industry), and the ability of the private sector to undertake such a project, particularly where other economic and social objectives were involved, namely Proton's role in spearheading industrialization by supporting local (Malay) component manufacture.

Proton's technology acquisition was affected by political considerations, namely the need to promote Malay (and bypass domestic Chinese) capital, and the legacy of the NEP which compromised learning. This affected negotiations for technology transfer and the learning process, creating additional problems for Proton as a late comer, and subsequently also affecting its performance after privatization. Negotiations with Mitsubishi, Proton's technical partner, were compromised by inexperienced (HICOM) officials and the highly centralized and secretive nature of negotiations, led by Mahathir, which excluded Malaysian Industrial Development Authority (MIDA) officials and (Chinese) Malaysian firms with experience in CKD pricing, technology transfer and local content (Doner 1991). As a result, the contract left several areas vague (including future local content levels, CKD unit prices, royalty payments, local content, technology transfer, and exports), providing gains 'far more secure for Japan and Mitsubishi than for Malaysia' (*Far Eastern Economic Review*, 20 April 1989; Doner 1991).[25]

Moreover, Proton did not have the right management or engineering expertise to meet learning requirements, and opted to use existing components and make modifications to the existing body instead of gradually developing its own technology (*Malaysian Business*, 16 October 2002; also see *Business Times*, 10 January 1992). According to Proton's managing director Mohd Nadzmi, technology transfer was slow because 'no one knew how to go about it' and Proton's management initially did not understand the business thoroughly (*Malaysian Business*, 1 July 1994: 14). As a result, progress was slow and Proton essentially remained a (Malay) assembler, relying on Mitsubishi technology and essentially rebadging old Mitsubishi models. In-house engine assembly only began in 1990, six years after commencement of operations, and the high cost of using Mitsubishi's engines and ongoing royalty payments affected Proton's competitiveness.[26]

Proton's original and subsequent production targets (after privatization) were substantially below industry estimates for economies of scale, with the government underestimating the capital and technological requirements, and time needed to develop a Malaysian car. While it sought to emulate South Korea's car industry, the government did not account for global conditions (including overcapacity) and industry forecasts made in the 1970s, as well as ongoing trends towards industry rationalization. Capacity expansion was further constrained by domestic market size and the lack of international competitiveness, particularly in the context of global overcapacity.

Proton's original and subsequent production targets (5,000 units in 1985, 120,000 by the 1990s, and 500,000 by 2000) were well below industry levels for economies of scale. Its planned capacity of 80,000 in 1985 was also uneconomical, while actual capacity in 1985 was even lower at 40,000. These figures were significantly below Hyundai's first production planned for 1976 (55,000) and 1978–1979 (120,000). By 1987, Hyundai was producing 670,000 cars (Bloomfield 1991). Proton's planned capacity expansion was ambitious and depended on substantial sales growth which only a large export market could provide. Hyundai's breakthrough as a major exporter came when it entered the North American market, selling 169,000 cars in 1986 and 263,000 in 1987, allowing it to increase production capacity from 150,000 (in 1984) to 700,000 (1988) (Gwynne 1991).

In comparison, the Malaysian government did not even have export plans for Proton to be able to duplicate these economies of scale, and the original agreement in fact incorporated a de facto restriction on exports of the Saga (Doner 1991; Tharu 1994). Furthermore, Proton's Japanese management was apparently not interested in competing with Mitsubishi, and targeted markets that Mitsubishi had no interest in and which only required minor modifications to the car.[27] As a result, early attempts to enter the US market failed partly due to the need for expensive modifications. Instead, as late as 1995, Proton continued to rely on 'a very strong, very big, domestic base' for a 'competitive production volume' of 250,000–300,000 a year in 1995[28] when total passenger car sales for the entire country that year was only 285,792 (Malaysian Motor Traders Association, cited in *Business Times*, 31 January 1997).

On top of this, privatization did not change Proton's relationship with its local suppliers, and the company continued to find it difficult to reduce component costs due to government policies on Malay vendors. Proton had to support local industries, meet NEP objectives by promoting Malay participation, and sustain employment. Its workforce increased from 3,104 in 1991 to an estimated 6,000 in 1998 and it was not allowed to retrench (*Business Times*, 10 January 1992). Multiple government objectives created conflicting requirements. While Proton's competitiveness required the rationalization of parts suppliers, the VDP sought to support more local (Malay) vendors, undermining economies of scale and preventing Proton from sourcing cheaper components elsewhere (*The Edge*, 6 December 1999; Bando 2000). Proton's competitiveness was thus closely related to the performance of local vendors, who remained inefficient and protected by the VDP, and whose efficiency was further constrained by their inability to export in order to benefit from economies of scale. Even the price of Proton's cars were subject to government approval, and it was not allowed to raise prices following the currency crisis and rising costs after 1997 (*The Star*, 29 November 1999; *The Edge*, 6 March 2000).

Crucially, privatization was undertaken without a clear understanding of the main problems Proton faced, and did not appear designed to address these issues. On the other hand, the privatization was consistent with the government's strategy of promoting (Malay) capital accumulation targeted at parties close to the political leadership by providing the opportunities for both short-term profits (from sales in a protected domestic market) and long-term profits (from exports). The subsequent actions of Proton's parent company DRB-HICOM suggest that it may have been more interested in pursuing short-term rents.

### *Ex post failure*

In the context of the ex ante failures discussed above, the government's capacity to ensure that long-term profits were pursued through technology acquisition and greater competitiveness was crucial for the success of Proton. The failure to do so represented an ex post failure, and this was evident in the government's inability to reduce protection levels, suggesting that privatization did not fundamentally alter the institutional relationship between the government and enterprise. Furthermore, while Proton made some progress towards greater efficiency, important changes were implemented only after its renationalization, indicating that the private owner did not have the financial capacity to sustain the required capital investment, and that the government was unable to design and implement a credible subsidization strategy to ensure that capital investment and learning took place.

The constraints of insufficient production scale are related to technology acquisition necessary for product competitiveness. Sub-optimal volumes of production arising from small domestic markets can limit technological diffusion in the auto industry in developing industries given the high costs (Odaka 1983; *The Edge*, 24 June 2000; *New Straits Times*, 22 July 2000; *Business Times*, 13 September 2000). As such, it is more useful to analyse the problems of economies of scale in terms of the lack of efficiency and competitiveness needed to capture a larger market. In the case of an infant industry such as Proton, competitiveness depends on the success of the government's technology acquisition strategy through conditional subsidies. The failure of Proton's privatization reveals that the real limitations of Malaysia's technology acquisition strategy (compared to South Korea) was in its management of learning rents, particularly the absence of a clear strategy and time frame for the removal of protection, and lack of strict performance targets such as exports which would be a clear indication of increasing competitiveness.

As noted in Chapter 3, this lack of disciplinary capacity appears to be an ongoing problem and, in this case, was reflected in the government's continued (ex post) failure to enforce conditionality. Technology upgrading was thus arguably much slower in Malaysia because the government lacked a credible strategy of providing conditional subsidies that could be effectively withdrawn if performance was poor. This could have been partly due to the limitation of having only one major car manufacturing unit which limited the institutional capacity of the state to play a 'carrot and stick' game with the enterprise. The government's disciplinary capacity was also likely to have been constrained by the nature of patronage relationships, which personalized regulation. This was compounded by the Prime Minister's personal interest in the project. While the government did previously display the capacity to sack the (Malay) management before privatization, it appeared unwilling to discipline Proton's private owners.

Privatization therefore did not improve the state's ability to enforce conditions despite Proton being provided with substantial learning rents. There was no clear timetable to make Proton competitive in terms of tariff exemptions, even as late as 2002 (two years after securing the postponement of AFTA) with the government failing to outline a strategy (*Business Times*, 1 February 2002). Instead, Mahathir announced that the government had not gradually reduced import duties because it was confident that Proton would be efficient and cost-effective by 2005 (*New Straits Times*, 7 May 2002). The subsequent announcement that Malaysia would start reducing import tariffs on foreign cars assembled in ASEAN as early as 2003 was equally vague (*Business Times*, 17 December 2002). This may have been due to the depth of the technological challenges (which in turn suggests privatization did not significantly improve Proton's efficiency) but also the political consequences of failure, particularly given that this was a Malay company and the Prime Minister's 'pet project' (*Asian Wall Street Journal*, 23 November 1998).

Furthermore, the government continued to own a significant stake in the company, and was represented on the board, with the Prime Minister consulted on all major decisions, including major appointments (*The Star*, 16 March 1996). However, government intervention was weak and often personalized, and Proton was not exposed to greater competition or the real threat of bankruptcy. The absence of regulation was mirrored by Mahathir's continued personal intervention in Proton's affairs, from suggesting new markets to apparently vetoing the sale of Proton shares. While Proton's long-term survival lay in making strategic affiliations with foreign car manufacturers in order to secure a global production network, Mahathir continued to resist this in order to preserve Proton's 'national identity' as letting 'foreigners decide what automobile production would be in Malaysia . . . would be detrimental to Malaysia' (*The Star*, 7 October 2000; *Business Times*, 23 June 1998).[29] He also continued to intervene even after stepping down as Prime Minister in 2003, announcing his own appointment as Proton's adviser in 2004 (shortly after Proton's largest shareholder Khazanah attempted to remove four directors including the chief executive Mahaleel) which led to several Proton board members threatening to resign (*Asian Wall Street Journal*, 19 April 2004; *The Economist*, 8 May 2004).

Technology acquisition was also constrained by the substantial capital costs involved which were beyond the owner's financial capacity. The costs involved in enhancing Proton's technological and production capabilities were substantial, with the company needing at least US$1.05 billion for R&D in 1998 and RM300 million to RM1 billion a year (or 5–11 per cent of its revenue) on product development (excluding vendor costs) (*The Edge*, 28 December 1998; *Business Times*, 10 April 2003). While the total development cost of the final version of the Saga, Proton's first (rebadged) model, was RM12.5 million, the Waja cost almost RM1 billion to develop (including RM600 million for the platform alone) with each new model estimated at a further RM1 billion (*The Edge*, 12 April 1999; *New Straits Times*, 27 May 2000; *The Star*, 8 February 2001). By May 2001, the total cost of the national car project was RM14 billion (*The Star*, 28 May 2001). Proton also expected to spend RM1.2–RM1.5 billion in capital expenditure for capacity expansion for 1996–2000, and the cost of raising capacity to 500,000 cars a year with the construction of Proton City was estimated at RM4 billion, later revised to RM5–RM6 billion over three to four years (to produce one million cars by 2010) (*Business Times*, 19 August 1996; *The Edge*, 16 September 1996; *The Star*, 24 July 1997; *The Sun*, 25 September 1997).

Proton's owner was unable to sustain this level of capital investment. The decision to sell Proton in late 1998 was in part to help pay DRB-HICOM's mounting debts (estimated at around RM3 billion) but it also coincided with Proton's steady loss of domestic market share, the downturn in car sales in 1998 (although Proton's sales growth started declining in 1997), the poor outlook for the auto sector, the looming AFTA deadline, and a requirement for increasingly substantial capital investment. Monthly national car sales slowed down from 9,356 units (December 1997) to 4,857 (January 1998) and was expected to fall by 40–65 per cent in the second half of the 1998 financial year due to weak demand, increased export competition, and the higher cost of Japanese raw material (*The Star*, 27 June 1998; *The Edge*, 6 July 1998, 2 March 1998). Proton's own sales were expected to fall by 60 per cent in 1998 (*The Star*, 1 December 1997; *Business Times*, 19 March 1998).

Although Proton was financially healthy with RM900 million in cash, a relatively low debt–equity ratio of 1:5 (as at March 1998), and a 9.1 per cent increase in turnover to RM6.8 billion, net profit fell by 40.6 per cent for the 1998 financial year (*The Edge*, 6 July 1998). By July 1998, Proton reduced its production from 4,500 to 2,000 cars a week and was faced with an inventory of 25,000 cars and vendor problems (*The Edge*, 13 July 1998, 10 August 1998). Higher component costs (as a result of the ringgit's depreciation) and a fall in car sales forced Proton to further reduce production from 20,000 to 5,000 cars a month, resulting in a RM82 million pre-tax loss for the six months ending 30 September 1998 (*Business Times*, 4 December 1998, 10 August 1998).

Following Proton's privatization, DRB-HICOM aimed to become 'a major industrial group which is global and highly diversified' where 'manufacturing, financial services and construction would continue to remain [its] core business' (*Business Times*, 19 August 1996). Despite this, about 75 per cent of its total sales (RM829 million in 1997) came from Proton cars, with few of its other subsidiaries able to generate cash flow let alone profit (see *New Straits Times*, 19 March 1998; *The Edge 12*, April 1999, 7 February 2000; *Malaysian Business*, 1 April 2000). HICOM's operating profit was insignificant after stripping out earnings from EON and Proton, and by 1999, only its automotive segment was making money (*Malaysian Business*, 1 April 2000; *The Edge*, 7 February 2000). The timing of the decision to sell Proton back to the government suggests that the owner may have preferred rents from a highly protected domestic market rather than invest in technology acquisition and production capacity needed to compete internationally. DRB-HICOM continued to distribute Proton and EON's substantial profits through its national dealership of Proton further suggests that this may have been a more important source of profit than manufacturing. This was reflected in DRB-HICOM's subsequent organizational restructuring and focus post privatization, shifting towards other non-competitive sectors of the economy.

After the sale of Proton (along with Proton Edar and Gadek Capital), the company amalgamated four listed companies to form the DRB-HICOM Group, focusing on three core divisions – automotive, property and construction – which generated 50, 17 and 33 per cent of the group's revenue respectively (*New Straits Times*, 2 May 2002). The focus on property and construction was consistent with the pattern of Malaysia's privatization and the preferences of (Malay) capital for non-tradable sectors. EON contributed two thirds of automotive earnings, but this was expected to decline as both it and Proton lost market share. DRB-HICOM subsequently secured the franchise for Honda and Chevrolet cars. Although it started out as an industrial conglomerate, the company shifted its focus to securing government contracts including the supply and maintenance of military vehicles for the Ministry of Defence, and construction, with RM2 billion worth of contracts, mainly in the construction of Phase 1 of the electrified double-tracking railway project between Ipoh and Rawang (*New Straits Times*, 2 May 2002).

This suggests that DRB-HICOM's main interest in Proton may have been in the sale (rather than manufacture) of cars through EON's exclusive distributorship. However, as Proton's (and EON's) market share declined, and substantial capital investment was required, DRB-HICOM chose to dispose of Proton and shift its focus to non-competitive sectors (property and construction), with its interest in automotive restricted to the assembly and distribution (rather than R&D and manufacturing) of more competitive imported brands.

Proton itself also sought to diversify into new areas of growth and announced a major revamp in 2003 in response to technology acquisition problems, substantial capital costs, increasing competition (from Honda and Toyota) and delays in its new model launches. The revamp was to transform Proton from a manufacturer of vehicles to a provider of a wide range of products and services, focusing on four core areas (manufacturing, sales and marketing, engineering services and ancillary products) (*Investors Digest*, 16 June 2003). Parts of the state bureaucracy also believed Proton was not viable, with an attempted boardroom coup by Proton's largest shareholder, Khazanah, on 7 April 2004 aimed at removing chief executive Mahaleel[30] and selling off Proton's substantial assets (Reuters, 8 April 2004). The evidence suggests that the government's ex post failure was in part due to the economic significance of the project and personal interest and intervention of the Prime Minister which constrained the state's capacity to enforce conditionalities.

## Conclusion

In this chapter, we examined why the government privatized Proton, why privatization failed, and what was needed to make privatization work. Proton was created as an infant industry to address technological challenges and meet NEP goals. Privatization aimed to overcome inefficiencies under state ownership as well as develop Malay capitalists. The data from the brief period before and after privatization, supported by evidence over the longer term between 1996 and 2000/3, reveal that Proton's performance did not improve in the crucial areas after privatization. It was unable to increase efficiency and competitiveness as measured by its production capacity, exports, technology acquisition and local content. Increasing turnover and profits were the result of a growing domestic market which Proton dominated through tariff and import duty exemptions. Even then, its market share had started declining after 1995. More crucially, while it made some progress technologically, privatization did not improve Proton's technology acquisition process sufficiently as reflected in its continued uncompetitiveness internationally, with exports declining as a share of total sales. This clearly shows that Proton was unable to address technological challenges and continued to rely on a protected domestic market for its profits. Furthermore, technology acquisition took longer and cost more than the owner could bear, and important changes only took place after renationalization.

Proton's poor performance was due to both types of government failure that we have identified in our case studies. Ex ante failure occurred at the project's inception, and again when Proton was privatized. In both instances, the government failed to determine project viability or introduce measures to achieve viability. It also did not account for the substantial cost of investment in capital and R&D, and the lack of incentives for the owner to continue meeting these costs in the context of significant industry challenges. Instead, Proton received ongoing protection without performance criteria or conditionality, and the government was unable to enforce discipline. This meant that Proton's competitiveness after privatization depended on the government's ability to better manage learning rents. As technology acquisition requires an effective rent-management strategy in this sector, success is then dependent on whether enforcement of conditionality is easier or more difficult with private ownership.

The answer clearly is that if the fundamental problem was a failure to enforce conditional subsidies in the first place, privatization by itself is not likely to make much of a difference. Proton's failure thus highlights the limitations of the government's technology acquisition and capital accumulation strategies given the nature of Malaysia's patron–client relations, legacy of the NEP and characteristics of the capitalist class. As discussed in Chapter 3, the government's lack of a credible strategy to enforce conditional subsidies has been a historical feature. The government's disciplinary capacity was partly affected by the nature of patron–client networks and the status of Proton as the sole national car company. This created a moral hazard problem given the personalized patronage relationships and Proton's size and economic significance which made it difficult to enforce credible sanctions.

This failure can be located within the wider context of government failure to promote (Malay) capital accumulation in dynamic sectors. This was evident in the continued preference of DRB-HICOM for rents through its monopoly distributorship of Proton (through EON) rather than manufacturing, and its subsequent shift into non-manufacturing sectors, including real estate and government contracts. Here, the timing of the decision to sell Proton back to the government, and DRB-HICOM's subsequent corporate focus, suggest that the owner may have preferred earning rents from a protected domestic market rather than addressing technology acquisition problems in order to become internationally competitive. This was in turn arguably a legacy of the government's previous capital accumulation strategies under the NEP discussed in Chapter 3, and its ongoing lack of disciplinary capacity. In this case, while the government's ex post political capacity – its capacity to correct earlier mistakes – was crucial to the success of Proton, this was significantly affected by ex ante failure.

# 8 Summary and conclusion

This book set out to explain the failure of four Malaysian case studies by asking three questions: Why privatize in developing countries? Why may privatization fail? What is needed to make privatization work? We have argued that privatization can be motivated by economic and political factors and will often be intrinsically tied with state efforts to promote capital accumulation and develop entrepreneurial capacity in developing countries. Furthermore, the very fact that it is the government which decides on privatization makes it an inherently political process, with potentially large distributive and political consequences (e.g. see Vickers and Yarrow 1991; Fine 1997). In addition, a lack of entrepreneurial capacity in developing countries can paradoxically lead to intense political competition for privatized assets as there are many potential entrepreneurs whose entrepreneurial capacity has not been tested. This then presents a very different set of problems and conditions for successful privatization which is directly related to the state's capacity to facilitate the transition of candidates into capitalists.

There are two related claims in this book. The first is that privatization is not sufficient for ensuring efficient economic outcomes for a variety of reasons. These reasons include the financing constraint of infrastructure and large-scale investments in general, the possibility that the enterprise operates in a monopolistic or oligopolistic market, the absence of pre-existing entrepreneurs with adequate management skills, technology-learning issues, political transfers necessary for stability, and public unwillingness to pay cost-covering tariffs. All these have necessitated state financing (most recently through public–private partnerships) and subsidies for learning and welfare. As a result, privatization does not improve incentives because the quality of residual control (management effort exerted by owners) is not uniquely aligned with residual returns (profit). This brings us to our second claim. Given the ongoing need for subsidies and regulation to deal with a variety of constraints that prevents the alignment of residual control with residual returns, the success of privatization depends on the institutional and political conditions that allow or constrain the implementation and management of regulations and subsidies. This means that privatization does not reduce the likelihood of state intervention, and in the case of developing countries, may necessitate an expanded role for the state. Regulation will be necessary in the context of monopolies and as subsidies will be needed to help meet the high cost of capital expenditure, where cost-covering tariffs cannot be implemented, and where the shortage of entrepreneurial capacity necessitates learning rents. In this context, an important condition for successful privatization is the state's regulatory capacity which needs to be conceived beyond what regulation conventionally involves in developed countries.

Regulatory capacity depends both on the state's institutional and political capacity. However, as institutions are also the outcome of political factors, effective regulation will depend more so on the state's political rather than institutional capacity. This is because any effective system of regulation implicitly assumes there are effective sanctions the state can use. Hence, even if we can design such a system, the state must be able to enforce it through a credible threat of penalties, e.g. by imposing heavy personal fines or transferring the company to someone else. In the Western context, there is a credible threat for non-delivery where the state simply gives the contract to someone else, and the company that failed to deliver goes bankrupt. In developing countries, the scarcity of capital and social costs of bankruptcy often means that the threat of bankruptcy is often not a credible threat. In addition, the nature of resource allocation through patron–client networks will further constrain the state's disciplinary capacity. The failure of privatization can thus be due to different combinations of institutional and political constraints that add up to specific state failures in different cases.

Here, we have distinguished between institutional and political failure to examine the composition of state failure in a number of different examples of privatization failure in Malaysia. Ex ante failure refers to mistakes made before or during the privatization process and is often related to information or institutional constraints, although it can also be affected by political factors. Ex post failure refers to the state's failure to correct these mistakes and to ensure the viability of privatization, and is usually political in nature. The longer the time frame, the more likely it is that ex post failures are political, because institutions and policies can be changed over time, and if they are not, it is usually because of some underlying political constraints. Because ex ante mistakes will often be unavoidable (given the shortage of entrepreneurs and as information is asymmetric), it becomes even more important for the state to be able to correct these ex post through the appropriate regulatory policies and by enforcing conditionality.

These theoretical considerations, discussed in Chapter 2, allow us to make sense of Malaysia's extensive privatization programme examined in Chapter 3. By applying our three central questions to the Malaysian case, we are able to establish the political motivations behind the government's decision to privatize, the reasons why the performance of privatization as a whole has been mixed, and what conditions are necessary for successful privatization. Privatization in Malaysia was motivated by both economic and political factors. However, it was the latter that was more important as this affected the character and outcome of privatization. Changes in social relations, namely the emergence of a new Malay middle class, increased political contests within UMNO, the Malay ruling party. As a result, the allocation of resources, previously centralized through UMNO's control of the state, became increasingly personalized around a few political leaders. This was reflected in the privatization programme, which was characterized by a personalized, non-transparent selection process, weak regulation, and limited complete divestitures, together with continued state intervention and presence in many privatized former state enterprises.

Gauging the performance of Malaysia's privatization is hampered by methodological, data and measurement problems. One alternative is to measure performance against official objectives. Here, privatization is argued to have relieved the government's financial and administrative burden, improved efficiency, contributed to economic growth, reduced the size and presence of the public sector, and helped meet New Economic Policy (NEP) redistributive targets. However, the evidence is patchy, incomplete and inconclusive, and our brief review of privatization between 1985 and 2000 suggests that:

1 savings in government expenditure are largely on paper and need to be balanced against the provision of soft loans and loss of revenue;
2 the evidence of efficiency gains is mixed and not comprehensive;
3 the impact of privatization on economic growth is difficult to establish;
4 there was no significant reduction in the level of government spending (as a percentage of GNP); and
5 privatization increased the private individual Malay share of capital and control of publicly listed companies (as opposed to state ownership on behalf of Malays) but did not reduce Malay dependence on government support.

This last point is of particular relevance to our discussion given ongoing government attempts to create Malay capitalists through economic redistribution which involved education, (public) employment and business opportunities. Central to this was the learning process in terms of managerial training in SOEs and through learning rents in specific sectors. The state's failure to create an independent Malay capitalist class (reflected in continued state intervention which included subsidies, protection and bail-outs) illustrates the ongoing difficulties in promoting learning. Failure here can be traced back to the government's ex ante and ex post failures. The former is related to ethnic considerations and patronage, which compromised the choice of privatizations and candidates. However, these problems are part of the political reality and are inevitable given the intense competition for resources which follow any state attempt to develop entrepreneurial capacity. As such, it is more important for the state to ensure that selected candidates meet performance targets. The failure to do so, either by implementing appropriate policy, or enforcing discipline or conditionality, represents the government's ex post failure and provides a more important explanation for the failure of privatization. Evidence shows that the Malaysian government has historically lacked disciplinary capacity, failing to withdraw subsidies or protection, for example. Here, privatization did not improve the government's disciplinary capacity, which continued to be constrained by existing patron–client relationships, the scarcity of capital and social costs of bankruptcy.

The discussion of Malaysia's political economy in Chapter 3 allows us to locate the four case studies that follow. The evidence from each of the case studies supports the two claims made in this book. In each case, privatization necessitated some form of state financial support due to high capital costs. State support was also required either because cost-covering tariffs or fares could not be implemented (IWK, LRT) or learning rents were needed (Proton). IWK needed state loans in order to keep sewerage charges low and publicly acceptable. The three LRT operators all relied on generous state loans which accounted for between 32 and 78 per cent of project financing at favourable interest rates and lengthy loan periods. MAS was entirely financed by commercial loans based on implicit state guarantees, but despite this, the private owner was unable to finance the airline's fleet expansion. Proton relied heavily on state support in the form of import duty exemptions, subsidies and tax breaks to finance its capital investment.

Poor performance in each case was partly due to the government's ex ante failure to determine project or privatization viability and the degree of necessary state support that would be required either over the short term or over the longer term in each case. Such an ex ante analysis may have enabled the identification of the institutional mechanisms that would be necessary in each case to ensure that the subsidies were not wasted, and owners had the best mix of incentives and compulsions to maximize their management effort. Thus, in the case of IWK, privatization proceeded without sufficient information on the economic viability requirements of sewerage treatment plants given the constraints on pricing. This prevented the operator from covering operating and capital costs, and the government from determining appropriate tariff levels. Poor data on asset condition and performance raised operating costs and affected the concessionaire's ability to meet service and environmental targets. Inappropriate tariff levels led to bill collection problems that ultimately undermined the operator's ability to meet capital investment targets. IWK's experience here also illustrates the difficulties in setting tariffs, which often have to be negotiated rather than set according to strict economic criteria. The privatization of the LRT system was based on the assumption that urban rail systems can be privately financed and are commercially viable whereas this has rarely been the case. To make matters worse, this was based on grossly overoptimistic ridership projections (arguably to secure project approval). This led to operational losses which could not be sustained by the operators of Systems 1 and 2. The LRT case again demonstrates the fact that tariffs or fares usually have to be negotiated, as has been the case in Singapore, Bangkok and Manila.

Similarly, MAS was privatized despite well-known industry problems related to high capital costs and the cyclical nature of the airline industry. Furthermore, the privatization was poorly structured, based entirely on loans which created an unpayable debt burden and affected the owner's ability to finance the airline. Proton was poorly conceived as a project and failed to take into account industry characteristics, global trends (towards industry rationalization) and the substantial technological and financial challenges. As Proton's success depended crucially on the technology acquisition process and hence, on the state's management of learning rents, privatization was an inappropriate policy response.

The fact that privatization proceeded despite these problems strongly suggests that it was motivated by political considerations. This could then explain some of the choices made in terms of candidates and privatization method. With the exception of LRT System 1 (which was owned by state agencies), all the other privatizations were awarded to individuals closely associated with a few political leaders, in particular, the Prime Minister Mahathir Mohamad and former Finance Minister Daim Zainuddin (see Chapter 3, Table 3.07). As discussed in Chapter 3, this was related to the growing political contest within UMNO which saw the increasingly personalized allocation of resources as a means of securing political support. At the same time, the political leadership also sought to continue to develop entrepreneurial capacity through the privatization process. The success of this depended on the government's disciplinary capacity to ensure that any efficiency trade-off was only temporary. However, the government's disciplinary capacity has historically been constrained by the legacy of the NEP's preferential treatment policies, which undermined the process of learning-by-doing, and led to a preference for easy rents. This affected the nature of privatized projects that were concentrated in non-competitive sectors, largely centred on infrastructure construction, with each of the privatization cases here providing opportunities for economic rents.

Despite the lack of information, the privatized national sewerage system was widely regarded as profitable based on the original and even revised tariffs. This is why each subsequent new owner was prepared to pay a premium for control of IWK even after the government revised tariffs downwards, and indeed, each sale netted the previous owner substantial profits. Moreover, control of IWK increased the parent company's share price and facilitated 'signalling' on the stock market to secure more bank credit on better terms. In the case of the LRT, the government chose to privatize both the construction and operation of the LRT system to the same concessionaire because profits were at least guaranteed in the former. This would have provided strong incentives for the operator of System 2 to meet the construction deadline, and may explain why the foreign (technical) partner for System 1 sold its stake back to the state upon completion of the project. The higher cost per kilometre for all three LRT systems, and in particular System 3, compared to similar lines in Singapore and Manila, provides evidence that rents may have been earned from construction. Similarly, reports of impropriety at MAS suggest that rents could have been earned from the purchase of new aircraft (through a third party) and relocation of the airline's hub in Germany, and through the creation of separate cargo and catering divisions. Finally, the owner of Proton was either more interested in earning rents through the sale (as opposed to manufacture and export) of Proton cars in a protected domestic market, or was unwilling/unable to invest further to improve technological and productive capacities. This was illustrated by the timing of the sale of Proton back to the government, and the company's subsequent move into non-competitive sectors.

However, while these problems affected performance, failure in each case was ultimately due to the government's ex post (political) failure to correct these mistakes. The government lacked the political capacity to override business and consumer interest groups necessary to implement a viable subsidization strategy and, more crucially, to enforce the payment of tariffs in the case of IWK. It failed to integrate both the LRT and public transport system, and reduce the use of private cars (all of which were central to increasing the LRT's ridership and commercial viability) because it was unable to enforce conditionalities on the concessionaires, override private sector recalcitrance and obstructionism, and centralize planning and authority in order to implement a coherent transport policy. It failed to address problems related to the airline industry (e.g. high capital costs and periodic downturns) and implement a credible subsidization strategy (in the case of MAS's loss-making domestic sector), and did not intervene despite being aware of mismanagement and impropriety. (The fact that these problems were addressed only after the airline's renationalization further suggests that the government's disciplinary capacity was constrained.) And it failed to enforce discipline by reducing protection levels for Proton.

The question is then: what constrained the government's ex post capacity? Understanding the sources of state capacity and failure is important if we are to establish why privatization failed and what conditions are necessary for successful privatization. Theories addressing state failure and the literature on the developmental state provide a more useful framework to analyse factors that are important for effective state intervention, based on the experiences of the East Asian developmental states which Malaysia sought to emulate. State theories generally highlight the importance of autonomy or insulation from social forces necessary for the state to develop and implement policy. At the same time, the state must also be connected to productive groups in society (i.e. capitalists), in order to promote development. This approach grounds state capacity within an analysis of social relations and the balance of power in society.

However, developing countries often lack a capitalist class to undertake economic investment. This means that the state's connection with society will be with non-capitalist groups which are also often 'unproductive'. The state will then have to create capitalists, usually through the creation of new property rights (e.g. through privatization) and by providing rents for learning. The success of this will depend on the state's ex post capacity to discipline candidates by imposing conditionalities. The developmental state literature suggests that effective state intervention depends on the compatibility of institutions and patterns of intervention with the balance of political power in society determined by the nature of social relations. The strength of the state in relation to various competing groups in society will determine the outcome, whether it is able to resist challenges by losers, and whether critical incentive structures can be effectively enforced.

In the case of Malaysia, the state's disciplinary capacity was constrained by the personalized nature of patron–client networks which was the outcome of increasing political contest in UMNO. The case studies highlight different political constraints faced by the state, and provide evidence of constraints posed by patron–client networks. In the case of the LRT, both Systems 2 and 3 were privatized to parties closely associated with either the Prime Minister or Finance Minister. This may account for the government's failure to discipline the owner of KL Monorail who failed to meet the original target and deadline, and instead successfully renegotiated the concession. It may also explain why the owner of MAS received twice the market price for his 30 per cent stake in the airline even after running up substantial debts, and despite the government already controlling the airline through ownership of almost half the shares.

The government was unable to discipline the owner of Proton by reducing protection levels, partly because of the enterprise's national and economic significance but also because of the owner's relationship with the Prime Minister and the latter's personal interest in the creation of a Malay-owned national car. In the case of IWK, the government's political failure to enforce payment of tariffs (for industry and households) illustrates the basic fact that the operation of any private sector activities requires an underlying state enforcement of rights and contracts.

This brings us to the conditions for successful privatization. Much of the literature on privatization has been preoccupied mainly with the link between privatization and performance. Poor privatization performance in developing countries has been largely blamed on weak public institutions, the problems of patronage and corruption associated with these, and arbitrary state intervention. Proposed solutions thus usually involve strengthening relevant institutions to promote transparency and accountability, including a regulatory framework which safeguards the private sector from political intervention and which promotes competition. While these institutional preconditions are important and were not met in the case of Malaysia, the specific conditions of developing country economies mean that even if these institutions existed, privatization by itself would not necessarily have resulted in the appropriate improvements in economic performance. We have argued that it is more pertinent to ask why a different set of institutional failures persisted which compromised the management of regulatory structures and of ongoing subsidies that were arguably necessary for the performance of the enterprises in the sectors we have looked at. We were concerned to explain why the government failed to rectify these issues, and for that matter, why it proceeded with privatization in these sectors despite institutional inadequacies. Our answer was to point out a range of institutional and political constraints that operated both ex ante and ex post, and which collectively point to the importance of political constraints in the performance of privatization in Malaysia. Effective regulation and the management of subsidies was undermined by institutional problems, but even more so, by the government's failure to enforce sanctions and take corrective measures where needed. Successful privatization thus depends not just on an appropriate institutional design that addresses the specific problems faced by the industries being privatized, but also by the state's political capacity to enforce and implement the necessary regulatory structure, investments and financing.

Privatization should therefore only be undertaken if the state has both the necessary institutional and political capacity to devise and enforce credible regulatory and subsidization strategies. This means that the sectors appropriate for privatization and the extent of privatization that is feasible depends on pre-existing institutional and political structures. The identification of the limits of viable privatization can only be based on a country-specific case study approach in order to examine the nature of social relations and distribution of power, and the specific technological and financial requirements of the sectors being privatized. This approach may better inform the design of privatization strategies in developing countries in the future.

# Notes

## 2 Privatization, rents and rent-seeking

1 A more uncompromising view is that uneconomic services (e.g. loss-making but socially desirable transport routes) do not make sense and should be abolished (e.g. see Hakim *et al.* 1996b). However, the alternative of addressing equitable access through a coupon system merely sidesteps the issue of who should pay for essential services.
2 Bardhan (2000) provides a critical discussion.
3 Price cap regulation 'caps' prices and pegs price increases to an independent measure, usually determined by reference to the inflation rate and an assessment of the potential for efficiency improvements (i.e. a retail price index, possibly adjusted for expected efficiency gains). Rate of return regulation establishes an acceptable profit on the firm's regulatory asset base after allowing for efficient capital and operating costs (Parker 2001: 14).
4 The developmental state 'establishes as its principle of legitimacy its ability to promote and sustain development, understanding by development the combination of high rates of growth and structural change in the productive system' (see Castells 1992: 56).
5 See Kessides (2004: 112) and Stottmann (2000).

## 3 Institutional and political failure: privatization in Malaysia

1 Malay businessmen have been variously categorized as independently wealthy (e.g. aristocrats), government proxies or rentiers (Tan T.W. 1982: 291); politicians or aristocrats or those with close political connections with such people (Lim 1981; Lim 1985: 54); and figurehead capitalists, executive professional and executive-trustee directors, functional capitalists and bureaucrats-turned-businessmen) (Searle 1999: 81).
2 Even though Malay businessmen in parliament were small in absolute terms, their numbers were high relative to their proportion in Malay society (Neuman 1971). Similarly, Malay politicians were overrepresented among Malay company directors, with the highest representation from UMNO (Lim 1981). For example, in 1972, 13.2 per cent of Malaysian directors were politicians, a 'very high percentage' given the small size of MPs. Furthermore, 26 per cent of Malay directors (rising to 50 per cent if we include civil servants), compared to 6 per cent of non-Malay directors, had political backgrounds (Lim 1981: 55–61).
3 Malay classes have been categorized by income, with the middle class at RM3,600–RM7,000 per household per year and upper income at RM 12,000 (Aris Othman 1977: 106).
4 The frustration of this group at making inroads into the modern sector was

directed primarily at the Chinese, and later, at the UMNO-led Alliance government (Searle 1999: 40).

5 Ethnic Malay business associations largely represented medium-scale enterprises dependent on bureaucratic patronage (Felker 1999: 103).

6 Many Malay businessmen were present or past high-level UMNO officials and top civil servants.

7 This group demanded Malay as the sole medium of instruction in order to benefit from higher education and government employment opportunities. Not coincidentally, UMNO's heads of branches and committee members at the time of Independence were mainly teachers (Ahmad 1985: 90).

8 The system of ethnic recruitment which became the basis of quotas and privileged access for Malays to the higher administrative positions was first introduced by the British for its Malay Administrative Service (Means 1986).

9 Malays were also designated a 'priority group' which required a minimum of 20 per cent of new loans be allocated to Malay individuals or Malay-controlled companies (Searle 1999).

10 For example, loans below RM5,000 did not require collateral or a guarantor.

11 Companies controlled by the government were skewed towards those with larger paid-up capital and higher gross profits (Tan T.W. 1982).

12 The government bailed out Bank Rakyat (after losses of RM65 million) in 1976 and Bumiputra Malaysia Finance (RM2.5 billion) in 1983 (Ismail and Osman 1991: 88; also see e.g. Daim 1990: 32).

13 These were doctors, lawyers, engineers, veterinary surgeons, dentists, accountants, surveyors and architects.

14 Malay managers increased from 7,400 in 1971 to over 61,000 (1985) (Ismail and Osman 1991: 39).

15 This included the Economic Planning Unit (EPU), Public Service Department (PSD) and the Implementation and Coordination Unit (ICU).

16 These figures are argued to have been grossly underestimated to justify continued redistributive policies under the NEP (Jomo 1990).

17 E.g. Pernas (the National Corporation), the Urban Development Authority (UDA) and State Economic Development Corporations (SEDCs).

18 Protests against economic reform and liberalization by this group led to resolutions at the Bumiputra National Economic Symposium (organized by the Malay Chamber of Commerce and Industry) calling on the government to establish a trust fund to prevent the forfeiture of property used as collateral for loans and 'changing the rules of the game if necessary' to make loans for Malays easier (Searle 1999: 53).

19 This included the transfer of profitable enterprises under Pernas (headed by the Minister of Trade Tengku Razaleigh Hamzah who contested the UMNO presidency) to PNB (which answered directly to Mahathir).

20 On the other hand, even when these proposals involved the private sector taking over the management/operation of existing state-run facilities, they were classified as new projects developed by the private sector (e.g. sewerage and garbage disposal, construction) (see Ismail and Lee 1990).

21 Nominees were used to hide ownership identities. In 2001, the government stopped this practice in order to improve transparency.

22 This (incomplete) list provided details of 171 privatizations between 1983 and 1998, and was released at the 1998 UMNO General Assembly in response to allegations (by Anwar supporters) that privatizations were mainly awarded to supporters of Mahathir and Daim.

23 Eric Chia was authorized to run the state steel company Perwaja as if he owned it, and regularly reported directly to Mahathir who had to personally approve any project (Bernama, 20 September 2004). Perwaja was bailed out after incurring

huge losses and Chia was arrested and charged with dishonestly authorizing the payment of RM76.4 million to another company after Mahathir stepped down as Prime Minister.

24 It is unclear whether savings in capital expenditure includes RM8.2 billion of infrastructural development from 1983 to February 1991 through BOT and BO contracts (Malaysia 1991b).

25 An estimated RM362 million was foregone from the sale of MAS (RM68.25 million), MISC (RM221 million), Tradewind (RM33.73 million) and Sports Toto (RM39.26 million) (Ismail and Lee 1990; Ismail 1991).

26 This was mainly in construction and real estate, where NPLs increased from 16.8 and 8.3 per cent respectively by the end of 1998 to 29.7 per cent for both sectors by the end of 1999 (Chin and Jomo 2001: 125–126).

27 The breakdown is as follows: 53,718 (1983–90); 43,038 (1991–95); 17,442 (1996–2000).

28 Powertek, Lingkaran Transkota, YTL Power International, Puncak Niaga and Digi.com.

29 By 12.6 per cent from RM37 billion (1995) to RM59 billion (1999) (Malaysia 2001b).

30 From 26 per cent (1995) to 26.7 per cent (1999) (Malaysia 2001b).

31 From RM4.15 billion (21.7 per cent) in 1983 to RM8.58 billion (25.6 per cent) as at December 2000 (Malaysia 2001b).

32 The NEP widened intra-ethnic inequality among Malays, concentrating wealth and control of corporations in the hands of a very small number of Malay individuals (Tan T.W. 1982; Schlossstein 1991). Of the two million Malay investors in the National Unit Trust Scheme (ASN), less than 2 per cent managed to acquire shares above RM5,000 in 1990 (Ismail and Osman 1991).

33 According to Mahathir, 'They must not be the kind of people who would sell their shares for quick gains' (Mahathir 1998a: 29).

34 It closed down two subsidiaries of the Lembaga Kemajuan Johor Tenggara (South East Johor Development Authority) (KEJORA) in 1981 following huge losses for several years; served notices to other SOEs to perform; and later ordered forty-one subsidiaries of various SEDCs to shut down (Tan C.K. 1984).

35 HICOM was also arguably driven by the personal preferences of Mahathir (then Minister of Trade and Industry) for large-scale, often prestige projects, and his desire to promote Malay industry. This may explain why the government opted for South Korea's heavy industrialization model rather than Taiwan's focus on small- and medium-scale industries (SMIs) which were dominated by Chinese firms in Malaysia.

## 4 Universal access and private provision: Malaysia's national sewerage system

1 JKR was responsible for the planning, design and construction of infrastructure projects; operation and maintenance of water supplies and specific government buildings; and offered technical expertise to the various levels of government.

2 DOE monitored and enforced environmental standards such as pollution.

3 United Utilities, NWW's parent company, had previously secured a contract in 1989 to upgrade a water treatment plant in Ipoh.

4 Berjaya Group was owned by Vincent Tan, a beneficiary of several privatization projects, including Sports Toto (the state lottery) and the Kuala Lumpur monorail system.

5 According to a former IWK director, as the project was an unsolicited proposal to the government, there was no guarantee it would be accepted and it depended on government legislation (personal interview, 2003).

6 IWK was incorporated as Indah Water Management (M) Sdn Bhd, changing its name to Indah Water Konsortium Sdn Bhd (IWK) on 13 May 1993.

7 AIMS Worldwide was controlled by Berjaya Group executive director Ghazi Hasbullah Ramli, who was also IWK's executive chairman and a close friend of Ahmad Sebi (who later purchased IWK).

8 There is insufficient data on actual population coverage for the 48 major and 96 smaller towns to separately determine whether these targets were met.

9 For example, IWK was later expected to provide treatment for ammonia pollution in 5,200 plants which was estimated to involve an additional RM1 billion in capital expenditure (*New Straits Times*, 14 March 1998).

10 These included Jelutong, Bayan Baru and Padang Matsirat, and STPs and pipe networks in Teluk Kemang and Sungala, Port Dickson. The STP in Kuah, Langkawi, was only 90 per cent constructed; connected sewerage services had not been implemented aside from Seremban Municipal Council; and 42 biosoil STPs had yet to be replaced (National Audit Department, Malaysia 2000).

11 IWK's performance compared favourably with local authorities, where only 20 per cent of the population was connected in Kelantan, and 3.2 per cent of septic tanks desludged in 1999 (National Audit Department, Malaysia 2000).

12 The number of contravention licences, however, went down from 3,263 in 1997 to 2,762 in 1998 (*Water & Environment International*, March 2000, 9 [66]).

13 This figure was reduced to RM84 million when LTAT opted for a moratorium for its portion (20 per cent) of the guaranteed profit.

14 IWK appointed three new directors (Jaganath Sabapathy, Surendran Palachandran and Albert Cheok) and retained five former directors (Ishak Ismail, Zulkifli Abdul Rahman, Ramli Ibrahim, Lodin Wok Kamaruddin and Gordon Tregaskis).

15 Personal interview (2003).

16 According to the Sewerage Services Department, Malaysia (1998) and National Audit Department, Malaysia (2000) respectively.

17 According to a former IWK director, if the concessionaire exceeded the rate of returns the amount charged would be reduced, and if it fell below a 'neutral window' it could increase charges (personal interview, 2003).

18 'There were no records because local authorities never visited the plants, performed maintenance or paid electricity for any of the plants' (ibid).

19 Ibid.

20 Ibid.

21 The pricing mechanism was determined by the DGSS, initially by agreement, which he could then adjust. Provisions were made for tariff reviews every five years or so in line with inflation and IWK's capital works programme. The concession did not provide for a mechanism for arbitrating disputes (ibid).

22 'Local and state authorities took the opportunity to increase their revenues even though it was likely that most local councils never budgeted for sewerage treatment in the first place' (ibid).

23 Ibid.

24 Personal interview (2003).

25 According to the Deputy DGSS, this was based on sample audits by the DSS and a quantitative audit was being put in place in late 2003 (personal interview, August 2003).

26 Each DSS branch was staffed by only three to six employees who were expected to cover large areas, including entire states.

27 Profit guarantee agreements were very difficult to enforce, and most of the guarantor companies had no money. Both the Royal Malaysian Police Investment Cooperative and Armed Forces Savings Board (LTAT) refused to pay the profit guarantees as it was against their constitutions.

28 According a former IWK director (personal interview, 2003).

29 This excludes LTAT's share.
30 This ranged from RM10 per month to RM11,500 (unconnected) and RM15,000 (connected).
31 According to the Deputy DGSS (personal interview, 2003).
32 According to a former IWK director (personal interview, 2003).
33 The highest number of debtors was in Johor (RM34 million) and lowest in Kuala Lumpur (RM8.6 million) (*The Sun*, 8 March 1999) where customers were used to paying as this was included in their assessment charges, according to a former IWK director (personal interview, 2003).
34 According to a former IWK director, there was a reluctance and some suspicion at the MoF, and IWK's nominees were unable to 'open doors' as would have normally been the case. 'The government didn't lend it the money it promised, and at the end of the day, the government brought it back into public ownership in order to protect the position on operating expenditure; and the capital refurbishment had not really taken place' (personal interview, 2003).
35 Ibid.
36 According to a former IWK director and the Deputy DGSS (personal interviews, 2003).
37 According to a senior executive at PUB in 2000 and former IWK executives in 2001 (e.g. see *Far Eastern Economic Review*, 27 September 2001).

## 5 The myth of privatized urban rail: Kuala Lumpur Light Rail Transit

1 This comprised US$548 million from Siam Commercial Bank (32.9 per cent majority owned by the Thai Ministry of Finance), US$424 million from Kreditanstalt für Wiederaufbau (KfW) (the German development bank), and US$80 million from the International Finance Corporation (IFC) (the World Bank's investment arm), with US$676 million from equity contributors (including a further US$20 million from the IFC).
2 This is an extensive system at 31.75 km with 57 stations.
3 According to a senior manager at the Ministry of Finance (MoF) Special Task Force for Public Transport in the Klang Valley (personal interview, 2003).
4 These included the contract for Metrolink, the first stage of the LRT, awarded to an Australian consortium in 1987, and a monorail project proposed by Hitachi of Japan in the 1980s.
5 The company had worked in Malaysia for around 40 years and became aware of the project through its local contractor Teamwork. According to TaylorWoodrow International Operations Director, other bids were excluded in this period while the company created a financial appraisal 'to allow the equity investors to think they were making a good investment'. This took several years. The government wanted System 1 to be created in a stand-alone manner and independently financed, with a guaranteed income from operating revenue (personal interview, 2003).
6 Adtranz provided the rail system and trains for System 1. It was later bought by Bombardier.
7 This covered the construction cost, financing and pre-operating expenses from Jalan Ampang to the city centre.
8 This was issued by the Infrastructure Development Corporation, wholly owned by the MoF.
9 Renong was to pledge PLUS (the North South Highway concessionaire) as security (*The Edge*, 12 October 1998).
10 This comprised RM719.8 million government support loans, RM466.6 million government loan, RM32.7 million Khazanah loan, and RM1.29 billion EPF loan.

11 This comprised EPF (20 per cent); Lembaga Urusan Tabung Haji (15 per cent); KWAP (5 per cent); LTAT (5 per cent); and Khazanah (5 per cent).
12 Renong also received RM1.2 billion as part of the government's RM5.1 billion of soft loans allocated to privatized projects (*New Straits Times*, 30 October 1996; *The Edge*, 17 November 1997).
13 This was repayable in 30 instalment between 2008 and 2022 at 5 per cent interest (STAR; *The Edge*, 15 January 2001; 5 June 2001).
14 This point was raised by several local and international consultants (personal interviews, 2002–3) and more recently in the press, e.g. see AFP, 15 September 2005 ('Malaysian Construction Sector Riddled with Corruption').
15 The internal rate of return was 15 per cent (STAR) and 11 per cent (PUTRA).
16 According to a senior manager at the MoF Special Task Force for Public Transport in the Klang Valley, the government left it to operators to determine optimum fares based on market sensitivity tests and was confident that fares would not be underpriced (personal interview, 2003).
17 Ibid.
18 According to Tai Tuck Leong, Perunding Traffik Klasik (the consultant for the LRT system after renationalization) and a senior manager at the MoF Special Task Force for Public Transport in the Klang Valley (personal interviews, 2003); also see Hilmi (2003).
19 Personal interwiews as in n. 18, and Hilmi (2003).
20 According to STAR CEO Zainal Ghani, STAR's problem was in repaying RM2.1 billion in bank loans and RM685 million in government support loans (*The Edge*, 19 July 1999).
21 PUTRA was also affected by its parent company's debt load of around RM6.8 billion. Renong was estimated to need to set aside at least RM1.8 billion in 1998–99 primarily to subscribe to Commerce Asset's rights issue (RM179 million), and to complete Phase 2 of LRT System 2 (RM1.3 billion). Renong's debt problem was the consequence of embarking on several capital-intensive projects, including System 2, simultaneously (*The Edge*, 13 July 1998).
22 According to the auditors' report in KL Infrastructure Group's financial statements for the year ended 30 April 2006.
23 Ibid, p. 8.
24 According to Tai Tuck Leong (personal interview, 2003).
25 According to a senior manager of the MoF Special Task Force for Public Transport in the Klang Valley (personal interview, 2003).
26 In addition, the government decided to extend a line south (Phase 2) for the 1998 Commonwealth Games through a sparsely populated area. As compensation, STAR received approval for a 3-km extension north into a high-density residential area (from Sultan Ismail to Sentul Timur) (Hilmi 2003).
27 The land was jointly owned by a Malaysian and a Singaporean company, the latter reported to be unwilling to allow access, according to a senior manager of the MoF Special Task Force for Public Transport in the Klang Valley (personal interview, 2003).
28 Ibid.
29 According to Tai Tuck Leong (personal interview, 2003).
30 Feeder bus operator Intrakota cited poor financial returns servicing these routes (*New Straits Times*, 26 March 1998). STAR took over the feeder bus service in April 1998 (*Business Times*, 26 March 1998; *Malay Mail*, 27 March 1998).
31 According to a senior manager of the MoF Special Task Force for Public Transport in the Klang Valley, commercial bus operators were represented by different political factions, each with its own political backers (personal interview, 2003).
32 Ibid.

33 DBKL and the government conducted separate studies for an ARP in 1991 (*New Straits Times*, 6 August 1991; *Business Times*, 20 November 1991). In 1993, the central bank's annual report pointed out that the LRT system should be complemented with traffic restrictions in the city centre to effectively reduce congestion (Bank Negara Malaysia [1993], cited in *Malay Mail*, 31 March 1993).
34 Local by-laws did not allow DBKL to dictate rates for private car park operators but this was recently amended and DBKL can now specify parking charges. The result has been a gradual increase in parking fares in the city centre.
35 According to Tai Tuck Leong (*New Straits Times*, 12 October 1995).
36 According to DBKL Urban Transportation Division Director Mahfix Omar (*Business Times*, 17 February 1993).
37 According to a senior manager of the MoF Special Task Force for Public Transport in the Klang Valley, establishing a transport authority was difficult, even after 20 years. The absence of a central transport authority and laws also complicated the introduction of ARP as it was unclear who would receive revenues collected (personal interview, 2003).
38 Ibid.
39 For example, one of the Ministry of [Malay] Entrepreneur Development's objectives was to encourage the development of small businesses (such as Kuala Lumpur's mini buses), but it was also responsible for implementing the policy for two lead bus operators (Halcrow Consultants 1999).
40 For example, a three-ministry task force set up in 1996 to conduct a comprehensive study on the public transport sector comprised the Ministries of Transport, Entrepreneur Development, and Culture, Arts and Tourism (*Business Times*, 22 March 1996).
41 According to a senior manager of the MoF Special Task Force for Public Transport in the Klang Valley (personal interview, 2003); also see *Business Times*, 5 February 1997.

## 6 Perverse incentives: Malaysia Airlines

1 The company is registered as Malaysian Airline but is officially known as Malaysia Airlines as stated on its logo.
2 According to court documents filed by the owner in his countersuit of Danaharta, the state asset management company, in 2006 (see *The Sun*, 6 July 2006).
3 According to industry sources, there is suggestion that some banks were instructed to lend while others willingly did so in the context of rapid economic growth and projections of MAS share prices rising from RM8 to RM15 (personal interviews, 2003).
4 According to a former MoF representative on the MAS board, aircraft were bought at a very high cost through a third party related to the new owner, and many similar transactions were at uncompetitive rates and went through the owner's companies. This was also raised by several investment analysts (personal interviews, 2002–3).
5 Between the peninsular states and Sabah and Sarawak in east Malaysia.
6 The residual value is the scrap value of an asset. By increasing the scrap value, the amount to be depreciated falls, so there is less to be depreciated over the same number of years, leaving more for profits. Simple depreciation is calculated by subtracting the residual from the asset value and then dividing by the number of years. Therefore, by increasing the residual value, the amount to be depreciated (asset value minus residual) over the same number of years becomes smaller.
7 Corporatization is seen as the first stage of divestiture.
8 This involved the sale of 35 million existing ordinary shares for RM63 million, 70

million new ordinary shares for RM126 million, and an estimated RM283 million from a second sale to foreigners at a considerably higher price.

9 According to court documents filed by Tajudin in his countersuit of Danaharta (see *The Sun*, 6 July 2006).

10 Through KWAP (the state pension fund) (11.6 per cent), Skim Amanah Saham Bumiputra (9.8 per cent) and the Employees Provident Fund (EPF) (5.8 per cent). Another 5 per cent was owned by the State Secretary of Sabah, on behalf of that state government.

11 This followed KWAP increasing its stake in MAS to 20.04 per cent through the purchase of an additional 9 per cent (72.12 million) MAS shares from the Brunei Investment Agency at RM4 each for RM280 million (*Business Times*, 4 December 2000, 12 December 2000; *The Edge*, 11 December 2000).

12 This figure uses combined data from ICAO and MAS due to the unavailability of ICAO data for 1992–93.

13 ATK per employee is dependent on the cost of employees in relation to the output they generate, and not number of employees; hence, ATK per employee per US$1,000 labour costs would be more indicative of productivity if the data was available.

14 According to a private consultant responsible for the post-privatization restructuring of MAS (personal interview, 2003).

15 Average debt ratio = (long-term debt + leases) divided by (LTD + equity + leases).

16 Average debt equity ratio = LTD + (leases divided by equity).

17 Average interest cover = operating profits divided by interest.

18 Return on assets (ROA) = EBIT minus tax divided by average total sales (i.e. revenue).

19 According to Tajudin in court documents filed in 2006 (*The Sun*, 6 July 2006).

20 Note that debt figures quoted here may differ from figures in the tables depending on the actual date.

21 This increased from US$7 a barrel in August 1995 to a three-year high at US$27.50 in December 1995 (*Business Times*, 13 December 1995).

22 According to the former head of the Corporate Debt Restructuring Committee [CDRC]) (personal interview, 2003).

23 This point was raised by industry consultants, investment analysts and business journalists (personal interviews, 2002–3).

24 Tajudin was general manager of UDA Merchant Bank, which no longer exists.

25 According to a former MoF representative on the MAS board (personal interview, 2003).

26 This comprised one (of 52) Boeing 747–400, 18 Boeing 737–400, two (of six) Boeing 737–500, one de Havilland Canada DHC-6 (Malaysia Airlines 1993).

27 This comprised 21 Boeing 737–400/500 and six Boeing 747–400.

28 This comprised 10 Boeing 747–400 and 15 Boeing 777–200ER.

29 This was first reported by *Asian Wall Street Journal* (25 September 1995).

30 According to a private consultant responsible for the post-privatization restructuring of MAS (personal interview, 2003).

31 This was also raised by a former MoF representative on the MAS board, private consultant responsible for the post-privatization restructuring of MAS, and *Asian Wall Street Journal* journalist (personal interviews, 2002–3).

32 According to a private consultant responsible for the post-privatization restructuring of MAS (personal interview, 2003).

33 ACL operated a cargo facility in Hahn, Germany, that MAS contracted to use as its global cargo hub in 1999. However, the Hahn cargo centre was 110 kilometres by road to Frankfurt International Airport.

34 Tajudin faced similar allegations following his resignation from Celcom, where the new management lodged a police report over RM260 million of fictitious invoices

made to the group between 1998 and 1999, and sought to recover RM185 million from share deals and around RM50 million in unauthorized payments made to three former directors (including Tajudin) for termination of services and a company car (*The Star*, 13 September 2002).

35 According to a former MoF representative on the MAS board (personal interview, 2003).

36 Financial benchmarks included targets for passenger revenue, load factors, fuel cost and consumption, comparing pre-budget and actual data, with variances to be shared between MAS and the state-owned PNB on a pre-determined basis (with a range of 10–50 per cent depending on the item). Operational benchmarks covered safety, security, punctuality and service (Nomura Asian Equity Research, 29 November 2002).

## 7 Rents and industrial upgrading: Proton

1 This eventually led to EON's majority shareholder UMW (which also owned the Toyota franchise) being bought out by the Ministry of Finance (MoF), MC and MMC in February 1989.

2 Eleven assemblers produced 25 makes and 122 models of commercial and passenger vehicles, with local content at 8 per cent (Doner 1991).

3 HICOM was initiated by Mahathir Mohamad, as Minister of Trade and Industry, and established with three priority investments: an integrated steel plant, a cement factory and an automotive plant.

4 Daihatsu later became technical partner in Perodua, the second national car project, which essentially involved the assembly and rebadging of Daihatsu cars restricted to below 1,000cc.

5 Its main shareholders were HICOM (29.2 per cent), the MoF (17.8 per cent), MC (8.7 per cent), MMC (8.7 per cent), and PNB, the National Equity Corporation (2.9 per cent) (*Business Times*, 10 January 1992).

6 HICOM's share price was RM4.52–RM4.78 in the week before and after the privatization. The deal was financed through an offshore bank in Labuan (*New Straits Times*, 20 October 1995, 7 August 1999).

7 Yahaya was regional/general franchise manager at Wearnes Brothers and executive director at Wira Wearnes. He started up Automotive Corporation (M) Sdn Bhd in 1979, auto assembler Master-Carriage (with Saleh Sulong) in 1980, Master Radiators Sdn Bhd, Master Seats Sdn Bhd, Auto Elegance Car Centre Sdn Bhd (later renamed USPD), Automotive Manufacturers (M) Sdn Bhd (AMM), and Auto Prominence (M) Sdn Bhd.

8 This was reported to have boosted Yahaya's bid for Proton, allowing him to beat a management buyout by previous Proton managing director Mohd Nadzmi and other senior Proton executives (*The Star*, 16 March 1996; *Asiaweek*, 11 April 1997).

9 See *The Edge*, 29 September 1997, 1 December 1997, 4 September 1998, 11 September 1998.

10 There were no indications that any of Proton's 6,000 staff was retrenched, according to a former Proton senior marketing executive (personal interview, 2003) and TA Securities (11 June 1998). Also see *Business Times* (10 January 2002).

11 Around 40 per cent of Proton's cost was in yen.

12 According to Proton's alternate director Fumio Yoshimi (*New Straits Times*, 22 July 2000).

13 JIT aims to reduce inventory costs and capital for warehouses by supplying goods just as needed.

14 According to a former Proton senior marketing executive (personal interview, 2003).

15 Proton's market share was expected to shrink from 65 to 55 per cent upon implementation of the CEPT, and then to 30 per cent over five years (if the CEPT was introduced in 2003), and to drop to 50 per cent immediately and decline to 20 per cent over the next seven years (if the CEPT was introduced in 2000) (DRB-HICOM circular to shareholders, 8 September 2000; *Business Times*, 8 September 2000; TA Securities, 26 July 2000).

16 Toyota Vios 1.5 (RM72,607), Honda City 1.5 (RM76,676), Kia Spectra (RM69,000), Hyundai Accent 1.5 (circa RM50,000) and Chevrolet Aveo 1.5 (RM65,000).

17 According to a former Proton senior marketing executive (personal interview, 2003).

18 According to Leonard Khong, a Malaysian motoring journalist (personal interview, 2003).

19 This was in collaboration with Michigan Automotive Research and German company EDAG Engineering and Design.

20 According to Peter Chong (auto analyst at SalomonSmithBarney) (personal interview, 2003); also see *The Edge*, 22 July 2002.

21 See e.g. Auto Trader <http://ces.autotrader.co.uk/ces/roadtest.do?usedCar=0&capcode=PRG216GSX5HPIM%20%20%20%20%20%20&rtid=211080&price=10406> and the Automobile Association <http://www.theaa.com/allaboutcars/carsearch/carsearch_cartest_reports.jsp?carTest=carTest&latestReports=n&modelID=A8&modelName=GEN-2&makeName=Proton> (both accessed 3 February 2007).

22 According to Peter Chong (personal interview, 2003).

23 Proton later acquired another 15 per cent of USPD from Khazanah for RM81 million.

24 This entailed a minimum order of 100,000 cars a year, with Proton able to appoint other 'super dealers'.

25 Mahathir later complained that the Japanese were 'dragging their feet' on technology transfer, with Proton having to pay royalties for incomplete technology (*Business Times*, 20 May 1993; *Asiaweek*, 4 November 1997).

26 An imported engine block constituted 40 per cent of final cost.

27 According to a former Proton senior marketing executive (personal interview, 2003).

28 According to Proton managing director Mohd Nadzmi (*The Star*, 23 January 1995).

29 According to DRB-HICOM chairman Saleh Sulong, offers by Ford and DaimlerChrysler were not accepted, as 'shareholding has to be majority Malaysian because it is a national car company' (*Malaysian Business*, 1 April 2000).

30 Proton's board of directors was eventually able to sack Mahaleel in July 2005 (AutoAsia E-newsletter, 26 July 2005).

# References


Adam, C. and Cavendish, W. (1995) 'Early Privatizations', in Jomo K.S. (ed) *Privatization in Malaysia: Rents, Rhetoric, Realities*, London: Westview Press.

Ahmad Atory Hussain (1985) *Pembentukan Dasar Awam Malaysia [Malaysia's Public Policy Formation]*, Kuala Lumpur: Utusan Publications.

Alavi, H. (1982) 'State and Class Under Peripheral Capitalism', in H. Alavi and T. Shanin (eds) *Introduction to the Sociology of 'Developing Countries'*, London: Macmillan Press.

Alavi, R. (1996) *Industrialisation in Malaysia: Import Substitution and Infant Industry Performance*, London: Routledge.

—— (1998) 'Management of Protection Policy: Lessons from Malaysian Experience', in Ishak Yussof and Abdul Ghafar Ismail (eds) (1998) *Malaysian Industrialisation: Governance and the Technical Change*, Bangi: Penerbit Universiti Kebangsaan Malaysia.

—— (1999) 'Rents, Technological Innovation and Firm Competitiveness in a Bumiputra Malaysian Firm', in Jomo K.S., G. Felker, and R. Rasiah (eds) *Industrial Technology Development in Malaysia: Industry and Firm Studies*, London: Routledge.

Alchian, A. and Demsetz, H. (1972), 'Production, Information Costs, and Economic Organisation', *American Economic Review*, 62: 777–795.

Amsden, A. (1989) *Asia's Next Giant: South Korea and Late Industrialization*, New York: Oxford University Press.

Aoki, M., Kim, H.K. and Okuno-Fujiwara, M. (eds) (1997) *The Role of Government in East Asian Economic Development: Comparative Institutional Analysis*, Oxford: Clarendon Press.

Applebaum, R. and Henderson, J. (eds) (1992) *States and Development in the Asian Pacific Rim*, London: Sage Publications.

Arab-Malaysian Merchant Bank [AMMB], Arthur D. Little, Nik Saghir and Ismail (1995). *Government of Malaysia: Post Privatization Study*, Volume I, Centre for Policy Studies, October.

Aris bin Othman (1977) 'Growth, Equality and Poverty in Malaysia, 1957–1980', PhD dissertation, Boston University.

Arrow, K. (1962) 'The Economic Implications of Learning by Doing', *Review of Economic Studies*, 29: 155–173.

Asia Equity (1997) 'Proton', stock analysis, March.

Aston, T.H. and Philpin, C.H.E. (eds) (1985), *The Brenner Debate: Agrarian Class Structure and Economic Development in Pre-Industrial Europe*, Cambridge: Cambridge University Press.

Aziz Zariza Ahmad (1997) *Mahathir's Paradigm Shift*, Taiping: Firma.

Bagwell, P. (2004) 'The Sad State of British Railways: The Rise and Fall of Railtrack, 1992–2002', *Journal of Transport History* 25 (2).

Bailey, E. and Pack, J. (eds) (1987) *The Political Economy of Privatization and Deregulation*, Aldershot: Edward Elgar.

Bando, T. (2000) 'Future of the Malaysian National Car Project', *Asian Economic Review*, 4th Quarter.

Barclays de Zoete Wedd (1994) 'Malaysia Airlines', stock analysis, April–June.

Bardhan, P. (ed) (1989a) *The Economic Theory of Agrarian Institutions*, Berkeley: University of California Press.

—— (1989b) 'Alternative Approaches to Theory of Institutions in Economic Development', in P. Bardhan (ed) *The Economic Theory of Agrarian Institutions*, Berkeley: University of California Press.

—— (1997) 'Corruption and Development: A Review of Issues', *Journal of Economic Literature*, September (35): 1320–1346.

—— (2000) 'The Nature of Institutional Impediments to Economic Development', in M. Olson, and S. Kähkönen (eds) *A Not-so-Dismal Science: A Broader View of Economies and Societies*, Oxford: Oxford University Press.

Barraclough, S. (2000), 'The Politics of Privatisation in Malaysia', *Contemporary Southeast Asia*, 22 (2): 344–357.

Barrett, T. (1999) 'PPPs in the Financing of European Transport Infrastructure', European Conference of Ministers of Transport (ECMT) Seminar on Public-Private Partnerships (PPPs) in Transport Infrastructure Financing, Paris, 12 January <http://www.cemt.org/online/ppp99/Barrett.pdf> (accessed 13 February 2007).

Bates, R. (2001) *Prosperity and Violence*, New York: W.W. Norton & Company.

Batley, R. (1996) 'Public-Private Relationships and Performance in Service Provision', *Urban Studies*, 33 (4–5): 723–751.

Bell, M., Rosa-Larson, B. and Westphal, L. (1984) 'Assessing the Performance of Infant Industries', *Journal of Development Economics*, 16: 101–128.

Bhagwati, J. (1982) 'Directly Unproductive, Profit-Seeking Activities', *Journal of Political Economy*, 90 (5): 988–1002.

Bienen, H. and Waterbury, J. (1989) 'The Political Economy of Privatization in Developing Countries', in P. Cook and C. Kirkpatrick (eds) (2000a) *Privatization in Developing Countries, Volume II*, Cheltenham: Edward Elgar Publishing.

Bishop, M. and Kay, J. (1989) 'Privatization in the United Kingdom: Lessons From Experience', *World Development* 17: 643–657.

Biswas, A.K. (2000) 'Water For Urban Areas of the Developing World in the Twenty-First Century', in J. Uito and A.K. Biswas (eds) *Water for Urban Areas: Challenges and Perspectives*, New York: United Nations University Press.

BKWPPLK (Bahagian Kemajuan Wilayah Persekutuan dan Perancang Lembah Klang) (1988) 'Wilayah Lembaga Klang Maklumat Asas' [*Klang Valley General Information*] (Volume III), Kuala Lumpur: Prime Minister's Department.

Bloomfield, G. (1978) *The World Automotive Industry*, Newton Abbot: David and Charles.

—— (1991) 'The World Automotive Industry in Transition', in C.M. Law (ed) (1991a) *Restructuring The Global Automobile Industry*, London: Routledge.

Bowie, A. (1988) 'Redistribution with Growth? The Dilemmas of State-Sponsored Economic Development in Malaysia', in J. Ravenhill, (ed) (1995) *Singapore,*

*Indonesia, Malaysia, The Philippines and Thailand Volume I*, Aldershot: Edward Elgar Publishing.
—— (1991) *Crossing The Industrial Divide (State, Society and the Politics of Economic Transformation in Malaysia)*, New York: Columbia University Press.
Boycko, M., Shleifer, A. and Vishny, R. (1996) 'A Theory of Privatization', *The Economic Journal*, 106 (435): 309–319.
Brenner, R. (1976) 'Agrarian Class Structure and Economic Development in Pre-Industrial Europe', *Past and Present*, 70 (Feb): 30–75.
—— (1985) 'The Agrarian Roots of European Capitalism', in T.H. Aston and C.H.E. Philpin (eds), *The Brenner Debate: Agrarian Class Structure and Economic Development in Pre-Industrial Europe*, Cambridge: Cambridge University Press.
Brownbridge, M. and Kirkpatrick, C. (2000) 'Financial Regulation in Developing Countries: Survey Article', *Journal of Development Studies*, 37 (1): 1–24.
Bruton, H. (1992) *Sri Lanka and Malaysia*, Washington: Oxford University Press.
—— (1998) 'A Reconsideration of Import Substitution', *Journal of Economic Literature*, 36, June.
Buchanan, J. (1980) 'Rent Seeking and Profit Seeking', in J. Buchanan, R. Tollison and G. Tullock (eds) *Toward A Theory of Rent Seeking Society*, Austin: Texas University Press.
Buchanan, J., Tollison, R. and Tullock, G. (eds) (1980) *Toward A Theory of Rent Seeking Society*, Austin: Texas University Press.
Campos, J.E. and Esfahani, H.S. (1996) 'Why and When Do Governments Initiate Public Enterprise Reform?', in P. Cook and C. Kirkpatrick (2000a) *Privatization in Developing Countries Volume I*, Cheltenham: Edward Elgar Publishing.
Castells, M. (1992) 'Four Asian Tigers with a Dragon Head: A Comparative Analysis of the State, Economy and Society in the Asia Pacific Rim', in R. Applebaum and J. Henderson (eds) *States and Development in the Asian Pacific Rim*, London: Sage Publications.
Cathay Pacific Airways (1995) *Annual Report*, Hong Kong: Cathay Pacific Airways.
—— (1996) *Annual Report*, Hong Kong: Cathay Pacific Airways.
—— (1997) *Annual Report*, Hong Kong: Cathay Pacific Airways.
—— (1998) *Annual Report*, Hong Kong: Cathay Pacific Airways.
Chang H.J. (1993) 'The Political Economy of Industrial Policy', *Cambridge Journal of Economics*, 17: 131–157.
—— (1999) 'The Economic Theory of the Developmental State', in M. Woo-Cummings (ed) *The Developmental State*, London: Cornell University Press.
—— (2002). *Kicking Away the Ladder: Development Strategy in Historical Perspective*, London: Anthem Press.
—— (ed) (2003) *Rethinking Development Economics*, London: Anthem Press.
Chang H.J. and Singh, A. (1992) 'Public Enterprises in Developing Countries and Economic Efficiency', Geneva: United Nations Conference on Trade and Development.
—— (1993) 'Public Enterprises in Developing Countries and Economic Efficiency: A Critical Examination of Analytical, Empirical and Policy Issues', Geneva: UNCTAD Review 4.
—— (1997) 'Can Large Firms Be Run Efficiently Without Being Bureaucratic?', *Journal of International Development*, 9 (6): 865–875.

Chee P.L. and Fong C.O. (1983) 'Ancillary Firm Development in the Malaysian Motor Vehicle Industry', in K. Odaka (ed) *The Motor Vehicle Industry in Asia*, Singapore: Singapore University Press.

Chin K.F. and Jomo K.S. (2000) 'Financial Sector Rents in Malaysia', in M.H. Khan and Jomo K.S. (eds) *Rents, Rent Seeking and Economic Development*, Cambridge: Cambridge University Press.

—— (2001) 'Financial Liberalisation and System Vulnerability', in Jomo K.S. (ed) *Malaysian Eclipse: Economic Crisis and Recovery*, London: Zed Books.

Choi B.S. (1993) 'Financial Policy and Big Business in Korea: The Perils of Financial Regulation', in S. Haggard, Lee, C.H. and S. Maxfield (eds) *The Politics of Finance in Developing Countries*, London: Cornell University Press.

City Hall Kuala Lumpur (undated) *Draft Structure Plan Kuala Lumpur 2020*, Kuala Lumpur: City Hall Kuala Lumpur.

Clague, C. (1997a) *Institutions and Economic Development*, London: The Johns Hopkins University Press.

—— (1997b) 'The New Institutional Economics and Economic Development', in C. Clague (ed) *Institutions and Economic Development*, London: Johns Hopkins University Press.

Clague, C., Keefer, P., Knack, S. and Olson, M. (1997) 'Democracy, Autocracy, and Institutions Supportive of Economic Growth', in C. Clague (ed) *Institutions and Economic Development*, London: Johns Hopkins University Press.

Clarke, T. and Pitelis, C. (eds) (1993) *The Political Economy of Privatisation*, London: Routledge.

Cobb, M.J. (2004) 'Mass Transit System: Planning & Financing the 'Mega Projects'', IDC International Development Consultants, LLC <http://www.idcworld.com/bangkok.htm> (accessed 13 February 2007).

Cook, P. (1997) 'Privatization, Public Enterprise Reform and the World Bank: Has 'Bureaucrats in Business' Got It Right?', in P. Cook and C. Kirkpatrick (eds) (2000a) *Privatization in Developing Countries Volume II*, Cheltenham: Edward Elgar Publishing.

—— (1999) 'Privatization and Utility Regulation in Developing Countries: The Lessons So Far', *Annals of Public and Cooperative Economics*, 70 (4): 549–587.

Cook, P. and Kirkpatrick, C. (1988) 'Privatisation in Less Developed Countries: An Overview', in P. Cook and C. Kirkpatrick (eds) (2000a) *Privatization in Developing Countries Volume I*, Cheltenham: Edward Elgar Publishing.

—— (1995) 'Privatisation Policy and Performance', in P. Cook and C. Kirkpatrick (eds) (2000b) *Privatization in Developing Countries Volume II*, Cheltenham: Edward Elgar Publishing.

—— (eds) (2000a) *Privatization in Developing Countries Volume I*, Cheltenham: Edward Elgar Publishing.

—— (eds) (2000b) *Privatization in Developing Countries Volume II*, Cheltenham: Edward Elgar Publishing.

Cook, P. and Minogue, M. (1990) 'Waiting for Privatisation in Developing Countries: Towards the Integration of Economic and non-Economic Explanations', in P. Cook and C. Kirkpatrick (eds) (2000b) *Privatization in Developing Countries Volume II*, Cheltenham: Edward Elgar Publishing.

Cook, P. and Uchida, Y. (2003) 'Privatisation and Economic Growth in Developing Countries', *Journal of Development Studies*, August, 39 (6): 121–154.

Cornia, G.A. (2003) 'Globalization and the Distribution of Income Between and

Within Countries', in H.J. Chang (ed) *Rethinking Development Economics*, London: Anthem Press.
Correia, F. (ed) (1998) *Institutions for Water Resources Management in Europe Volume 1*, Rotterdam: A.A. Balkema.
Cox, W. (1997) 'New Urban Rail In America: Exorbitant Costs, Negligible Benefits', *Engineering News Record*, December 16. <http://www.publicpurpose.com/pp-rail.htm> (accessed 13 February 2007).
Crone, D.K. (1995) 'State, Social Elites and Government Capacity in Southeast Asia', in J. Ravenhill (ed) *Singapore, Indonesia, Malaysia, The Philippines and Thailand Volume I*, Aldershot: Edward Elgar Publishing.
Crouch, H. (1992) 'Authoritarian Trends, the UMNO Split and Limits to State Power', in J. Kahn and F. Loh (eds) *Fragmented Vision: Culture and Politics in Contemporary Malaysia*, Sydney: Allen and Unwin.
—— (1993) 'Malaysia: Neither Authoritarian Nor Democratic', in K. Hewison, R. Robison and G. Rodan (eds) *Southeast Asia in the 1990s: Authoritarianism, Democracy and Capitalism*, Sydney: Allen & Unwin.
—— (1996) *Government and Society in Malaysia*, New York: Cornell University Press.
Daim Zainuddin (1990) 'The Malaysian Economy in 1990', in Daim Zainuddin (1996) *Daim Speaks His Mind*, Petaling Jaya: Pelanduk.
—— (1996) *Daim Speaks His Mind*, Petaling Jaya: Pelanduk.
Daniels, R. and Trebilcock, M. (2000) 'An Organisational Analysis of the Public-Private Privatization', in P. Rosenau (ed) *Public-Private Policy Partnerships*, London: The MIT Press.
Davies, R.E.G. (1964) *A History of the World's Airlines*, London: Oxford University Press.
Doganis, R. (1991) *Flying Off Course: The Economics of International Airlines*, London: Harper Collins Academic.
Doner, R. (1991) *Driving a Bargain: Automobile Industrialization and Japanese Firms in Southeast Asia*, Berkeley: University of California Press.
Dunn, J. Jr. (2000) 'Transportation: Policy-Level Partnerships and Project Based Partnerships', in P. Rosenau (ed) *Public-Private Policy Partnerships*, London: The MIT Press.
Edgren, G. (ed) *The Growing Sector: Studies of Public Sector Employment in Asia*, New Delhi: ILO-ARTEP.
Edwards, C. (1992) 'Managing Structural Change and Industrialisation: Foreign Investment and Industrialisation in Malaysia', paper presented at the ISI-HIID Conference on the Malaysian Economy, June 1–13.
Estache, A. (2003) 'Privatization in Latin America: The Good, The Ugly, and The Unfair' (first draft, August 14), The World Bank and ECARES, Université Libre de Bruxelles.
Evans, P. (1994) 'The State as Problem and Solution: Predatory Developmental, and Other Apparatuses: A Comparative Political Economy Perspective on the Third World State', in A. Kincaid and A. Pates (eds) *Comparative National Development, Society and Economy in the New Global Order*, Chapel Hill: University of North Carolina Press.
—— (1995) *Embedded Autonomy*, Cambridge: Policy Press.
Fayard, A. (1999), 'Overview of the Scope and Limitations of Public-Private Partnerships', Paris: Seminar on Public-Private Partnerships (PPPs) in Transport Infrastructure Financing, European Conference of Ministers of Transport.

Felker, G. (1993) 'Political Economy and Malaysian Technology Policy', in Jomo K.S. (ed) *Industrialising Malaysia: Policy, Performance, Prospects*, London: Routledge.

—— (1998) 'Political Economy and Malaysian Technology Policy', in Ishak Yussof and Abdul Ghafar Ismail (eds) *Malaysian Industrialisation: Governance and the Technical Change*, Bangi: Penerbit Universiti Kebangsaan Malaysia.

—— (1999) 'Malaysia's Innovation System', in Jomo K.S. and G. Felker (eds) *Technology, Competitiveness and The State: Malaysia's Industrial Technology Policies*, London: Routledge.

Fine, B. (1997) 'Privatization: Theory and Lessons from the UK and South Africa, *Seoul Journal of Economics*, 10 (4), 373–414.

—— (2003) 'Beyond the Developmental State: Towards a Political Economy of Development', in Hirakawa, H, Noguchi, M. and Sano, M. (eds) *Beyond Market-Driven Development: A New Stream of Political Economy of Development*, Tokyo: Nihon Hyoron Sha.

Flyvbjerg, B., Holm, M.S. and Buhl, S. (2002) 'Underestimating Costs in Public Works Projects: Error or Lie?', *APA Journal*, 68 (3) Summer.

Galal, A. and Shirley, M. (1994) *Does Privatization Deliver?: Highlights from a World Bank Conference*, Washington DC: World Bank.

Galal, A., Jones, L., Tandon, P. and Vogelsang, I. (1994a) *Welfare Consequences of Selling Public Enterprises*, Washington DC: Oxford University Press (The World Bank).

—— (1994b) 'Divestiture: Questions and Answers', in A. Galal, L. Jones, P. Tandon and I. Vogelsang *Welfare Consequences of Selling Public Enterprises*, Washington: Oxford University Press (The World Bank).

Gale, B. (1981) *Politics and Public Enterprise in Malaysia*, Singapore: Eastern Universities Press.

Ghosh, B.N. (1999) 'Privatization: The ASEAN Experience', *Indian Journal of Economics*, January.

Goh C.T. (1971) *The May Thirteenth Incident*, Kuala Lumpur: Oxford University Press.

Goh, W. and Jomo K.S. (1995). 'Efficiency and Consumer Welfare', in Jomo K.S. (ed) *Privatizing Malaysia: Rents, Rhetoric, Realities*, Boulder: Westview Press.

Gomez, E.T. (1990) *Politics in Business: UMNO's Corporate Investments*, Kuala Lumpur: Forum Enterprises.

—— (1991) *Money Politics in the Barisan Nasional*, Kuala Lumpur: Forum.

—— (1994) *Political Business: Corporate Involvement in Malaysian Political Parties*, Queensland: James Cook University.

—— (1997) 'Privatised Patronage: The Economics and Politics of Privatisation in Malaysia', *Journal of the Asia Pacific Economy*, 2 (2): 178–200.

—— (1999) *Chinese Business in Malaysia*, Surrey: Curzon Press.

—— (ed) (2002a) *Political Business in East Asia*, London: Routledge.

—— (2002b) 'Introduction: Political Business in East Asia', in E.T. Gomez (ed) (2002a), *Political Business in East Asia*, London: Routledge.

—— (2002c) 'Political Business in Malaysia: Part Factionalism, Corporate Development, and Economic Crisis', in E.T. Gomez (ed) (2002a), *Political Business in East Asia*, London: Routledge.

Gomez, E.T. and Jomo K.S. (1997) *Malaysia's Political Economy: Politics, Patronage and Profits*, Cambridge: Cambridge University Press.

Gouri, G. (1991) *Privatisation and Public Enterprises: The Asia-Pacific Experience*, New Delhi: Oxford University Press and IBH Publishing.

Gouri, G., Sankar, T.L., Reddy, Y.V. and Shams, K. (1991) 'Imperatives and Perspectives', in G. Gouri (ed) *Privatisation and Public Enterprise: The Asia-Pacific Experience*, New Delhi: Oxford University Press and IBH Publishing.

Gwynne, R. (1991) 'New Horizons? The Third World Motor Vehicle Industry in an International Framework', in C.M. Law (ed) (1991a) *Restructuring The Global Automobile Industry*, London: Routledge.

Haggard, S. (1997) 'Democratic Institutions, Economic Policy, and Development', in C. Clague (ed) *Institutions and Economic Development*, London: Johns Hopkins University Press.

Haggard, S. and Maxfield, S. (1999) 'Political Explanations of Financial Policy in Developing Countries', in S. Haggard, Lee C.H. and S. Maxfield (eds) *The Politics of Finance in Developing Countries*, London: Cornell University Press.

Haggard, S., Lee C.H. and Maxfield, S. (eds) (1999) *The Politics of Finance in Developing Countries*, London: Cornell University Press.

Hakim, S., Seidenstat, P. and Bowman, G. (1996b) 'Review and Analysis of Privatization Efforts in Transportation', in S. Hakim, P. Seidenstat and G. Bowman (eds) *Privatizing Transportation Systems*, London: Praeger.

—— (eds) (1996a) *Privatizing Transportation Systems*, London: Praeger.

Halcrow Consultants (1999) 'Kuala Lumpur Public Transport Restructuring Final Report', Kuala Lumpur: Corporate Debt Restructuring Committee.

Harriss, J., Hunter, J. and Lewis, C. (eds) *The New Institutional Economics and Third World Development*, London: Routledge.

Harris, N. (1999) 'Competitive Strategies for Railways in the UK: A Corporate Perspective', *Transport Reviews*, 19 (2): 191–202.

Heilman, J. and Johnson, G. (1992) *The Politics and Economics of Privatization*, London: University of Alabama Press.

Hemming, R. and Mansoor, A. (1988) 'Privatization and Public Enterprises', in P. Cook and C. Kirkpatrick (eds) (2000a) *Privatization in Developing Countries Volume II*, Cheltenham: Edward Elgar Publishing.

Henderson, J. and Applebaum, R. (1992b) 'Situating the State in the East Asian Development Process', in R. Applebaum and J. Henderson (eds) *States and Development in the Asian Pacific Rim*, London: Sage Publications.

—— (1992a) *States and Development in the Asian Pacific Rim*, London: Sage Publications.

Hill, H. (ed) (2002) *The Economic Development of Southeast Asia Volume IV*, Cheltenham: Edward Elgar Publishing.

Hilmi Mohamad (2003) 'Rail Transportation in Kuala Lumpur', *Japan Rail & Transport Review*, July, 35.

Ho K.L. (1988) 'Indigenizing the State: The NEP and the Bumiputra State in Peninsular Malaysia', PhD dissertation, Ohio State University.

Hochstein, A. (1996) 'Strategies for Improving Port System Performance', in S. Hakim, P. Seidenstat and G. Bowman (eds) *Privatizing Transportation Systems*, London: Praeger.

Hua W.Y. (1983) *Class and Communalism in Malaysia: Politics in a Dependent Capitalist State*, London: Zed Books.

Huber, E., Rueschemeyer, D. and Stephens, J.D. (1993) 'The Impact of Development on Democracy', *Journal of Economic Perspectives*, 7 (3) Summer.

International Air Transport Association (IATA) (2001) *World Air Transport Statistics*, London: International Air Transport Association.

—— (2002) *World Air Transport Statistics*, London: International Air Transport Association.
International Civil Aviation Organization (ICAO) (1991) *Civil Aviation Statistics of the World 1990*, Montreal: International Civil Aviation Organization.
—— (1992) *Civil Aviation Statistics of the World 1991*, Montreal: International Civil Aviation Organization.
—— (1993) *Civil Aviation Statistics of the World 1992*, Montreal: International Civil Aviation Organization.
—— (1994) *Civil Aviation Statistics of the World 1993*, Montreal: International Civil Aviation Organization.
—— (1995) *Civil Aviation Statistics of the World 1994*, Montreal: International Civil Aviation Organization.
—— (1996) *Civil Aviation Statistics of the World 1995*, Montreal: International Civil Aviation Organization.
—— (1997) *Civil Aviation Statistics of the World 1996*, Montreal: International Civil Aviation Organization.
—— (1998) *Civil Aviation Statistics of the World 1997*, Montreal: International Civil Aviation Organization.
—— (1999) *Civil Aviation Statistics of the World 1998*, Montreal: International Civil Aviation Organization.
Ismail Salleh (1991) 'The Privatisation of Public Enterprises: A Case Study of Malaysia', in G. Gouri (ed) *Privatisation and Public Enterprise: The Asia-Pacific Experience*, New Delhi: Oxford University Press and IBH Publishing.
Ismail Salleh and Lee, T.H. (1990) 'Privatisation: The Process So Far', Kuala Lumpur: ISIS.
Ismail Salleh and Osman Rani (1991) 'The Growth of the Public Sector in Malaysia', Kuala Lumpur: ISIS.
Jacobsson, S. (1993) 'The Length of the Infant Industry Period: Evidence from the Engineering Industry in South Korea', *World Development*, 21 (3): 407–419.
Japan International Cooperation Agency (JICA) (1997) 'Financial Analysis and Perspectives', Integrated Urban Transportation Strategies for Environmental Improvement in Kuala Lumpur (SMURT-KL).
—— (1998a) 'Progress Report II', Integrated Urban Transportation Strategies for Environmental Improvement in Kuala Lumpur (SMURT-KL), March.
—— (1998b) 'Clues on Sources From Institutional Arrangements', Integrated Urban Transportation Strategies for Environmental Improvement in Kuala Lumpur (SMURT-KL).
Japan International Cooperation Agency (JICA) and Urusetia Perancang Lembah Klang (1986) 'Klang Valley Transportation Study Technical Report E-3 Public Transport Study', December.
Jesudason, J. (1989) *Ethnicity and the Economy: The State, Chinese Business, and Multinationals in Malaysia*, Singapore: Oxford University Press.
Johnson, C. (1982) *MITI and the Japanese Miracle*, Stanford: Stanford University Press.
—— (1999) 'The Developmental State: Odyssey of a Concept', in M. Woo-Cummings (ed) *The Developmental State*, London: Cornell University Press.
Jomo K.S. (1986) *A Question of Class: Capital, the State and Uneven Development in Malaya*, Singapore: Oxford University Press.
—— (1990) 'Whither Malaysia's New Economic Policy?', *Pacific Affairs*, 63 (4): 469–499.

—— (1993a) 'The Way Forward?: The Political Economy of Development Policy Reform in Malaysia', Kuala Lumpur: University of Malaya.
—— (ed) (1993b) *Industrializing Malaysia: Policy, Performance, Prospects*, London: Routledge.
—— (1994) *U-Turn? Malaysian Economic Development Policy After 1990*, Queensland: James Cook University.
—— (1995) *Privatizing Malaysia: Rents, Rhetoric, Realities*, London: Westview Press.
—— (ed) (1999a) *Rethinking Malaysia*, Hong Kong: Asia 2000.
—— (1999b), 'A Malaysian Middle Class?: Some Preliminary Analytical Considerations', in Jomo K.S. (ed) *Rethinking Malaysia*, Hong Kong: Asia 2000.
—— (ed) (2001) *Malaysian Eclipse: Economic Crisis and Recovery*, London: Zed Books.
—— (2002) 'Privatization's Distributional Impact in Malaysia', New York: Initiative for Policy Dialogue Task Force Working Paper. <http://www0.gsb.columbia.edu/ipd/programs/item.cfm?prid=22&iyid=13&itid=477> (accessed 13 February 2007).
Jomo K.S. and Edwards, C. (1993) 'Growth and Structural Change in the Malaysian Economy', *Development and Change*, April 24 (2).
Jomo K.S. and Felker, G. (eds) (1999) *Technology, Competitiveness and the State: Malaysia's Industrial and Technology Policies*, London: Routledge
Jomo K.S. and Gomez, E.T. (2000) 'The Malaysian Development Dilemma', in M.H. Khan and Jomo K.S. (eds) *Rents, Rent Seeking and Economic Development*, Cambridge: Cambridge University Press.
Jomo K.S. and Hamilton-Hart, N. (2001) 'Financial Regulation, Crisis and Political Response', in Jomo K.S. (ed) *Malaysian Eclipse: Economic Crisis and Recovery*, London: Zed Books.
Jomo K.S. and Tan K.W. (1999) *Industrial Policy in East Asia: Lessons for Malaysia*, Kuala Lumpur: University of Malaya Press.
Jomo K.S., Felker, G. and Rasiah, R. (eds) (1999) *Industrial Technology Development in Malaysia: Industry and Firm Studies*, London: Routledge.
Jones, L. (1994) 'Malaysia', in A. Galal and M. Shirley (eds) *Does Privatization Deliver?: Highlights from a World Bank Conference*, Washington DC: World Bank.
Jones, L. and Fadil Azim Abbas (1992) 'Malaysia: Background, Malaysian Airlines, Kelang Container Terminal, Sports Toto', paper presented at the World Bank Conference on The Welfare Consequences of Selling Public Enterprises, Washington DC, 11–12 June.
—— (1994) 'Sports Toto', in A. Galal, L. Jones, P. Tandon and I. Vogelsang (eds) *Welfare Consequences of Selling Public Enterprises*, Washington: Oxford University Press (The World Bank).
Jones, L. and Mason, E. (1982) 'Role of Economic Factors in Determining the Size and Structure of the Public Enterprise Sector in Less-Developed Countries With Mixed Economies', in P. Cook and C. Kirkpatrick (eds) (2000a) *Privatization in Developing Countries Volume I*, Cheltenham: Edward Elgar Publishing.
Kamal Salih and Zainal Aznam Yusoff (1989): 'Overview of the NEP and Framework for a Post-1990 National Economic Policy: Options', *Malaysian Management Review* 24 (2): 13–61.
Kamal Salih (1989) 'The Malaysian Economy in the 1990s: The Alternative Scenarios', *MIER [Malaysia Institute of Economic Research] Discussion Paper* 27, August.
Kennedy, J.C. (2002) 'National Economic Action Council Executive Director Dato'

Mustapa Mohamed on Economic Growth and Investment in Malaysia', in *Academy of Management Executive*, 16 (3).

Kessides, I. (2004) *Reforming Infrastructure: Privatisation, Regulation and Competition*, Washington DC: World Bank.

Khan, M.H. (1997) 'State Failure in Weak States', in J. Harriss, J. Hunter and C. Lewis (eds) *The New Institutional Economics and Third World Development*, London: Routledge.

—— (1998) 'Patron-Client Networks and the Economic Effects of Corruption in Asia', *European Journal of Development Research*, 10 (1): 15–39.

—— (2000a) 'Rent-Seeking as Process', in M.K. Khan and Jomo K.S. (eds) *Rents, Rent-Seeking and Economic Development*, Cambridge: Cambridge University Press.

—— (2000b) 'Rents, Efficiency and Growth', in M.H. Khan and Jomo K.S. (eds) *Rents, Rent-Seeking and Economic Development*, Cambridge: Cambridge University Press.

—— (2000c) 'The Political Economy of Industrial Policy in Pakistan 1947–1971', *SOAS Department of Economics Working Paper Series*, 98.

—— (2004) 'State Failure in Developing Countries and Strategies of Institutional Reform', in B. Tungodden, N. Stern and I. Kolstad (eds) *Toward Pro-Poor Policies: Aid Institutions and Globalization*, Proceedings of Annual World Bank Conference on Development Economics, Oxford: Oxford University Press and World Bank.

—— (forthcoming) 'Analysing Corruption as Process: Competing Paradigms in Economics and Political Economy'.

—— (undated) 'The New Political Economy of Corruption', Department of Economics SOAS.

Khan, M.H. and Jomo K.S. (eds) (2000) *Rents, Rent-Seeking and Economic Development*, Cambridge: Cambridge University Press.

Khoo B.T. (1995) *Paradoxes of Mahathirism*, Kuala Lumpur: Oxford University Press.

Khoo K.J. (1992) 'The Grand Vision: Mahathir and Modernisation', in J. Kahn and F. Loh (eds) *Fragmented Vision: Culture and Politics in Contemporary Malaysia*, Sydney: Allen and Unwin.

Khor K.P. (1986) 'Industrial Policy in Malaysia – Problems and Prospects', *Kajian Ekonomi Malaysia*, 23 (1) June: 5–26.

Kikeri, S., Nellis, J. and Shirley, M. (1994) 'Privatization: Lessons from Market Economies', in P. Cook and C. Kirkpatrick (eds) (2000b) *Privatization in Developing Countries Volume II*, Cheltenham: Edward Elgar Publishing.

Kim L. (2004) 'The Multifaceted Evolution of Korean Technological Capabilities and its Implications for Contemporary Policy', *Oxford Development Studies*, 32 (3): 341–363.

KL Infrastructure Group (2006) Financial statements for the year ended 30 April 2006.

Koo H. and Kim E.M. (1992) 'The Developmental State and Capital Accumulation in South Korea', in R. Applebaum and J. Henderson (eds) *States and Development in the Asian Pacific Rim*, London: Sage Publications.

Kraemer, A. (1998) 'Public and Private Water Management in Europe', in F. Correia (ed) *Institutions for Water Resources Management in Europe Volume 1*, Rotterdam: A.A. Balkema.

Krueger, A.O. (1974) 'The Political Economy of Rent-Seeking Society', *American Economic Review*, 64 (3): 291–303.

—— (1990) 'Government Failures in Development', *Journal of Economic Perspectives*, 4 (3) Summer: 9–23.
Kuo C.T. (2000) 'New Financial Politics in Thailand and Malaysia', *Issues & Studies*, 36 (6): 139–176.
Lall, S. (1995) 'Malaysia: Industrial Success and the Role of the Government', in H. Hill (ed) (2002) *The Economic Development of Southeast Asia Volume IV*, Cheltenham: Edward Elgar Publishing.
—— (2003) 'Symposium on Infant Industries: Roberts on Infant Industry Protection – Another Comment', *Oxford Development Studies*, 31 (1): 14–17.
Law, C.M. (ed) (1991a) *Restructuring the Global Automobile Industry*, London: Routledge.
Leary, S. (1998) 'Malaysia: Continuing Role in Economic Life', *Privatisation International Yearbook 1998*.
Lee K.H. and Nagraj, S. (eds) (1991) *The Malaysian Economy Beyond 1990*, Kuala Lumpur: Persatuan Ekonomi Malaysia.
Lee, C. (2004) 'Regulating Competition in Malaysia', P. Cook, C. Kirkpatrick, M. Minogue and D. Parker (eds) *Leading Issues in Competition, Regulation and Development*, Cheltenham: Edward Elgar Publishing.
Lee J. (1997) 'The Maturation and Growth of Infant Industries: The Case of Korea', *World Development*, 25 (8): 1271–1281.
Lee Y.F. (1997) 'The Privatisation of Solid Waste Infrastructure and Services in Asia', *Third World Planning Review*, 19 (2): 139–162.
Leftwich, A. (2002) 'A Contradiction in the Politics of Economics', *New Political Economy*, 7 (2): 269–273.
Leigh, M. (1992) 'Politics, Bureaucracy, and Business in Malaysia: Realigning the Eternal Triangle', in A. McIntyre and J. Kanishka (eds) *The Dynamics of Economic Policy Reform in Southeast Asia and South West Pacific*, Singapore: Oxford University Press.
Leong C.H. (1991) 'Late Industrialisation Along with Democratic Politics in Malaysia', PhD thesis, Harvard University.
Levy, B. and Spiller, P. (1993) 'Regulation, Institutions and Commitment in Telecommunications: A Comparative Analysis of Five Country Studies', in P. Cook and C. Kirkpatrick (eds) (2000a) *Privatization in Developing Countries Volume II*, Cheltenham: Edward Elgar Publishing.
Light Rail Transit Association (UK Development Group) (1997) 'Asia's Urban Rail Congress', Fact Sheet 45.
Lim L.L. and Chee P.L. (eds) (1984) *The Malaysian Economy at the Crossroads: Policy Adjustment or Structural Transformation*, Kuala Lumpur: Malaysian Economic Association and Organisational Resources.
Lim M.H. (1981) *Ownership and Control of the 100 Largest Corporations in Malaysia*, Singapore: Oxford University Press.
—— (1985) 'Contradictions in the Development of Malay Capital: State, Accumulation and Legitimation', *Journal of Contemporary Asia*, 15 (1).
Linder, S. (2000) 'Coming to Terms With Public-Private Partnerships', in P. Rosenau (ed) *Public-Private Policy Partnerships*, London: The MIT Press.
Lubeck, P.M. (1992) 'Malaysian Industrialisation, Ethnic Division and the NIC Model: The Limits of Replication', in R. Applebaum and J. Henderson (eds) *States and Development in the Asian Pacific Rim*, London: Sage Publications.

Lum W.K. (1994) 'Privatisation of Sewerage Services in Malaysia: The Way Forward', Kuala Lumpur: Department of Sewerage Services, Malaysia.
Mackie, J.A. (1995) 'Economic Growth in the ASEAN Region: The Political Underpinnings', in J. Ravenhill (ed) *Singapore, Indonesia, Malaysia, The Philippines and Thailand Volume I*, Aldershot: Edward Elgar Publishing.
Mahathir Mohamad (1986) *The Challenge*, Petaling Jaya: Pelanduk Publications. [Translated from *Menghadapi Cabaran*, Kuala Lumpur: Pustaka Antara, 1976].
—— (1998a) *The Way Forward*, London: Weidenfeld & Nicolson.
—— (1998b) *The Challenges of Turmoil*, Subang Jaya: Pelanduk Publications.
Malaysia (1981) *Fourth Malaysia Plan, 1981–1985*, Kuala Lumpur: Government Printers.
—— (1983a) *Industrial Master Plan*, Kuala Lumpur: Government Printers.
—— (1983b) *Malaysian Industrial Policy Study*, Kuala Lumpur: Government Printers.
—— (1985) *Guidelines on Privatization*, Kuala Lumpur: Government Printers.
—— (1986) *Fifth Malaysia Plan, 1986–1990*, Kuala Lumpur: Government Printers.
—— (1989) *Mid-Term Review of the Fifth Malaysia Plan*, 1986–1990, Kuala Lumpur: Government Printers.
—— (1991a) *Sixth Malaysia Plan, 1991–1995*, Kuala Lumpur: Government Printers.
—— (1991b) *Privatization Master Plan*, Kuala Lumpur: Government Printers.
—— (1996) *Seventh Malaysia Plan, 1996–2000*, Kuala Lumpur: Government Printers.
—— (2001a) *Eighth Malaysia Plan, 2001–2005*, Kuala Lumpur: Government Printers.
—— (2001b) 'White Paper: Status of the Malaysian Economy', Kuala Lumpur: Economic Planning Unit, 30 November.
—— (2002) Sewerage Services Act 1993 (Incorporating all Amendments up to 28 February 2002), Kuala Lumpur: The Commission of Law Revision, Malaysia.
Malaysia Airlines (1991) *Annual Report*, Kuala Lumpur: Malaysia Airlines.
—— (1992a) *Annual Report*, Kuala Lumpur: Malaysia Airlines.
—— (1992b) 'Circular to Shareholders in Relation to the Proposed Rights Issue of 350,000,000 New Ordinary Chares', 5 August.
—— (1993) *Annual Report*, Kuala Lumpur: Malaysia Airlines.
—— (1994) *Annual Report*, Kuala Lumpur: Malaysia Airlines.
—— (1995) *Annual Report*, Kuala Lumpur: Malaysia Airlines.
—— (1996) *Annual Report*, Kuala Lumpur: Malaysia Airlines.
—— (1997) *Annual Report*, Kuala Lumpur: Malaysia Airlines.
—— (1998) *Annual Report*, Kuala Lumpur: Malaysia Airlines.
—— (2002) 'Reorganization of the Group Corporate Structure', public announcement, 30 July [prepared by Bina Fikir Consultants].
Malek Merican (1986) 'Review of the NEP from a Private Sector Perspective', paper presented at GEMAPUTRA, Kuala Lumpur.
Mandell, R.W. (1979) *Financing the Capital Requirements of the US Airline Industry in the 1980s*, Lexington: Gower Press.
Martin, S. and Parker, D. (1997) *The Impact of Privatisation: Ownership and Corporate Performance in the UK*, London: Routledge.
Marx, K. (1979 [1867]) *Capital Volume 1*, Harmondsworth: Penguin Books.
McVey, R. (1995) 'The Southeast Asian Entrepreneur', in J. Ravenhill (ed) *Singapore, Indonesia, Malaysia, The Philippines and Thailand Volume I*, Aldershot: Edward Elgar Publishing.

Means, G. (1986) 'Ethnic Preference Policies in Malaysia', in N. Nevitte and C.H. Kennedy (eds) (1986) *Ethnic Preference and Public Policy in Developing States*, Colorado: Lynne Rienner Publishers.

Meerman, J. (1979) *Public Expenditure in Malaysia*, New York: Oxford University Press.

Mehmet, O. (1988) *Development in Malaysia: Poverty, Wealth and Trusteeship*, Kuala Lumpur: Insan.

*Melitz, M.* (2005) 'When and How Should Infant Industries Be Protected?',
*Journal of International Economics,* 66 (1): 177–196.

Millward, R. and Parker, D. (1983) 'Public and Private Enterprise: Comparative Behaviour and Relative Efficiency', in P. Cook and C. Kirkpatrick (eds) (2000a) *Privatization in Developing Countries Volume I*, Cheltenham: Edward Elgar Publishing.

Milne, R. and Mauzy, D. (1999) *Malaysian Politics Under Mahathir*, London: Routledge.

Mohamad Sheriff (1991) 'Privatisations', in Lee K.H. and S. Nagraj (eds) *The Malaysian Economy Beyond 1990*, Kuala Lumpur: Persatuan Ekonomi Malaysia.

National Audit Department, Malaysia (2000) *Laporan Ketua Audit Negara Mengenai Penyata Akaun Awam Serta Aktiviti-aktiviti Kementrian dan Agensi Kerajaan Persekutuan [Report of the National Auditor General on the Accounts and Activities of Federal Government Ministries and Agencies],* Putrajaya: Government Printers.

Neuman, S. (1971) 'The Malay Political Elite: An Analysis of 134 Malay Legislators, Their Social Backgrounds and Attitudes', PhD dissertation, New York University.

Nevitte, N. and Kennedy, C.H. (eds) (1986) *Ethnic Preference and Public Policy in Developing States*, Colorado: Lynne Rienner Publishers.

Nomura Asian Equity Research (2002) 'Malaysian Airlines System', stock analysis, 29 November.

Odaka, K. (ed) (1983) *The Motor Vehicle Industry in Asia*, Singapore: Singapore University Press.

Olson, M. (1997) 'The New Institutional Economics: The Collective Choice Approach to Economic Development', in C. Clague (ed) *Institutions and Economic Development*, Baltimore: Johns Hopkins University Press.

—— (2000) 'Dictatorship, Democracy and Development', in M. Olson and S. Kahkonen (eds) *A Not-So-Dismal Science*, Oxford: Oxford University Press.

Olson, M. and Kahkonen, S. (2000) 'Introduction: The Broader View', in M. Olson and S. Kahkonen (eds) *A Not-So-Dismal Science*, Oxford: Oxford University Press.

Oster Jr, C. and Strong, J. (2000) 'Transport Restructuring and Reform in an International Context', *Transportation Journal*, 39 (3) Spring: 18–32.

Paribas Capital Markets (1994) 'Malaysian Airlines', stock analysis.

Parker, D. (2001) 'Economic Regulation: A Preliminary Literature Review and Summary of Research Questions Arising', Manchester: Centre on Regulation and Competition Working Paper Series No. 6.

Parker, D. and Kirkpatrick, C. (2002) 'Researching Economic Regulation in Developing Countries: Developing a Methodology for Critical Analysis', Manchester: Centre on Regulation and Competition Working Paper Series No. 34.

—— (2003) 'Privatisation in Developing Countries: A Review of the Evidence and the Policy Lessons', Manchester: Centre on Regulation and Competition Working Paper Series No. 55.

Payson, W. and Steckler, S. (1996) 'Developing Public-Private Partnerships in Infrastructure', in S. Hakim, P. Seidenstat and G. Bowman (eds) *Privatizing Transportation Systems*, London: Praeger.
Pempel, T.J. (1999) 'The Development Regime in a Changing World Economy', in M. Woo-Cummings (ed) *The Developmental State*, London: Cornell University Press.
Plane, P. (1997) 'Privatization and Economic Growth: An Empirical Investigation from a Sample of Developing Market Economies' in P. Cook and C. Kirkpatrick (eds) (2000a) *Privatization in Developing Countries Volume II*, Cheltenham: Edward Elgar Publishing.
Pongsiri, N. (2001) 'Regulation and Public-Private Partnerships', Manchester: Centre on Regulation and Competition Working Paper Series No. 12.
Poole, R. (1996) 'Privatisation for Economic Development', in T. Anderson and P. Hill (eds) *The Privatization Process*, London: Rowman and Littlefield Publishers.
Prime Utilities (1995) *Annual Report*, Kuala Lumpur: Prime Utilities Bhd.
—— (1996) *Annual Report*, Kuala Lumpur: Prime Utilities Bhd.
—— (1997) *Annual Report*, Kuala Lumpur: Prime Utilities Bhd.
—— (1998) *Annual Report*, Kuala Lumpur: Prime Utilities Bhd.
—— (1999) *Annual Report*, Kuala Lumpur: Prime Utilities Bhd.
—— (2000) *Annual Report*, Kuala Lumpur: Prime Utilities Bhd.
Proton (2001) *Annual Report*, Kuala Lumpur: Proton Bhd.
Przeworski, A. and Limongi, F. (1993) 'Political Regimes and Economic Growth', *Journal of Economic Perspectives*, 7 ( 3).
Puthucheary, J. (1960) *Ownership and Control in the Malaysian Economy*, Singapore: Eastern University Press.
Puthucheary, M. (1984) 'The Political Economy of Public Enterprise in Malaysia', in Lim L.L. and Chee P.L. (eds) *The Malaysian Economy at the Crossroads: Policy Adjustment or Structural Transformation*, Kuala Lumpur: Malaysian Economic Association and Organisational Resources.
Ranis, G. (2003) 'Symposium on Infant Industries: A Comment', *Oxford Development Studies,* 31 (1): 33–35.
Rasiah, R. (1998) 'Capital Expansion, Cronyism and Contraction', *Journal of the Asia Pacific Economy*, 3 (3): 358–378.
—— (2001) 'Pre-Crisis Economic Weaknesses and Vulnerability', in Jomo K.S. (ed) *Malaysian Eclipse: Economic Crisis and Recovery*, London: Zed Books.
Rasiah, R. and Ishak Shari (2001) 'Market, Government and Malaysia's New Economic Policy', *Cambridge Journal of Economics*, 25: 57–78.
Ravenhill, J. (ed) (1995) *Singapore, Indonesia, Malaysia, The Philippines and Thailand Volume I*, Aldershot: Edward Elgar Publishing.
Rhys, D.C. (1972) *The Motor Industry. An Economic Survey*. London: Butterworths.
Rodrik, D. (1995) 'Getting Interventions Right: How South Korea and Taiwan Grew Rich', *Economic Policy* 20.
Roland, G. (1994) 'On the Speed and Sequencing of Privatisation and Restructuring', *Economic Journal, Royal Economic Society*, 104 (127): 1158–1168.
Rosenau, P. (2000b) 'The Strengths and Weaknesses of Public-Private Partnerships', in P. Rosenau (ed) *Public-Private Policy Partnerships*, London: The MIT Press.
—— (ed) (2000a) *Public-Private Policy Partnerships*, London: The MIT Press.
Rosli Nekmat and Ooi P.H. (1993) 'Application of EMME/2 in Transit Forecasting

for Kuala Lumpur Light Rapid Transit (LRT) Project', paper presented at the 8th International EMME/2 Users' Conference, Seattle, Washington, November 3–5.
Rowthorn, B. and Chang, H.J. (1993) 'Public Ownership and the Theory of the State', in T. Clarke and C. Pitelis (eds) T*he Political Economy of Privatisation*, London: Routledge.
Salleh I.M. and Meyanathan, S.D. (1993) 'Malaysia: Growth, Equity and Structural Transformation', in D. Leipsiger and V. Thomas (eds) *The Lessons of East Asia*, Washington DC: World Bank.
SalomonSmithBarney (2002) 'Malaysia Auto – Brave New World',
—— (2003) Proton Financial Data.
Sappington, D. and Stiglitz, J. (1987a) 'Privatisation, Information and Incentives', in E. Bailey and J. Pack (eds) *The Political Economy of Privatization and Deregulation*, Aldershot: Elgar Reference Collection.
—— (1987b) 'Information and Regulation', in P. Cook and C. Kirkpatrick (eds) (2000a) *Privatization in Developing Countries Volume I*, Cheltenham: Edward Elgar Publishing.
Schlossstein, S. (1991) *Asia's New Little Dragons*, Chicago: Contemporary Books.
Searle, P. (1999) *The Riddle of Malaysian Capitalism*, Honolulu: Allen & Unwin and University of Hawai'i Press.
Securities Commission, Malaysia (1999a) 'Revised Requirements for Listing, Reverse Take-Overs and Back-Door Listings and Flexibilities in the Issue Of Replacement Warrants and Fixing of Exercise Prices', press release, 30 April, Kuala Lumpur.
—— (1999b) 'SC Allows Flexibilities for Variations to Profit Guarantee, Sets Conditions to Protect Investors', press release, 30 September, Kuala Lumpur.
Sewerage Services Department, Malaysia (1998) *Sewerage Services Report 1994–1997*, Kuala Lumpur: Percetakan Nasional Malaysia.
—— (2001) *Sewerage Services Report 2001*, Kuala Lumpur: Percetakan Nasional Malaysia.
Shamsul A.B. (1986) *From British to Bumiputra Rule*, Singapore: ISEAS.
Shannon, R. and Lockshin, L. (2000) 'Bangkok's Skytrain: A Marketing Challenge', paper presented at the Australian and New Zealand Marketing Academy Conference.
Shaoul, J. (2004) 'Railpolitik: The Financial Realities of Operating Britain's National Railways', *Public Money & Management*, January.
Shirley, M. (1997) 'The Economics and Politics of Government Ownership' in P. Cook and C. Kirkpatrick (eds) (2000a) *Privatization in Developing Countries Volume II*, Cheltenham: Edward Elgar Publishing.
Shleifer, A. and Vishny, R. (1993) 'Corruption', *The Quarterly Journal of Economics*, 108 (3): 599–617.
Shoji, K. (2001) 'Lessons from Japanese Experiences of Roles of Public and Private Sectors in Urban Transport', *Japan Railway & Transport Review*, 29, December.
Singapore Airlines (1997) *1996/1997 Annual Report*, Singapore: Singapore Airlines.
—— (1998) *1997/1998 Annual Report*, Singapore: Singapore Airlines.
—— (1999) *1998/1999 Annual Report*, Singapore: Singapore Airlines.
—— (2000) *1999/2000 Annual Report*, Singapore: Singapore Airlines.
Singaravelloo, K. (1996) 'Employees Perceptions of Privatisation: The Case of Kelang Container Terminal Bhd', *Borneo Review*, VII (1): 23–41.
SMRT [Singapore Mass Rapid Transit] Corporation (2001) (SMRT) *Annual Report*, Singapore: SMRT Corporation Ltd.

—— (2002) (SMRT) *Annual Report*, Singapore: SMRT Corporation Ltd.
—— (2003) (SMRT) *Annual Report*, Singapore: SMRT Corporation Ltd.
—— (2004) (SMRT) *Annual Report*, Singapore: SMRT Corporation Ltd.
Stern, J. and Holder, S. (1999) 'Regulatory Governance: Criteria for Assessing the Performance of Regulatory Systems. An Application to Infrastructure Industries in the Developing Countries of Asia', *Utilities Policy*, 8: 33–50.
Stiglitz, J. (1971) 'The Theory of Economic Regulation', *Bell Journal of Economic and Management Science*, 2 (1): 3–21.
—— (1996) *Whither Socialism?* Cambridge: The MIT Press.
—— (1998) 'Private Uses of Public Interests: Incentives and Institutions', *Journal of Economic Perspectives*, 12 (2): 3–22.
Stittle, J. (2002) 'Regulatory Control of the Track Access Charges of Railtrack plc', *Public Money & Management*, January–March.
Stottmann, W. (2000) 'The Role of the Private Sector in the Provision of Water and Wastewater Services in Urban Areas', in J. Uito and A. Biswas (eds) *Water for Urban Areas: Challenges and Perspectives*, New York: United Nations University Press.
Supian Ali (1988) 'Malaysia', in G. Edgren (ed) *The Growing Sector: Studies of Public Sector Employment in Asia*, New Delhi: ILO-ARTEP.
TA Securities (1993) 'Malaysia Airlines', stock analysis.
—— (1996) 'Proton', stock analysis, 9 February.
—— (1998) 'Proton', company update, 11 June.
Tan, C. (1996) *Corporate Handbook Malaysia December 1996*, Singapore: Thompson Info (S.E. Asia).
Tan C.H. (1991) 'Privatization in Malaysia and Singapore: A Comparison', *Journal of Southeast Asia Business*, 7 (4) Fall: 12–25.
Tan C.K. (1984) *Without Fear or Favour*, Petaling Jaya: Eastern Universities Press.
Tan T.W. (1982) *Income Distribution and Determination in West Malaysia*, Kuala Lumpur: Oxford University Press.
Tatahi, M. (2003) 'Privatisation Performance in Major European Countries since 1980', PhD thesis, School of Oriental and African Studies, University of London.
Terry, F. (2001a) 'The Nemesis of Privatization: Railway Policy in Retrospect', *Public Money & Management*, January–March.
Terry, F. (2001b) 'Privatization and Public Enterprise Reform: The New Labour Agenda for Pubic Management in the UK', in A. Farazmand (ed) *Privatization or Public Enterprise Reform*, London: Greenwood Press.
Thai Airways International (1998) *Annual Report 1997/98*, Bangkok: Thai Airways International Public Company Limited.
—— (1999) *Annual Report 1998/99*, Bangkok: Thai Airways International Public Company Limited.
—— (2000) *Annual Report 1999/2000*, Bangkok: Thai Airways International Public Company Limited.
Tharu T. Tharumagnanam (1994) *The Making of The National Car*, Kuala Lumpur: TASMAG Publishing.
Townsend, C. (2003) 'In Whose Interest? A Critical Approach to Southeast Asia's Urban Transport Dynamics', PhD thesis, Western Australia: Murdoch University.
Tullock, G. (1967) 'The Welfare Costs of Tariffs, Monopolies and Theft', *The Western Economic Journal*, June.

Uito, J. and Biswas, A. (eds) (2000) *Water for Urban Areas: Challenges and Perspectives*, New York: United Nations University Press.
United Kingdom (2006) West Coast Main Line: Department of Transport Progress Report (May), London: DfT Publications.
Vartiainen, J. (1999) 'The Economics of Successful State Intervention in Industrial Transformation', in M. Woo-Cummings (ed) *The Developmental State*, London: Cornell University Press.
Vickers, J. and Wright, V. (1989) *The Politics of Privatisation in Western Europe*, London: Cass.
Vickers, J. and Yarrow, G. (1988) *Privatization: An Economic Analysis*, Cambridge, Mass; London: MIT Press.
—— (1991) 'Economic Perspectives on Privatisation', *Journal of Economic Perspectives*, 5 (2), 111–132.
—— (1995) *Privatization: An Economic Analysis*, London: The MIT Press.
Wade, R. (1990) *Governing the Market: Economic Theory and Role of Governance in East Asian Industrialisation*, Princeton: Princeton University Press.
—— (2003) 'Symposium on Infant Industries: Reply to John Roberts on Infant Industry Protection', *Oxford Development Studies*, 31 (1): 8–14.
Warr, P.G. (1987) 'Malaysia's Industrial Enclaves: Benefits and Costs', *The Developing Economies*, 25 (1) March: 30–55.
Weber, R. (2002) 'Do Better Contracts Make Better Economic Incentives?', *APA Journal*, 68 (1): 43–55.
Wedeman, A. (2002) 'Development and Corruption: The East Asian Paradox', in E.T. Gomez (ed), *Political Business in East Asia*, London: Routledge.
Weiss, L. (1998) *The Myth of The Powerless State*, Cambridge: Polity Press.
Weiss, L. and Hobson, J.M. (1995) *State and Economic Development: A Comparative Historical Analysis*, Cambridge: Polity Press.
Whitehouse, L. (2003) 'Railtrack is Dead – Long Live Network Rail? Nationalization Under The Third Way', *Journal of Law & Society*, 30 (2), June.
Williamson, O. (2000) 'Economic Institutions and Development', in M. Olson and S. Kahkonen (eds) *A Not-So-Dismal Science*, New York: Oxford University Press.
Wilson, R. (1999) 'The Political Economy of Financing Development in Malaysia', in B.N. Ghosh and Muhammad Syukri Salleh (eds) *Political Economy of Development in Malaysia*, Kuala Lumpur: Utusan Publications and Distributors.
Windsor, D. (1996) 'Creative Financing Options for Urban Transport Privatization', in S. Hakim, P. Seidenstat and G. Bowman (eds) *Privatizing Transportation Systems*, London: Praeger.
Woo-Cummings, M. (ed) (1999) *The Developmental State*, Ithaca: Cornell University Press.
World Bank (1994) *World Development Report 1994: Infrastructure for Development*, New York: Oxford University Press/World Bank.
Yarrow, G. (1986) 'Privatization in Theory and Practice', *Economic Policy*, 2: 324–364.
Yusoff, M. (1990) *Time for Change*, Kuala Lumpur: The Champ.
Zeufack, A. (2004) 'Assessing the Impact of Privatization: Lessons from International Experiences', ISIS, Kuala Lumpur, Malaysia, 19 February.

## Newspapers, magazines, websites and other sources


Agence France Presse (AFP)
*Asian Business Review*
*Asian Wall Street Journal*
*Asiaweek*
*AutoAsia*
*AutoTrader*
<http://ces.autotrader.co.uk/ces/roadtest.do?usedCar=0&capcode=PRG216GSX5HPIM%20%20%20%20%20%20&rtid=211080&price=10406> (accessed 3 February 2007)
*Automotive News*
*Autozine*
<http://autozine.kyul.net/Manufacturer/Korea.htm> (accessed 18 Dec 2005)
Bernama.com
Boeing Corporation
<*http://active.boeing.com/commercial/orders/summaries.cfm*> (accessed 2 June 2005)
*Business Times*
Companies Commission Malaysia
*Far Eastern Economic Review*
*Global Car Production Statistics Pages*
<http://www.geocities.com/MotorCity/Speedway/4939/korea.html> (accessed 3 February 2007)
*International Herald Tribune*
*Investors Digest*
Kowloon-Canton Railway Corporation
<http://www.kcrc.com/> (accessed 3 February 2007)
Light Rail Transit Authority (Manila)
<http://www.lrta.gov.ph/index.htm> (accessed 3 February 2007)
*Malay Mail*
*Malaysiakini*
<http://malaysiakini.com>
*Malaysian Business*
*Malaysian Industry*
*New Straits Times*
*PACIFIC Exchange Rate Service*
<http://pacific.commerce.ubc.ca/xr/data.html>
Reuters
*The Automobile Association*
<http://www.theaa.com/allaboutcars/carsearch/carsearch_cartest_reports.jsp?carTest=carTest&latestReports=n&modelID=A8&modelName=GEN-2&makeName=Proton> (accessed 3 February 2007)
*The Economist*
*The Edge*
<http://www.theedgedaily.com>
*The Star*
*The Sun*
*Water & Environment International* (March 2000, 9 [66])
<http://web.ebscohost.com/ehost/detail?vid=3&hid=120&sid=80dfd078–4901–4d34-a489–9ff0f8b01db2%40sessionmgr107> (accessed 7 February 2007)

# Index

For Product Safety Concerns and Information please contact our EU representative GPSR@taylorandfrancis.com
Taylor & Francis Verlag GmbH, Kaufingerstraße 24, 80331 München, Germany

www.ingramcontent.com/pod-product-compliance
Ingram Content Group UK Ltd.
Pitfield, Milton Keynes, MK11 3LW, UK
UKHW022133190926
475702UK00013B/1785

*9780415545372*

# Regulation in the European Electricity Sector

Since the very beginning of European integration, electricity has been within the legal sphere of the EU. Much of this is found within the binding European acts making up the framework of the Energy Packages. The established legal institutions have had a significant impact on the shape of the energy market in Europe. Nevertheless, the European energy market still seems to be developing, as demonstrated by the current lively discussion about the state of the Energy Union.

*Regulation in the European Electricity Sector* delves into European energy law and reflects on some of the primary issues related to the public legal impact on the European energy sector. The book offers a brief explanation of the background operation of the electricity sector, as well as liberalisation within the area, and traces the evolution of the EU's approach towards the issue of public law regulation within the electricity sector. Finally, the book presents an analysis of European and national laws, considering their interpretation, and explores the future of public law regulation.

Aimed at giving the reader a deep insight into the nature of the state's presence in the power sector, this book will be of great interest to students and scholars of EU energy law and policy.

**Maciej M. Sokołowski** is a Doctor of Law and a President of the ABC Institute. He was granted the Swiss Government Excellence Scholarship at the University of Basel (Europa Institute), the Swedish Institute Visby Programme Scholarship at the University of Gothenburg (School of Business, Economics and Law), and the Shanghai Municipal Government Scholarship at the Shanghai University.

**Routledge Studies in Energy Law and Regulation**

**Regulation in the European Electricity Sector**
*Maciej M. Sokołowski*